On the

Suppression of the

Society of Jesus

On the
Suppression of the
Society of Jesus

A Contemporary Account

GIULIO CESARE CORDARA, S.J.
(1704–1785)

Translation and notes by John P. Murphy, S.J.

an imprint of
Loyola Press

Chicago

an imprint of
Loyola Press
3441 North Ashland Avenue
Chicago, Illinois 60657

© 1999 John P. Murphy, S.J.

Cover and interior design by Amy Evans McClure

Cover illustration: Pope Clement XIV presents a copy of the Decree of Suppression of the Society of Jesus to Spanish ambassador Giuseppe Moniño, count of Floridablanca, to deliver to King Charles III. Unknown French engraver, c. 1774. Museo di Roma, Istituto Centrale per il Catalogo e la Documentazione, Ministero per i Beni Culturali e Ambientali (#418). Reproduced with permission of Dottoressa Calegari, Direttrice.

Library of Congress Cataloging-in-Publication Data
Cordara, Giulio Cesare, 1704-1785.
    [De suppressione Societatis Iesu commentarii. English]
    On the suppression of the Society of Jesus : a contemporary account /
by Giulio Cesare Cordara ; translation and notes by John P. Murphy.
       p.   cm.
    Includes bibliographical references and index.
    ISBN 0-8294-1295-6 (pbk.)
    1. Jesuits—Europe—History—18th century.   I. Murphy, John P.,
S.J. II. Title.
BX3715.C6713   1999
271'.53'009033–DC21   99-24712
                                           CIP

Printed in the United States of America
99 00 01 02 03 / 10 9 8 7 6 5 4 3 2 1

CONTENTS

ILLUSTRATIONS

TRANSLATOR'S PREFACE

Giulio Cesare Cordara begins his account of the suppression of the Society of Jesus by observing that this event would make 1773 the outstanding year in the eighteenth century. Yet when he wrote, a quarter of the century remained, the American Revolution was unfolding, and the French Revolution would not occur until the next decade. These two revolutions introduced the modern world and the modern, secular state, and they certainly marked the end of the *ancien regime*. Absolutist monarchs of the century had brought down the Society of Jesus, but their own falls were in the offing. Though the Society of Jesus did offer support to the existing governments (Cordara's work shows a decided, not to say, exaggerated, deference to the person and office of king), Jesuits were seen as champions of the pope and the Church and opponents of the absolutist claims of the enlightened eighteenth-century monarchs. The eighteenth century saw the humiliation of the papacy by Catholic powers and the nineteenth century was to see the culmination of this hostile attitude in imprisonment of both Pius VI (1799) and Pius VII (1809–14) by France and Napoleon.

The authoritarianism and regalism of the Spanish and Portuguese patronages viewed the Society of Jesus suspiciously, for the Society was the champion of the pope's powers and privileges. Further, the Society was a genuinely international organization, transcending national boundaries and interests. The ministers who advised the kings were hostile to the Society's influence with the aristocracy, from whose ranks came many Jesuits and whose sons were trained in Jesuit colleges. Portugal and Austria attempted state control of education before the end of the century, but all governments had to make some provision for replacing the Jesuit schools, even if only by allowing the Jesuits to continue to teach as secular priests. It is well known that Frederick II in his realms (Silesia) and Catherine the Great in Russia refused to have the decree of suppression, *Dominus ac Redemptor*, promulgated, precisely because they wanted to keep the Jesuit schoolmasters.

The eighteenth century also saw the continuance of the struggle between England and France. Queen Anne's War (1702–13), the War of the Austrian Succession (1740–48), and the Seven Years War (1756–63) saw France's overseas possessions fall, mostly to England and some to Holland. Louis XV of France enjoyed a long reign (1715–74), but he is generally considered weak and ineffective, subject to the influence of his mistresses and ministers. France did try to put its house in order, but could not overcome the inequalities in distribution of wealth and burdens of taxation. The Church was the major landholder in France and its wealth tempted the monarch and royal cabinet members. As the theory of popular sovereignty was growing and asserted itself dramatically in the French Revolution, so also the once dominant clerical and ecclesiastical orders saw the *ancien regime* passing away.

Another feature of the eighteenth century was the rise of Prussia under Frederick II and of Russia under Catherine II. These monarchs' predecessors had, to be sure, started their nations' rise, but under these two sovereigns, Prussia and Russia became new forces on the European political scene. Though Frederick and Catherine showed the same absolutist behavior as their Catholic counterparts, and though they too were influenced by the *philosophes* and the Enlightenment (Voltaire, for example, spent three years in the early 1750s with Frederick), they protected the Society of Jesus and did not badger the pope for its suppression. As Prussia and Russia rose in the European political scene, Spain and Portugal declined.

The encyclopedists and *philosophes* were in correspondence with monarchs, ministers, and even ecclesiastics. They sometimes wrote in terms of the need to destroy the Church and, in order to do this, they proposed first to attack the Society of Jesus. Both the Church and the Society were seen as blocks to the advance of reason. It is not clear that there was any concerted effort on the part of the *philosophes* to eradicate the Society and to destroy the Church, but they did want greater emphasis on natural science and an almost total neglect of theology. They delighted to see the internecine struggle between Jansenists and Jesuits, and exulted when the Jansenists prevailed in France and the Society was outlawed there in 1762.

Within the Church, the eighteenth century also marked the end of the disputes concerning the Malabar and Chinese rites when Benedict XIV spoke definitively on the topic with the bull *Ex Quo Singulari* (1742). These disputes caused bitterness between the Society and other religious orders. Bad feeling and outright animosity continued and undoubtedly motivated some within the Church to advocate the suppression of the Jesuits or at least to be willing to acquiesce in it.

The struggle between Jesuits and Jansenists was another interecclesial source of tension in the early eighteenth century. A circle of persons in Rome was influenced by rigorist tendencies and considered the Jesuits too lax in their moral teaching. Cordara describes meetings of these anti-Jesuit churchmen and the steps they took to disseminate anti-Jesuit pamphlets in the Eternal City. In France, the struggle with the Jansenists had taken on a political cast. The Jansenists tended to champion the Gallican Church and to back the Parlement in its clash with Louis XV, who tried in vain to halt the Parlement's harsh anti-Jesuit measures.

A carryover from the Jansenist controversy was the tension between Jesuits and some Augustinians. In fact, the Augustinian general at the time of the suppression, Francisco Xavier Vazquez, was among the most active anti-Jesuit ecclesiastics in Rome. The issues here were the alleged laxity of many Jesuit moral theologians, the Society's unflinching opposition to Jansenism, and its wholehearted support of the bull *Unigenitus* (1713), which condemned Jansenism. Many in France and in Italy, therefore, were hostile to the Society because of its stance in these matters.

Cordara takes up almost all these topics as he recollects his personal experience of the suppression. He does not write with scholarly apparatus nor does he use extensive quotations. Rather, he addresses his brother in a conversational manner, interjecting personal reflections at times and anecdotes that involve himself. His essay is a complement to the studies of the suppression which are made on the basis of letters and archival materials. It is by no means a definitive account of the suppression of the Society of Jesus, but it certainly is a valuable contemporary document. The purpose of this translation is to make Cordara's commentary more readily available for the Latinless students of the history of the Society of Jesus.

I wish at this point to thank the officials of Loyola Press, especially my editors, Dr. Ruth E. McGugan, Amy Schroeder, and Belinda Duvel, as well as the Press's readers who made suggestions to improve the manuscript. I wish to thank also the library staff of Loyola University Chicago, and especially the archivist and curator of the Rare Book Room, Brother Michael Grace, S.J. The librarians and archivists at the Jesuit Curia and Historical Institute in Rome also deserve my thanks. In particular, Father Ugo Storni, S.J., Father Thomas Reddy, S.J., and Father Joseph DeCock, S.J., made their expertise available to

me in my research. To these Jesuits and to their assistants, the present anno-
tated translation owes much, and I express my sincere gratitude to them.
Finally, I thank Father Charles Ronan, S.J., professor emeritus of Loyola
University Chicago, for suggesting the project and encouraging me as the
work progressed.

ABBREVIATIONS

Dammig   Dammig, Enrico. *Il movimento giansenista a Roma nella seconda metà del secolo XVIII.* Rome, 1945.

DdC   Berton, Charles. *Dictionnaire des Cardinaux.* Paris, 1857.

EC   *Enciclopedia Cattolica.* Città del Vaticano, 1948–54.

EI   *Enciclopedia italiana di scienze, lettere ed arti.* . . . Rome, 1929–39.

GE   *La grand encyclopédie.* Paris, 1885–92.

GL   *Grand Larousse.* Paris, 1960.

Rialp   *Gran enciclopedia Rialp.* Madrid, 1989.

SHSI   *Synopsis historiae Societatis Iesu.* Louvain, 1950.

Sommervogel   Backer, Augustin de. *Bibliothèque de la Compagnie de Jésus.* Carlos Sommervogel, ed. Louvain, 1960.

Giulio Cesare Cordara, S.J., 1704–85

Giulio Cesare Cordara, S.J.
(1704–1785)

Giulio Cesare Cordara, in a letter of 18 March 1779 to his former pupil and very close friend, Francesco Cancellieri, announced his intention of making an abstract which would treat the suppression of the Society of Jesus from his longer work entitled *De suis ac suorum rebus aliisque suorum temporum, usque ad occasum Societatis Iesu Commentarii.*[1] That work had been conceived and executed after the complete suppression of the Society of Jesus, which occurred in August 1773. Through Cordara's letters to Cancellieri, one can trace the progress of that rather extensive survey of the life and times of Cordara, for frequent allusions to the work occur in the letters from 1775 to 1779.

Cordara felt that the sensitive nature of much of the matter he was dealing with and the fact that some of the principals were still living, were reasons why the publication of his work should be delayed—if it were ever to be published at all. That is, in fact, what happened. An edition of some excerpts from the *De suis temporibus*, made by Johann J. Döllinger, appeared in 1882.[2] Then in the first part of the twentieth century, Giuseppe Albertotti, a renowned oculist and fellow townsman of Cordara, began publishing some of the all but lost works of Cordara. In the aforementioned collection of letters made in 1912 and 1916, there are extensive abstracts from the *De suis temporibus*, which, however, had to wait until 1933 for a complete edition.[3] In the intervening period, Albertotti had published in 1923 and 1925 the excerpted books on the suppression of the Society of Jesus.[4] That latter work is now translated into English in the present volume.

Francesco Galluzzi, S.J.

Early Years

Giulio Cordara (he himself took the name Cesare as a literary affectation), was born at Alessandria in northern Italy on 16 or 17 December 1704.[5] He was the second of three boys in the Cordara family. Francesco Maria, the oldest boy (one year older than Giulio), is the addressee of both the longer and excerpted commentaries. He was a successful and highly regarded government official in the kingdom of Sardinia. The younger brother, Guglielmo, died at age forty-five on 17 April 1755 while in the military service of his king. The family estate was at Calamandrana, a short distance from Alessandria, though they also lived at nearby Nizza Monferatto.

In 1715 after the death of their mother in 1710, the two older Cordara boys were sent to Rome for their studies and lived there with their clerical uncle Giacomo Cordara. Just short of eleven years of age, Giulio enrolled in the Jesuits' Roman College where he studied for three years and soon began to shine as a Latinist. The spiritual father of the college, Father Francesco Galluzzi, discerned in the young Giulio the makings of a Jesuit. At only fourteen years of age and against the inclinations of his father, Giulio sought and obtained the special permission of Father General Michelangelo Tamburini (generalate: 1706–30)[6] to enter the novitiate of San Andrea al Quirinale on 20 December 1718.

Jesuit Training

After the two-year period of the novitiate, Giulio excelled in the study of the classics, which he studied for two more years (1720–22). Three years of philosophy at the Roman College followed the humanistic studies of the juniorate (1722–25). At the conclusion of his philosophical studies, Giulio performed the grand act, a public defense of scholastic philosophy. Giulio then had a full five-year period of regency (1725–30), or teaching experience. He taught Latin poetry and rhetoric at Viterbo, Fermo, and Ancona. As a regent, Giulio dipped into satire. In 1730, Cordara returned to Rome for the study of theology and was ordained a priest in 1733. For two of his four years of theological study, Cordara lived at the German College, a contributing factor, no doubt, for his subsequent monograph on the history of that college. His tertianship, or third year of novitiate and spiritual formation, was done at Florence in 1734–35.

Teacher and Historiographer

Having completed the seminary course, Cordara's apostolic life as a priest began with a teaching assignment at Macerata where he further showed his penchant for satire and was subsequently silenced by Father General Francis Retz (generalate: 1730–50), and his work was placed on the Index.[7] As always and everywhere, Cordara showed his talent for making friends at Macerata. He next moved to Rome to teach philosophy, but found that discipline little to his taste. Even more distasteful was teaching canon law. It was then (1742) that Father General Retz decided that Cordara should continue the history of the Society of Jesus, taking the office of historiographer of the Society. Cordara's contribution was the Sixth Part, covering the first eighteen years of the generalate of Mucius Vitelleschi (Cordara's coverage was 1615–33; Vitelleschi died 9 February 1645). Because of bickering within the Society, the first volume of Cordara's history, covering the years 1615 to 1625, did not appear until 1750. The second volume, covering 1625–33, was not published until 1859, by which time the idea of a universal history of the Society had been abandoned.

At this period of his life, Cordara was cultivating the friendship of many Roman aristocrats and ecclesiastics. His commentaries *De suis temporibus* are filled with references to these nobles as well as to his other literary endeavors.[8] Cordara was living at the Jesuits' generalate, then located at the Gesù, and he enjoyed a close relationship with Lorenzo Ricci, who eventually became General in 1758 and thus was at the helm in the last years of the Society's pre-suppression existence until 1773. Cordara felt that his connections both outside of and within the Society gave him a unique and particularly valuable vantage point from which to view the momentous historical event of the suppression. He has the advantages and disadvantages of a contemporary witness. The advantage is that he was an eyewitness and the only eighteenth-century author to attempt an overview of all the events and to make an evaluation of the causes for the Society's suppression.[9] A disadvantage is that he made many mistakes in judging his friends' and acquaintances' attitudes toward the Society. Often those whom he judged to be friendly were strongly tinged with antipathy toward the Society, frequently derived from Jansenistic tendencies. Also, he never set foot outside Italy and thus at times, he lacked a broader perspective. Like most of us, he may have trusted his own judgment too much, and may have been harsh in his judgments of others and easy on himself. He certainly was unable to form an unfavorable opinion of the monarchs: He always represented them as led astray by wrong-headed ministers.

Final Years in Alessandria

Cordara busied himself with other literary efforts while composing his volumes on the history of the Society and kept a busy social calendar with visits to and from Roman and, later, Alessandrian notables. He was never of robust health and had to retire to the Alban hills for a few months in 1771. Since he had not fully recovered, he decided to return to Alessandria in 1772 to take his native air and hoped to regain enough of his physical health to be able to return to Rome, a wish that was not to come true. After an emotional good-bye to his close friend Father General Lorenzo Ricci, Cordara traveled to Turin and Alessandria, leaving behind forever the city of Rome where he had studied, lived, and worked for so many years. During this period of his life, 1772–85, he was, as indicated above, very active with literary matters and among other things produced the sixteen books of *De suis temporibus* and the eight-book précis entitled *De suppressione Societatis Iesu commentarii*. After a brief illness, Giulio Cesare Cordara ended his long, productive life on 6 March 1785.

On the
Suppression of the
Society of Jesus

Introduction:
A Momentous Event

The suppression of the Society of Jesus will make memorable for all time the seventy-third year of this century and the pontificate of Ganganelli, who was called by the name Clement XIV. Surely in the memory of man nothing more momentous was ever done in the Church, nothing more clamorous, nothing less expected. For that order was suppressed which was, in the common view, holier than the rest and more useful to the public. If people had been asked, all would prefer that that one Society be preserved rather than the other religious orders. I believe that a few years previously almost all the kings and princes of Europe would have thought the same thing. They were using no other guides of conscience than Jesuits and they seemed to prefer them by far to other orders.

Jesuits Esteemed

The esteem of the Jesuits was great and universal, and, I think, not undeserved. Their rules were holy; their morals upright; their efforts for the common good were many, varied, and constant. There was no kind of sacred ministry in any way profitable for their neighbor that they thought foreign to themselves. There was no race of men to whom they would not supply the helps for eternal salvation. They were training youth in schools and seminaries no less in letters than in good character. They were feeding the people with the food of the Divine Word. They fostered, in their own separate and proper sodalities, the growth of priests and laymen, nobles and commoners, merchants and workers. Some traveled through villages and towns on sacred missions. Others, in places of holy seclusion, were giving the Spiritual Exercises as prescribed by St. Ignatius. All, as occasion demanded, went day and night to the sick, to the hospitals, to the prisons. All heard confessions. You might say that in one college of the Society there was established a sort of arsenal of public assistance.

Yet the Jesuits had received special praise because of the missions in India and other foreign parts. They were the first to go to China, to Japan, to Paraguay. They were the first to bring the faith to the Abyssinians, to the Kaffirs. Many confirmed the faith by shedding their blood either amid the pyres of the Japanese or the daggers of the Malabars.[1] [13] In the vast, uncultivated tracts of Maranhão [in northern Brazil] and Paraguay, where formerly there was only a huge wasteland, they sought out the natives in their forest retreats and brought them together for life in common. They had founded new cities and had ordered them in a civic and Christian manner. They dared to do that which others had not even thought of. And now they were directing the colonies of newly baptized in such a way that more cultivated people could scarcely be found anywhere else. Surely the kings of Spain and Portugal had no more loyal and obedient subjects.

No less was the Society praised for its learning and sanctity. Libraries are full of excellent books by Jesuits in every kind of discipline. The learned praise these books and all posterity will also. No one is believed to have written more clearly and vigorously against heretics and for the power of the Supreme Pontiff. They number nine saints in their ranks, duly recognized as such.[2] No other order had so many in so short a time. To summarize briefly, the Jesuits (although a fairly recent institute, for from their inception they count a little more than two hundred years)[3] were almost equaling or even excelling the glory of the older orders and were far outdistancing the other, newer orders.

The number of the Jesuits was about 22,000. The majority were priests or clerics. For the lay brothers comprised scarcely one-sixth. In that number there was a flowering of talent and learning. There was much piety and nobility. There were not inconsiderable financial resources, but greater in appearances than in reality. Just about everywhere there were magnificent buildings for the colleges and very ornate churches. Jesuits' fare, however, was frugal and perfectly common; there was a marvelous modesty in their lifestyle. You would find no one unoccupied, no one completely unlettered and boorish, and almost no one who was not content with his lot. For they did not pronounce their solemn vows until they were thirty-three years of age. Before this time each was allowed, with the proper permission of the Father General, to return to his family. The General, however, retained no one against his will, and dismissed the disobedient even though they wished to stay. Further, the power of the General is complete and perpetual over the entire order. He alone appoints major and minor superiors and establishes provinces. By this means all opportunity for canvassing and subsequent discords which arise elsewhere out of ambition for offices is completely shut off. Finally, nations and cities extolled this Society with unbounded praises and held it dear and accepted above other orders. [14] Princes deemed it worthy of special favor. The supreme pontiffs protected it with particular regard as the beloved and most faithful of their legions and kept it safe against countless adversaries.

They were not only doing this, but also were enhancing it with ever greater honors and benefits. It would seem scarcely credible what I saw with my own eyes. Jesuits were prohibited by vow from accepting ecclesiastical dignities. Still, three cardinals from the Society were living in Rome at the same time.[4] All were forced by Clement XI to accept the honor.

Jesuits Envied

But there was as much envy as honor, and I am not sure whether there were more enemies than friends. Even granted that the friends were greater in number, surely the enemies excelled in hatred and in the desire to do harm. Other religious looked askance at the Society and as "Joseph's brothers, seeing that he was loved by his father more than the rest of his sons, hated him and could not speak peaceably to him," (Gen. 37.4) so other religious could not calmly bear that the Society be so approved and applauded beyond themselves, and they waited for an opportunity to destroy it; and when the opportunity was presented, they eagerly seized upon it. But we will discourse on these matters more fully elsewhere.

Meanwhile the Society was an order that was solidly founded on such holy laws and relying on so many and such great means of protection. Yet, when it seemed to have arrived at its peak of authority and glory and was above any mishap of fortune, it was, nonetheless, suddenly suppressed and abolished. The order, which a short time before outshone the others, now lies cast down upon the ground. It is the fate of some human things that the higher they ascend, the closer they are to danger and they fall from the slightest disturbance. The Society of Jesus has been snuffed out. That great ship, so well made, so often weathering storms and waves while sailing prosperously toward immortality under full sail, has met a pitiable shipwreck when the wind suddenly blew against it and it was swamped by waves. Alas! Others

have taken for their use our colleges, our expensive churches. Our inheritance
has been handed over to others.

But what you would marvel at more is that the princes were the authors of
this calamitous upheaval. The best of men and most just in themselves, they
previously had been well affected toward the Society. They seem to be far distant from oppressing it and would always be thus. But to pass over other
things, who would not think that Charles the Bourbon, the king of Spain,
would be farthest distant from suppressing the Society?[5] (Spain had given
Ignatius of Loyola to the light of day and for that reason, Spaniards are scarcely less proud of him than of Dominic de Guzman, the founder of the
Dominican order. Both orders, inasmuch as they were born of a Spanish
father, increase the renown of the people.) Who would believe that the king of
Spain would want to strip his nation of this glory? [15] Who would believe
that Charles, who drew his Farnese blood together with love for the Society
from his mother Elizabeth, would want the Society destroyed? For a Farnese,
Pope Paul III, was the first to approve the Society and to accept its Formula.
Other princes from the Farnese family have bestowed so many and such great
favors on the Society that they almost exceeded every limit of generosity. Yet
Charles wanted it destroyed. He accomplished its destruction with incredible
eagerness, with supreme effort. He demanded it with complete resoluteness
and did not rest until it was done.

To top off the wonder, the Supreme Pontiff snuffed out the Society which
was doing services for him with such great faithfulness and virtue. He ought
to have defended and protected the Society if not for love of us, at least for his
own practical benefit. What sort of pontiff was he? A Ganganelli nourished in
the Franciscan family, almost the only religious order that had always gotten
on well with the Society. A Ganganelli who in his private affairs had always
shown himself a very close friend of the Jesuits. A Ganganelli who was elected
to the college of cardinals for no greater reason than his well-attested friendship with the Jesuits; in fact, it seemed as if he were another Jesuit. We mourn
the suppression and extinction of the Society by the decree of this pontiff.
These things may seem quite remarkable and beyond all belief. So much the
more ought we in silence to look up to heaven and pay homage to the Divine
Will by which all mortal affairs are directed from on high.

Cordara's Motivation: To Tell the Naked Truth

My plan is to put these things down now in writing and to hand them over to
the memory of posterity. For such an important event, which was discussed

by all manner of men and which filled the whole world with admiration, ought not be forgotten. Without a doubt there will be others who will pick up the theme and will write in better Latin or Italian. But I do not know if there is anyone beside me who can unfold with greater truth all the things that must be said and who wants to do it with greater reliability. Externs did not know well enough the things that were done internally among ourselves, and they generally gathered information only from vulgar rumors and from the street corners. Few of Ours were grasping external affairs since each was intent upon his own ministry. Older fathers, who did know what was going on in the Society and outside it, do not easily bestir themselves to write either from distaste for the labor or from some other consideration. And many of them have already died. The reliability of all those who finally do write on these matters will be suspect. They will be compared to most men who want matters judged as their emotions and interests prompt them. In this case, you would scarcely find a neutral party [16] who could be judged free of all bias.

But I (let me speak with you, my brother Francesco, a little more freely), although I had no part in the public administration of the Society, still I was assigned to the Curia of Father General. I was a close friend of Father General, Lorenzo Ricci. I saw many intimate things which escaped the general run of Jesuits. Since I had great and almost daily contact with prominent men of the city and officials of the papal court, I likewise found out from them many secrets. Finally, nothing carried more weight with me, nothing was more important than the naked truth. I was as dedicated to the Society as anyone. Perhaps no one was more dedicated than I. This was proven in many situations and not without my personal risk. Nevertheless even among us, I was not approving many things and many things I freely and openly was condemning. But now that there is no Society any longer, I will write about these matters without rancor or bias and as if I had never been a member. In this frame of mind, I will subsequently touch on certain things which Jesuits perhaps would not want written and I am afraid they will accuse me of being debased. But I will say nothing that I did not see with my own eyes at Rome where all this material is collected or that I have taken from suitable authors.

Since therefore I have enough leisure and more than enough desire and opportunity, I turn to these *Commentaries on the Suppression of the Society* and I undertake the compiling of the whole history of this remarkable deed from its beginnings. I turn to an arduous task, as I see, and one full of danger so that that dictum of Horace seems to fit me: "You handle a task full of perilous luck and you walk through fire beneath which lie pain-inflicting embers" (*Odes* 2.1.6–8). For now princes are so sensitive that the things which they did in full view of the world, they cannot bear to be spoken of by others and to be bruited about. But my happy fate is to deal with most just men who in their fairness grant this favor to me that I think them to be men; men, I say, subject like any other men to error, and perhaps more subject than others since they yield to the flattery of courtiers and they ought necessarily to believe the accounts of their ministers, whatever sort of people they may be. If I obtain this favor, there is nothing I will fear. Whatever was done against the Society wickedly, maliciously, and fraudulently is to be thought assignable to the treachery of ministers and their crafty arts. The princes who slipped due to human error are excused from blame. That very fact our history will clearly show. [17]

Sebastian Joseph Carvalho, Marquis of Pombal

BOOK I

Portugal, Part 1
Carvalho's Enmity; Saldanha's Visit

The beginnings of our first undoing are to be sought in Portugal and in Sebastiâo José de Carvalho, the prime minister of King Joseph I. Later we will call him the Marquis of Pombal.[1] He is to be considered the first author and architect of the suppression. For when he expelled the Jesuits from Portuguese territory, he gave an example which other ministers, men with almost equal power but with a little less treachery than he, took up for imitation in France, in Spain, in the Duchy of Parma, and in both Sicilies. Afterwards when the Society had been expelled from so many places and was thoroughly shaken, the Bourbon kings easily prevailed upon the Supreme Pontiff to suppress and abolish the Society completely. Carvalho had once been, or had wanted to appear to be, most devoted to the Society; and so, since he showed great talent for diplomacy, with the support of Jesuits who were very powerful at court, he was, under King John V, sent first to England and then to Vienna with the title of Royal Legate. When John died his successor Joseph I, again with the recommendation and urging of Jesuits, chose that same man as his Minister for Internal Affairs. Joseph handed over to him the reins of government with so much authority conferred upon him alone that he was considered to be, and in fact, was, the powerful judge of all things.

But Carvalho, the ungrateful man, could not bear that the power of the Jesuits equaled his own. Although he had grown by their backing and favor, still he thought they should be taken down a rung or two. First he attacked the court confessors, good and God-fearing men. They were for that reason too weak adversaries to be able to stand up to that very powerful, cunning enemy who made no distinction between right and wrong. When the confessors were gotten out of the way, he declared impious war on the rest of the

Jesuits. He relentlessly pursued them now with calumnies and lies, now with open force until he ordered them stripped of all their property and deported a great distance. It is unsure why he was so angry. I will expound the more probable reasons just as they were being handed down.

Jesuits Accused as Authors of Rebellion in Paraguay

The kings of Portugal and Spain had already (1750) entered a pact [19] on exchanging certain tracts of land in South America. These lay next to Paraguay and on the boundaries of both kings. The king of Portugal was transferring to the power of the king of Spain, Colonia del Sacramento, an island situated at the mouth of the Rio de la Plata. In return the Spanish king ceded to the Portuguese seven colonies, that is to say, that number of cities of Paraguayan converts.

Although this exchange was detrimental to the interests of Spain, Queen Barbara, the sister of King Joseph of Portugal, had secretly promoted it. Consideration for her brother and her family carried more weight with her than the interests of her husband Ferdinand from whom she left no children behind her. But when it came to the actual transfer, the Paraguayan converts rose up in revolt and took up arms to repulse the Portuguese whom they thoroughly hated and to whose power they most stoutly refused to be subjected. Nor was the cause for resistance unjust. For beside an ingrained hatred of the Portuguese name, there remained fixed deeply in their memories injuries which they had often received from Brazilian Portuguese. And finally they had voluntarily given themselves to the king of Spain—voluntarily, when they lived as free men in the inhospitable forests and each was his own master. Then they had entrusted themselves to his good faith and accordingly they were professing their desire to remain in that good faith.

However that may be, many were easily convinced that the Jesuits were the authors of the uprising of Paraguayan converts because they had brought these peoples out of their forest hiding places, had drawn them together in towns, and had formed them to the ways of a Christian and societal life. Further, the Jesuits were still their directors and pastors and had them obedient to their words. Hence a story spread throughout Europe about a new king of Paraguay, Nicholas, and him a Jesuit. A coin was displayed to confirm this story. On one side the name of King Nicholas was inscribed, and on the obverse, the name Jesus. It is remarkable how one who wants a lie believed passes over nothing to make the lie feasible. Afterwards it was discovered how this was all falsely made up. Yet this was the first reason for Carvalho's anger at us. Because it had some semblance of respectability, Carvalho made a pretence of it as the one cause, as I shall relate. But there were other, more hidden and truer reasons which he did not want made public.

Moreiro Foils Hanover Marriage Plot

If the analysts of Joseph's reign tell the truth, one of the principal causes of Carvalho's anger at the Jesuits was this: The king of Portugal lacked male offspring. Many princes from all over Europe were favoring his oldest daughter Maria Francesca as the heir to the realm. It was a common wish among the Portuguese that the royal maid marry Peter, their king's brother. Then the offspring of royal Braganza blood would not be broken off nor would the realm—a thing at which the people stood aghast—pass to outsiders. [20] But Carvalho had fixed in his mind everything differently. Stirred by some hatred for Peter—perhaps because Peter seemed rather attached to the Jesuits—he made efforts to block Peter's marriage with his niece. He preferred that she be married to William Henry Hanover,[2] the brother of the king of England, despite the fact that he was heterodox. To better achieve this purpose, he made Peter suspect to the king, who was by nature timid and suspicious. He made out that Peter, buoyed by the favor of the people and relying on the resources of the Jesuits, was ambitioning a tyranny over the realm. Carvalho brought to the king's mind another Peter, his grandfather, who snatched from his brother Alphonsus both his kingdom and his wife by the evil (or so he was alleging) contrivances of the Jesuits and exiled him, once dethroned, to a distant island in the Atlantic Ocean. What, Carvalho added, would the king not have to fear from one who was the last prince of Braganza blood, who enjoyed such favor with the people and with the aristocracy, and who was completely under the control of the Jesuits? What would he not have to fear if he married the king's daughter, the heir of the realm and if he begot children from her? The English prince would dare no such thing. He would bring no birthright to the realm. He would be a consort to his wife Francesca, not on the throne but only in the bedroom.

Dinning these and similar things into the king's ears, Carvalho had almost persuaded him. The king, however, was still uncertain in mind, and before he made a decision on a matter of such grave importance, he thought he should consult his guide of conscience, the Jesuit Moreiro.[3] Moreiro so disapproved the plan of Carvalho that he even injected a scruple into the king over the matter of introducing into the family a prince who was not of the Roman faith.

Due to that single admonition of one Jesuit, there crashed to the ground the huge scheme which Carvalho had built up with such long labor and skilled crafting, and all his hope was frustrated. That man, proud beyond what can be described, reacted so furiously that he began to detest and to work havoc, not only for Moreiro but for anything having to do with the Jesuits.

Jesuits Report Mendoza's Crimes

A second cause of Carvalho's opposition is said to have been this. The Queen Mother, Mariana of Austria, was a very holy and zealous woman, whose biography has been published. Whenever Jesuits set sail for the missions in Maranhão, she again and again used to urge them not only to work hard and courageously in the interests of religion, but also not to hesitate to inform her by letter if they saw the king's governors doing wrong and acting illegally. She would see to it that remedies would be applied without the writers' names being disclosed and without danger to them. With this assurance, Jesuits were writing many things subsequently against Xavier de Mendoza, [21] Carvalho's brother, who was then ruling over Maranhão. (It is the custom in Portugal that each one takes the surname that he prefers. Hence in the same family, there are often as many surnames as there are brothers.)

Governors of provinces which are far distant from the court exercise a freer and greater power. So Mendoza sorely tried the people with no restraint of law nor respect for the king. He also impeded the propagation of religion in many places. The Queen Mother, informed of this by the Jesuits' letters, advised her son the king and he took care that the audacity of the unjust governor be checked. Carvalho was incensed with pain and rage. When he saw his brother thus accused, he could not divine the accusers. The Queen Mother meanwhile passed away. They say that then Carvalho confiscated all her letters and learned the source of the accusations. Thus he had conceived such a massive anger against the Jesuits that he planned for their destruction. If that is not the truth, it certainly is very much like it. For at the beginning Carvalho faulted only the Maranhão Jesuits, and seemed to hate only these. Other Jesuits he spared.

Jesuits Use Earthquake to Preach Repentance

In addition there occurred a most disastrous earthquake which will make 1 November 1755 a memorable day for all time at Lisbon. Hence stemmed another occasion for Carvalho's opposition, a new stimulus for his hatred of Jesuits. I leave to others to describe the destruction of buildings, the loss of life, the filth and squalor caused in that great city. What pertains to my theme is this. The survivors of that enormous disaster, both men and women, were frightened and pale with fear. They fled to the open fields and eked out a miserable existence, some in tents, others in the open air. The Jesuits thought this an opportune time, a fitting occasion, to instill piety. They divided up the roads and went out among the people. With a crucifix in the lead, they went through the surrounding area and gathered the general public for a sermon. They exhorted all to a detestation of their sins. They kept saying the offended Divine Power must be appeased, that the anger of heaven must be averted by salutary penances. Such a catastrophe was brought down upon the flourishing city not by human trickery nor by some fortuitous chance. It was a punishment inflicted by God for sins which outraged the Divine Majesty and which threatened even more grave punishments for the guilty unless they came to their senses in time.

Putting these thoughts in suitable sermons, they brought about abundant fruit for their labors. For very many were frightened out of their old habits of sin, and seeking peace with heaven, they threw themselves at the feet of the priests. They relieved their consciences of heavy burdens with many tears. So many flocked to confession that there were scarcely enough priests to hear them. [22]

The situation pleased the pious king, so much so that he thanked the Jesuit Provincial for such service and ordered money to be paid out of the royal treasury to repair the provincial house which had partly collapsed. But Carvalho thought completely otherwise. Two things greatly troubled him. One was that the king seemed mollified toward the Jesuits when Carvalho was secretly striving to alienate the king from them. The second was that the Jesuits attributed the unusual earthquake to the crimes of the city, as if more and graver sins than ever before were being committed at Lisbon under his administration. Carvalho considered that charge to be disgraceful and even spiteful toward himself. He began to insist openly that the necessary effects of natural causes were not a matter of heavenly wrath. Tremors of the earth come from gasses shut up in the ground, which are seeking an outlet. Those who ascribe them to God as a punisher of sin are not only ignorant and uncouth, but are also revolutionary and in their rebellion try to cover their perfidy with piety. They are misusing the confusion of the people to stir up the masses. With such words he was carping at the Jesuits and turning the people from piety.

Carvalho Attacks Malagrida

At that time there was at Lisbon a famous Jesuit, Gabriel Malagrida.[4] He was an Italian and a saint in everyone's view. He had gained the reputation for holiness from his great labors and accomplishments in Maranhão. Then he worked with sodalities and in giving the Spiritual Exercises of St. Ignatius. When Malagrida heard what Carvalho was claiming so openly and, I may say, so impiously, he was inflamed with zeal for the divine glory. He wrote a brilliant speech in which he proposed that, though earthquakes, pestilences, and droughts occur from natural causes, still God directs, guides, and plans them for punishing and correcting sinners. He clearly demonstrated his thesis from Sacred Scripture, the Fathers, and theological reflection. Nor was he concealing the fact that many things were being permitted in Lisbon, especially in religious houses, which were provoking the divine anger.

The oration was duly approved by the censors and printed. He sent it to the king and to the royal family, and he gave a copy to Carvalho himself. I do not say he was imprudent. For the prudence of saints is much different from our more common and ordinary prudence. The situation certainly led to Malagrida's ruin. The king, when he read the oration, was uneasy and silently reflected upon himself. He was debating whether he should make a retreat as soon as possible under the direction of Malagrida. [23] He considered Malagrida a truly saintly man and honored and esteemed him. If he had done that, no doubt all Carvalho's schemes would have been destroyed. And nothing would have been more proper than that this powerful man, like a Sejanus, should be removed from the pinnacle of power and reduced to the status of an ordinary citizen.

But Carvalho, that shrewd man, having sensed what was happening and out of fear and anger, met the crisis in this way. He goes to the king in a state of panic. He informs the king that he has uncovered a foul sedition of the people. It will soon break out unless it be repressed in time. The leader and fomenter of this sedition—a fact that ought to appear strange to him—is Malagrida. He has a big following because of his reputation for holiness. He has already sounded the trumpet of doom. The oration, which he spread among the people under the cloak of a false piety, now has led to his forming cadres of revolutionaries and under the safe name of Spiritual Exercises, he is concocting secret plans.

The king, as I said, was by nature timid. He was thoroughly shaken by such an unexpected denunciation. He asked what he should do. Then Carvalho said the head of the aroused throng must be destroyed. That troublesome man must be expelled from the city as soon as possible and sent far away. Otherwise the public peace and safety of the king himself cannot be provided for. The rest Carvalho will make his concern. The king, thus put on the spot, entrusted his safety to Carvalho alone and handed over all decision-making power solely to him. Nor did Carvalho delay in executing his evil designs. He wanted that hated and feared Malagrida driven far away on that very day. But in order that the city not take offense at the exile of such a man who enjoyed a reputation for holiness and whom all, both highborn and lowly, considered sent from heaven, and in order to deflect the deed's unpopularity, Carvalho wanted the matter handled by the Pontifical Legate, who at that time was Filippo Acciaiuoli.[5]

And so on the same day, Carvalho went to the Legate, and stating that the king had due cause to want Malagrida driven from the city, he pressed him with the authority of the royal name to order Malagrida to depart immediately and to go into exile to Setúbal, a town twenty-four miles distant from Lisbon. Malagrida did what he was ordered so obediently that he immediately broke off a retreat that he was giving to a group of women and went to Setubal without delay; nor did he ever leave there until three years later when he was called, as we will see below, to Lisbon to defend himself on the charge of treason. Carvalho, however, was believed to have designated Malagrida for such a blow since he had caused him so much fright. What punishment his audacity sought out will have to be told in its place.

Carvalho continued after this to violently assail those who attributed the earthquake to divine vengeance. He went so far in his madness [24] as to forbid prayers of petition and other public signs of penance which had begun to be commonly practiced to appease the divine will. But he had the ulterior motive of further instilling in the mind of the king a fear of sedition, and so he forbade public gatherings.

These were the principal causes that stirred Carvalho against the Jesuits. There were perhaps other minor reasons, but ones no less effective in exasperating that fierce, violent, easily insulted man. There were perhaps some Jesuits—as there always are in a large group—so imprudent as to speak too critically of Carvalho and who provoked him with their ill-considered remarks. They say that one Jesuit, when he was speaking in public, violently denounced a company of merchants which Carvalho, to his great profit, had set up to deal in port wine. The Jesuit openly condemned the company for exercising an unjust monopoly. If this denunciation was made, I certainly could not excuse the Jesuit's boldness and rashness.

Carvalho Continues Campaign Against Jesuits

Perhaps also, as the Jesuits fought at close quarters with Carvalho over power, they made attacks on his strength, and were trying to bring him back down to the level from which they had advanced him. I have no doubts that the Society's enemies—few though they be and this is to be reckoned a great plus—added fuel to the fire. They used the occasion to inflame Carvalho against the Jesuits in hate-filled conversations and false—may it please God— reports. They goaded him on when he was already galloping on his own.

Certainly after that foul earthquake at Lisbon, Alessandro Ratta returned from there to Rome. Up to that time he had been an auditor on the Pontifical Delegation. (Now he is an auditor for the Roman Rota, no less notable for his integrity than for his learning and wisdom.) He reported that another kind of earthquake was imminent in Portugal: the pressing fear that the Jesuits would be overwhelmed. Their affairs were in difficult straits. A huge rift had occurred between the court confessors and the prime minister of the realm, Carvalho. Nothing could be predicted about the outcome. The king was still wavering, uncertain in mind and fluctuating between the two sides. But if Carvalho gets the upper hand—may the powers above prevent it—the Jesuits will undoubtedly be reduced to the direst straits, given Carvalho's character. And he will easily win in the conflict since the Jesuits defend themselves with only honorable means while he, on the other hand, will use any device at all to crush the Jesuits.

I heard Ratta saying such things more than once, but Ours scarcely believed him. For at that time, the Jesuit Antonio Cabral was serving as ambassador of the king of Portugal to the Holy See. [25] He and the Jesuit court confessors were said to enjoy great favor and authority from the king. There was nothing they could not do. There was no indication of a change in the king's mind. But that Ratta spoke the truth was all too painfully borne out by what soon followed.

Joseph I Writes to Father General Centurione

Luigi Centurione was head of the Society in 1757 when the first rumblings of the growing storm in Portugal were heard.[6] Centurione suddenly received a letter from the king couched in kindly terms, but threatening something troublesome and causing him wonder and worry. The letter was full of complaints against explicitly named Jesuits who were caring for Christians in Maranhão.

That was all the more remarkable, for three years earlier when Centurione informed him of his election to the Generalate, the king praised all the Jesuits in his kingdom, but in a specially expansive manner those of Maranhão. It appeared that the king was obviously alienated and that after a spell, for no known reason, he had changed not only his good will toward, but also his assessment of, the Jesuits.

In response to this letter Centurione wrote back to thank the king first of all because he had informed him of such matters. He professed, however, that he knew nothing of these things. He hoped that whatever was wrong was not beyond remedy. He would see to it that any aberration that may have crept in among the Companions in Maranhão would be removed according to the king's wish. He was writing in this vein to the Father Provincial and he was giving him as appropriate mandates as he could. The General gave the mandates, but they had no effect. For Carvalho wanted not the correction, but the removal and destruction of the Companions—a plan which was already worked out in his mind. But Centurione did not see the evils that followed from these beginnings, for in the first days of October, he succumbed to an illness that he had contracted before and which gradually got worse. Worn out by the lingering illness, he died at the Society's villa at Castel Gondolfo on 2 October 1757.

Timoni Serves as Vicar-General

The Society's custom was that the General substitute, before his death, a vicar for the time of the interregnum until another General might be duly elected. That office Centurione had conferred upon Giovanni Antonio Timoni, a Greek by nationality.[7] He was a good, learned, and, so many thought, industrious man. He immediately took charge of the Society and called a General Congregation for the following year. [26]

Scarcely had things begun to settle, when a new sign of a storm in Portugal appeared. Cabral, who as I said before was serving as the king's ambassador to the Supreme Pontiff, was suddenly ousted by a letter of Carvalho. He was ordered to drop the office and title and to hand them over to a certain Portuguese named Almada. Almada was a man of no account, a relative of Carvalho. He was living at Rome in poor rather than moderate circumstances. It is easy to see how readily character is changed with fortune and how truly it has been said that there is nothing prouder or more arrogant than a poor man suddenly become rich. When Almada came into his wealth and position, though accustomed previously to openly fawn upon Cabral and to cadge some money off of him under the pretext of friendship, he had scarcely been marked off with the title of Royal Ambassador and received that income when he began to spurn Cabral with unbearable haughtiness, to disdain speaking to or looking at him, and even to show himself openly hostile. In addition Almada lashed out with reproaches and curses against the Society to which he previously professed himself to be absolutely devoted.

At the same time reports corresponding to these were being brought from Lisbon. Each ship that arrived from Maranhão carried Jesuits deported from there. The city was astonished at their return, for it previously had seen Jesuits frequently setting out for America; now Lisbon was beholding them returning in even greater numbers. Of course Mendoza, who, as I said, was in power in Maranhão, punished with exile all whom he knew to be opposed to his schemes, no matter their merits or their age. He would put them on ships and send them back to Europe.

But Carvalho was turning over in his mind even greater things. He understood there would always be a delay of his initiatives as long as the Jesuits had access to the king. He determined to block that access altogether inside an hour. In the quiet of the night after their retirement, the five Jesuit court confessors who were living in the palace were rousted from bed. Carvalho ordered them to be carried by carriage to houses of the Society. He then issued an edict to forbid them and any other Jesuit to go to the royal court. He laid down capital punishment for those who dared to do otherwise. Their many wealthy friends and supporters in the court he banished, not only from the palace but also from the city. He sent various ones off in various directions, even to the ends of Africa and America. Once that was done and there was no one left to plead the Jesuits' case with the king, the way was open to accomplish his other designs.

When this sequence of events was reported at Rome, Timoni saw that these acts of cruelty were just the beginning of something greater. Therefore to avert the storm, if he could, [27] he wrote a letter to the king, full of humble submission. He sought to soothe his anger and to be obliging. If the Jesuits had committed some fault, he would punish them severely. If the king wanted something among the Jesuits corrected, if he wanted something changed, all would immediately be corrected according to his wish, all would be changed. He would omit nothing that would serve to placate the king's anger. Timoni asked only that he moderate his anger and not allow his original good will toward the Society to lessen for whatever reason.

Timoni received no reply. But as if Centurione were still alive, the king responded not to Timoni but to Centurione's previous letters so that he seemed to be angry only with the Maranhão Jesuits. He alleged that they had committed many crimes and outrages which were unknown at Rome and were escaping the notice of the General. But in these letters too, the king treated Centurione nicely and respectfully.

Carvalho Publishes More False Accusations

Meanwhile an incriminating pamphlet began to be spread at Rome. Its title was *The Republic of Paraguay* and it stirred up great hatred for the Jesuits. In the pamphlet, Carvalho, or whoever else the author was, charged that since they were pastors and directors, the Jesuits stirred the people to sedition and steeled them to resistance by word and deed. The pamphlet depicted the pastors in military array. It asserted that armies were drafted by the Jesuits, battle lines drawn up, and machines of war deployed. It claimed that the war was so directed and led that the armies of two powerful kings, those of Spain and Portugal, could not, even with their joint forces, break the ferocity of those people.

These claims brought a smile to readers. But what is more remarkable, the author claims that the Portuguese Jesuits working in Maranhão agreed with the Spanish ones in this business. The contention is that the Portuguese, who are naturally opposed to the Spaniards, preferred to favor the Spanish king rather than their own and that they put aside their national traits because they were Jesuits.

Next, the pamphlet depicted all the Jesuit missions in black colors, both those in Maranhão and Brazil and those established in Paraguay. It asserted that the Jesuits had seized vast tracts of land under the pretext of spreading religion, had instituted a tyranny over vast provinces, and had so strengthened their power that they seemed invincible. Meanwhile they conduct themselves as kings. They judge the people. They administer public and private matters as they wish. They exercise a dominance that is subject to no laws, that is clearly unchecked. Thus the pamphlet was describing the form of that most just and admirable rule [28] which kings had ratified with their laws, which long experience approved, and which a writer of our times, Muratori, admires and praises so much in the book *Christianesimo felice*.[8]

Countless copies of this pamphlet were immediately spread through the whole city. Almada was passing them out and almost forcing them upon the unwilling. In every social group and gathering, the pamphlet was eagerly read.

Benedict XIV (Lambertini)

Most, however, marveled more at such horrendous things than believed them. The Jesuits endured the situation in silence. For they did not have the means to defend the reputation of their comrades who were so far away. But at Madrid the Fathers of the Holy Inquisition took up their defense by condemning in a solemn judgment the pamphlet as libelous and by ordering it to be burned by the hand of the executioner. Next, the above-mentioned Barbara, the queen of Spain, refuted in her way the pamphlet and declared it fictitious, not by her word, but by her deed: She was dying at this time and bequeathed to the Portuguese Jesuits 100,000 gold pieces for the use of the Maranhão missions.

Meanwhile the pope, Benedict XIV, worn out by sickness and old age, passed away. He died on 2 May 1758, on which day he did the Society a signal favor by a decree on the virtues of Francesco de Geronimo whom the Neapolitans call their apostle.[9] That event was not only a notable credit to our order, but also very opportune because of the conditions of the times. For de Geronimo had lived within our memory and proved that not just in the preceding century, as our foes were gratuitously contending, but also in these later times men of attested holiness had flourished in the Society.

Benedict XIV Appoints Saldanha Visitor

But the joy over the decree was cut short by information on an apostolic letter. By the letter the pontiff one month before had appointed Cardinal de Saldanha visitor and reformer of the Society in Portugal.[10] The King's minister had so skillfully elicited this letter that neither Timoni nor any other Jesuit at Rome had an inkling of it. As soon as it spread to the public, however, everyone saw the clever hand of Carvalho. When he had fixed it in his mind to attack the reputation, property, and standing of the Jesuits, he wanted to impress on the Portuguese people, who were religious by nature and revered the Society, that the attack was being made on the Society by the authority of the Supreme Pontiff. For he had Saldanha in his power and had no doubts he could sway him as he wished.

Benedict was afflicted with an incurable dysuria and distracted by other cares. There is doubt—and a reasonable doubt—whether he ever read or saw the letter, which, as we say, was in the form of a brief [29]. For there were certain things in the letter which the pontiff with his learning and insight was not about to approve. To pass over other things, at first Saldanha was forbidden to decide anything of major import without consulting the Holy See. Later a faculty was given him that had no limitations. Add the fact that Florio, who wrote the letter and signed it for Cardinal Passionei, Secretary of Briefs, may rightfully be considered guilty of deceit and fraud.[11] Indeed in the next pontificate we see him consigned to Castel Sant' Angelo though under no published charge, where he perished awaiting trial.

But however that may be, to the letter's Latin text which was written in broad, sweeping terms, Benedict had, on his own, added other remarks in the vernacular by which he clearly and eloquently explained what he wanted done. We received a copy from Giampedi of Ancona, a very good and honest man, who wrote the letter at the pontiff's dictation. The gist of the letter was this: At the outset the pontiff severely admonished Saldanha that he was not to use the power granted him except for the obvious good of the Society. Apostolic visitations of religious orders are undertaken only for renewal of discipline, should there be any decline. Benedict then said that the Jesuits were being accused by the king and many charges were leveled at them. But all seemed questionable. Accordingly Saldanha should not readily accept accusations. He should hear the accused, allow for exceptions, and hear defenses. He should not delegate for himself any as visitors unless they be respectable, above suspicion, and free of all bias. He should especially be careful that matters be conducted in secret so that there would be no leak of information that would do harm to the Jesuits' reputation. Let him recall that the order had served the cause of Christianity well. With its sweat and blood it had extended the name and faith of Christ to the ends of the world. At the end he was to send to Rome the *acta* of the visitation, duly signed, and he was not to issue any public decree which the Holy See had not approved beforehand. These were the pontiff's directives. What Saldanha in obedience to the pope did we will shortly see.

Jesuits Elect Father General Ricci

Six months had passed since the death of Centurione, and the elected Fathers were at Rome from every region to elect a new Father General. Only the Portuguese were absent. For Carvalho did not allow so many trumpeters and witnesses of his just deserts to come to the Eternal City. They observed properly all the legal and customary requirements, and all things considered, no one of that large group seemed worthier of the office than Lorenzo Ricci [30]. He had a great and obvious holiness. He was mild, genuine, candid, and highly prudent whether he was acting or speaking. He was of no ordinary learning as he had long shown in his teaching career at the Roman College in both secular and divine subjects. In addition to these qualities, he was of noble Florentine blood, the right age, closer to his prime than to declining years, and of pleasing exterior. Lack of experience was his only drawback. For before this he had held no office in the Society. But to counter this defect, he gave hope that he would undertake nothing without the advice of his consultors and would rule not so much by his judgment as by law.

I had a special love for the man, and perhaps he was the closest Jesuit friend I had. We had grown up together so that the bond of friendship could scarcely be tighter. I think you recall, brother, that when you were living at the Clementine College in Rome, I used to come to visit you, but never without Ricci. Already then he was the most intimate of my companions. He knew all my personal affairs and that same intimacy perdures till this day. But although that was the case, I wanted nothing less than that such a burden be placed upon such a man at such a time. I grieved that this innocent soul was tossed into a sea of such boundless turbulence and I sensed he would be easily overwhelmed by the force of the storm. I think he would have been most suitable

Lorenzo Ricci, S.J.

for ruling the Society if the sea were peaceful and calm. But I thought him less apt, because of his native placidity and calm, to be at the helm amid such stormy conditions. For I thought that unusual means had to be taken in those unusual circumstances, as those times were. Something extraordinary had to be ventured upon, something outside the usual.

Others felt far differently. They asserted that nothing should be put up against the growing storm except silence and patience. If you were to resist a bit, all would turn to the worse. That view prevailed. I still do not see what worse thing could have happened to the Society. And so when the Fathers inclined toward Ricci because they thought he would direct the community well and with success, on 21 May 1758 they elected him General of the Society by universal agreement.

Saldanha's False Accusations

A few days after this the first fruits of the Portuguese visitation appeared at Rome. A decree of Saldanha was printed that was most reproachful toward the Society. As many Jesuits as there were under the jurisdiction of the Portuguese King were alleged to be carrying on sordid commerce, and as if they were caught red-handed they were declared to be wicked violators of the sacred canons. The decree was issued on 2 May, the very day [31] that Benedict had died and one month after the letter of visitation was sent from Rome. So you see how promptly and exactly did Saldanha obey the Supreme Pontiff's order that the name and reputation of the Society were not to be harmed nor was Saldanha to issue public decrees which the Apostolic See had not duly reviewed and approved beforehand!

The following events were even more noteworthy. He issued the decree before he had interviewed any Jesuit or initiated any form of the apostolic visitation. Finally, it was not apparent what Saldanha meant by this decree of his. For in fact it was deciding nothing, and it appeared that this renowned reformer of religious orders wanted not to correct faults but to broadcast them. At least he might have restricted himself to spreading the bad report about the Jesuits only in Lisbon. But this man was shamefully sold out to Carvalho and had sent instructions to all the visitors in Portuguese territories that they should sign their names to that same decree and see to it that it be published in their respective provinces. Archbishop de Mattos of Bahia hesitated, declaring that it was not right to cast such aspersions upon religious men without their case being heard. Testimony of the most honest citizens cleared them of every taint of commerce. Accordingly Carvalho ordered de Mattos deposed from his see, and when he stripped the bishop of his property, he reduced him to beggary. But our treatment will return to this point below.

Meanwhile Saldanha's decree was translated into all the modern languages and spread through the whole world. Almada ordered a thousand copies to be printed immediately at Rome. Through his agents, many of whom were monks, he saw to its distribution to religious houses, including even convents of nuns. A certain Portuguese, Rodrigues by name, played a major role in this business. The foulest of persons, he was Almada's secretary and had recently left the Franciscans, the group they call Friars Minor Observant. The Jesuit Cabral, concerning whom I spoke above, had kindly helped Rodrigues financially when the latter wanted to be received into that religious family, but did not have the funds to purchase a habit. But it is, as it were, the fate of Jesuits that they often do kind deeds to the undeserving and find those whom they help to be ungrateful.

But it was not difficult to refute the lies of the decree and to answer the false accusation with a true rebuttal. For the Jesuits in Maranhão and Brazil did not buy what they sold and that is the essence of forbidden commerce. But they had fruit-bearing estates which were set aside to sustain them and the missions. From the produce that was left over they sold things and made necessary purchases for themselves and the missions [32] of things imported from Europe. Just as we turn grain, oil, and other things of that sort to our use, so they had in their possession cocoa plantations, sugar refineries, and other things of that type for the area's produce. And in some places the kings had granted fishing rights. Accordingly, they gathered into storehouses quantities of cocoa, sugar, dried fish, and foodstuffs of this sort. These they brought to the leading markets, especially Lisbon, where the profits were greater. The Jesuits had continuously done this after the missions in the New World had somewhat stabilized and this in full view not only of the people, but also of ecclesiastical superiors and even papal nuncios. No one had seen canons violated. No one had found fault with the system.

What is more, all the religious of the other orders who have missions in that part of America openly and publicly use the method. No one was complaining. That very scrupulous defender of the canons, Carvalho, was conniving at it. To be sure, the storehouses of the Jesuits were richer than the storehouses of others. But that was because they served with their holy missions more and larger provinces.

Ricci Forbids Jesuits to Refute Charges

If only these things were explained, the infamy from Saldanha's decree would undoubtedly have been dissipated. And there were some Jesuits who were ready to take up the pen for a precise answer; but Ricci forbade it. He thought the calumny would die on its own and he had settled in his mind not to oppose unjust attacks except through modesty, silence, and patience.

But Carvalho, on the other hand, kept advancing towards his goal. He piled still more unjust deeds upon his wicked beginnings. He was thinking that the decree had not sufficiently humbled the Jesuits' pride. For the people flocked to their churches no less than before. And because they seemed unjustly harassed, many nobles supported them that much more fervently and openly. Carvalho decided he had to do something to weigh the Jesuits down with more serious unpopularity and keep so many of the common people and the nobility from contact with the Jesuits. With this in mind he went to the Patriarch of Lisbon, Cardinal de Atalaja.[12] He said a few things on the subject and then reported that it pleased the king that the Patriarch forbid the Jesuits who were within the boundaries of the patriarchate the ministry of preaching and hearing confessions. Atalaja is said to have resisted stoutly and for a long time the issuing of such an interdict because it would bring harm to divine worship, the salvation of souls, and would meet with great resentment from the people. Nor, in truth, was he unaware that bishops were forbidden by a constitution of Clement X to submit an entire religious family to a penalty. Whatever excuse Atalaja offered, Carvalho would not brook being resisted, and finally he obtained by force and fear what he could not get by persuasion [33]. By alleging the king's indignation, he broke down the man's firmness; and so, though most unwilling, Atalaja signed the unjust decree. On the same day, to avoid seeing the sadness of his flock, he retired to his villa where three days later he passed away, worn out by illness.

Carvalho was extremely pleased with the successful outcome of his schemes. For the Jesuits had previously laughed at the empty declaration of Saldanha since they were buoyed by the people's favor and supported by their friendships with the nobles. He now saw them dejected and almost dispirited by this unexpected thrust. He was thinking that an altogether lethal blow had been inflicted.

Cardinals Elect Clement XIII

While these things were going on in Lisbon, the cardinals were meeting in conclave at Rome to elect a new pope. There was never such expectation in the city. The interests of men were never so various, never so keen. The city was almost split into factions. Some wanted a pope favorable to the Jesuits, others one who was hostile, according to how their inclinations affected them. Like a madman, Almada scurried about here and there with his followers and underlings. He tried to inflame with his crazed shouts every class of men against the Jesuits. The Jansenists, who were always plentiful in the city, thought this was their time, their opportunity. So now they were as alert as they could be to their advantages. The heads of the group sent some picked men from France to pursue vigorously the sect's interests. The Jesuits wavered between hope and fear.

But the cardinals were intent, as was fitting, only on the benefit of the Church. They determined that no one was to be elected who did not stand out for his wisdom, deliberation, and virtues. He was to be no less worthy of the highest office among men than capable of sustaining such a great burden. Eighteen of them—and this was a sufficient number to block any candidate— had bound themselves by oath to never agree to a man who was thought hostile to the Jesuits. My witness for this is the author of that agreement, Gianfrancesco Albani.[13]

For a long time the Fathers leaned toward Guidobono Cavalchini.[14] He was very upright and experienced. He was from Tortona and was all but elected. In the midst of this movement, Cardinal Luynes, who represented the name and authority of the French king, arose and intervened, saying Cavalchini was not at all acceptable to his king.[15] That one comment pushed that most deserving man from the pinnacle; but he, however, was not shaken by the blow.

Since Cavalchini was rejected, the eyes of the Fathers turned to Carlo Rezzonico. He was especially acceptable to those who had sworn for a pro-Jesuit candidate. There was nothing you would not approve of in this man. [34] His disposition was mild, his manner open, his personal habits most disciplined. In addition, his mien was dignified, his modesty remarkable, his kindness in dealing with others the highest. He had enormous experience in the conduct of public business and was often proven by trials, for as a young man he had administered with distinction several cities in the Papal States. Next he was elected to the Duodecimviral College which the Romans call the Sacred Rota. On that prestigious, international board, he administered justice for a long time with a most favorable reputation for judgment and prudence. Finally, he was chosen for the cardinalate and appointed to the see of Padua. He so directed that church for several years that he fulfilled in outstanding fashion all the duties and roles of the good and holy pastor.

Yet two things seemed to stand in the way of his being made pope. One was that he favored the Jesuits more earnestly than the spirit of the times required. The second was that he was a Venetian, for the Venetians had but recently passed some law or other of which Benedict did not approve. Benedict was more or less indulgent toward the power of princes, but he thought this law detracted too much from the papal dignity and therefore wanted it investigated and abrogated altogether. When the Venetians insisted on stoutly defending the law which they had passed and considering it valid, Benedict had desisted without accomplishing his aim. In this disagreement, however, it did not seem right to elect as pope one who had such close ties to the Republic of Venice.

Nor were the cardinals unaware of this. But if ever at any other time it was permissible to perceive that the election of the Supreme Pontiff was directed and guided by a certain divine inspiration and will, that evidently occurred now. There were altogether forty-four cardinals at the conclave. Twenty-nine of the cardinals agreed on Rezzonico. Only two votes were lacking for the required number, but there was no hope that Rezzonico could add them. Yet it was decided to make a trial ballot, not with any hope of completing the election, but to show, as often happens, the power of the faction. However, when the ballots were opened, thirty-one votes were found to be for Rezzonico, with only thirteen not for him. Since two-thirds was the required majority for election, what started out as a trial of strength ended up in the proper election of Rezzonico. In an inquiry into what had so surprisingly and unexpectedly happened, it was learned that two French cardinals had crossed over in order to have the glory of making the pope, but they communicated their intentions to no one. Secretly they transferred their votes to Rezzonico. This was done on 6 July 1758 and the new pontiff took the name Clement XIII. [35]

BOOK II

Portugal, Part 2
Anti-Jesuit Cardinals; Assassination Attempt

The Roman people rather coolly received the election of a pope who was Venetian by birth and who failed to receive thirteen votes. Yet the people cheered themselves with the thought that they would have an excellent leader and a very saintly one who was such in fact and not just in name, for the man's piety was commonly known. It would be hard to describe the great rejoicing for the Jesuits and the applause of those predicting all would be well under such a pope. They could scarcely hope for a pontiff who was better disposed to their interests. I had a particular and personal reason for rejoicing because I had dealings with Rezzonico in my private life and I was the teacher of philosophy at the Roman College for his nephew, his brother's son Charles, who would soon be a cardinal and an elector to the papacy. I was a friend of his and likewise of his brothers Ludovico, Giovanni Battista, and Abondio.

However, in the general rejoicing of the Jesuits, I was grieving, nor could I completely hide the grief. One of my companions, I recall, who noticed that I was somewhat dejected, asked me the reason. I answered him, "What do you want? Rezzonico will have the office and insignia of the papacy, but Spinelli will have the power." Cardinal Spinelli was in other respects a very irreproachable man, but he was secretly hostile to the Society and quite clever about hiding this animus.[1] He was so influential with the pope that it seemed the pontiff would do nothing without his advice and approval. What hope was left for us with this man as the overseer of events and policies?

Cardinals Archinto and Spinelli

The prime minister [2] of the new pope, Cardinal Archinto, was increasing my anxiety. He was a good and prudent man, but likewise, it was alleged, rather adverse to Jesuits.[3] Finally, the very goodness of the new pope was terrifying me, for when that gift is in excess, it is a fault in a prince. I would have preferred a less favorable pope, but one equally upright and a little more clever.

Nor did my presentiments deceive me. As soon as Spinelli had the opportunity to speak with the pontiff freely and without witnesses, he brought up the Jesuits. He pretended that he was deeply moved by their misfortunes, [37] and he said that such an illustrious order should be helped. Assistance should be offered to those who serve the Church so well and are now in peril. But this should be done gradually and cautiously so that the situation does not worsen. Loud protests are especially to be avoided. The king of Portugal appears to be sorely aggrieved. He must not be further exasperated. Perhaps he can be mollified by prudent subterfuge and patience. If the pontiff were to proceed in any other way, he, as things stood, would be entering upon rash designs to the great harm of the Church. It is prudent to endure some small evils in order that more serious ones not ensue.

His words were very just in appearance, but full of deceit and fallaciousness. Spinelli so captivated the pontiff's mind that, although the wounds inflicted on the Society demanded a quick and effective medicine, still he thought he had to be always careful. And so he did not apply remedies to the wounds except for some minor ones which alleviated the wounds somewhat but did not cure them. Thus Spinelli for a long time deluded the pope and his nephew Cardinal Rezzonico.[4] At length the pontiff saw through the man and withdrew himself from his influence, but later than was needed, for the situation had advanced to the point that the evil was beyond every remedy. But let us not break the thread of our narrative.

On the day on which Ricci first came to pay his respects to the new pontiff, he brought to him a pamphlet of petition in which he expounded the initiatives of both the visitor Saldanha and the patriarch Atalaja. He humbly begged the pontiff to use his authority to defend the Society thus oppressed. The petition was composed with such modesty and moderation of language that there was not a single word in it that the king of Portugal or his minister Carvalho could justly complain of. When the pontiff read the petition, he commended three things to Ricci which he wanted Jesuits to observe carefully: silence, patience, and holy prayers. They should entrust other things to Divine Providence. After saying several things on the matter in a kindly fashion, the pope sent Ricci away.

He then handed over the petition to the Congregation of the Holy Office since he was not about to undertake anything important on the matter except on its authority and recommendation. Whatever business is brought to that committee ought to remain a complete and total secret. The cardinals and their advisors are bound to this by oath. Yet on the same day a copy of the petition was brought to Almada. It is uncertain who violated the pledge of secrecy. For there were present at that session: Passionei, Tamburini,[5] Spinelli, Archinto, and the protector of Portugal, Corsini.[6] Perhaps there were some others who were either hostile to the Society or bound by some link to the king of Portugal. The result is that you would not know upon whom the suspicion ought to fall. Still more, what each of the cardinals thought on the matter was soon spread through the whole city.

Nothing seemed more just [38] than that Saldanha's power as visitor be taken away, for he was misusing it; and that their ministries be returned by pontifical authority to the Jesuits to counter Atalaja's decree. If these two things had been done immediately and fearlessly, without a doubt the plans of Carvalho would have been upset and the force of the fierce persecution blunted. But a different view prevailed. Although the cardinals admitted that Saldanha and Atalaja had acted falsely and too unjustly, they still denied that any vigorous step needed to be taken because of the matter. The king of Portugal could be offended by it. They pushed forward the example of England, which, once split off from the Church, had never returned to obedience to the Roman pontiff after so many centuries. With this example many today are wont to frighten the popes away from stoutly resisting with priestly firmness the princes who undertake every sort of injustice. They think that all the Catholic princes are so many Henrys, prepared like the English king to rush into every crime and to split off from the Church's faith. It is as if there were no promises of Christ that keep the Church safe for all time against all the power of hell or as if there were no trust in God's help when the Church's concerns are at stake.

However that may be, when the pontiff received the answer of the Congregation, he could not approve of nor hide what had been done against the Jesuits in Portugal. He thought he had to avoid using too sharp a remedy. So he took a middle way. He ordered Archinto to write only this and to send directives to the nuncio Acciaiuoli but in a kindly way and as if Saldanha were acting on his own initiative: the decree made by Saldanha against the Jesuits has displeased the Supreme Pontiff especially since it is said that it was made with no judicial form being observed and the visitation was not even duly initiated. In the same vein, he was to indicate to Atalaja (for at Rome they had not yet heard of his death) that by a law of Clement X it was not permitted to him to interdict sacred ministries to all Jesuits and therefore the interdict ought to be lifted. With these moderate measures, Clement XIII not only did not benefit the Jesuits, but he also inspired greater audacity in Carvalho since Clement was revealing the fear that gripped him.

Anti-Jesuit Pamphlets

It was a matter of the greatest importance to Almada that Ricci's petition, about which I have been speaking, be forever buried since it disclosed the crimes of the Portuguese cardinals. Yet a few days later he ordered the petition published but with some explanatory notes added. He had purchased the pen of Urbino Tosetti to compose these notes.[7] Tosetti was from the Poor Clerics Regular of the Mother of God Congregation, a Piarist, and considered among his own as an eloquent author. He was truly a good writer, but also arrogant and sarcastic. Nicola Pagliarini, a leading printer of Rome, supplied the plates for the printing. For this reason, [39] as we will see below, he was condemned to the galleys.

When Ricci's petition first began to be distributed in the city, there was no one who did not marvel at Almada's blatant obtuseness. Because of his efforts, there were passing through men's hands accounts of so many and such manifest crimes of his people. Good men praised highly the modesty and prudence of Ricci. On the other hand, Tosetti's additional notes, which made up the bulk of the work, made the readers angry. In them there was nothing about Saldanha's decree, nothing about the Patriarch's interdict. They contained nothing pertinent. They contained only the charges that were now so stale—warmed up a hundred times over, refuted a hundred times—charges about regicide, about the Chinese rites, about illicit commerce, about moral teaching. It would seem that the poor commentator had nothing to say against Ricci's document. Otherwise he would have been more sparing of the slanders which he boldly spewed out upon the Jesuits.

It was most just that that pamphlet, which attacked a religious order so blatantly and wantonly with so many calumnies, be proscribed and placed on the index of forbidden books. Every law and the custom of the city called for this. But out of regard for the king of Portugal, this step was not taken. This lack of punishment made the Piarist all the bolder and barefaced in scattering his libels. The shameless slanderer added an appendix to his vile work because, I suppose, a second book was needed since he had not exhausted all sources of revilement. The inept fool tried to show in this work that Jesuits had always been disobedient and insubordinate to the Supreme Pontiffs and always hostile and dangerous for kings. He wanted thus to make the Society hateful to both the sacred and secular authority.

He counted up at least twenty kings and other princes who had been killed by the Jesuits either by the sword or by poison. And because Cardinal Archinto had passed away suddenly a few days before, he included that prelate in the number. Finally, in order to block every sort of interchange with the Jesuits, he attacked by name anyone in the city whom he knew to favor the Jesuits. Though they were excellent men in their status, wealth, and service, still he heaped horrible calumnies upon them. This son of a filthy fishmonger had such boldness, had such nerve because he was wearing the Piarist habit of Calasanctius.[8] The Jesuits were protesting in vain. The man and his work went unpunished by the pope in order to avoid provoking the king of Portugal.

By now (1759) it was absolutely clear that the pontiff had made a deliberate decision to make no move in the cause of the Jesuits that would, rightly or wrongly, offend the king of Portugal. This decision gave heart to the Society's enemies, whose heads and leaders were in the city to continue what they had begun. And then for the first time, perhaps, they began to think of suppressing the Society not only in Portugal, but also, if any way possible, in France and Spain. [40] There were certain indications of this dark conspiracy to mention which I think is apposite to my theme.

Jesuits Alleged to Be in Disfavor

The new pope had two nephews in the Roman College, Giovanni Battista and Abundio Rezzonico, very gifted young men. The pontiff himself had once been educated by the Jesuits at Xavier College in Bologna. The directors of the Roman College decided to hold games for the people in honor of the recently elected pontiff. The students were to perform both equestrian exercises and literary ones. Thus the courtyard was covered and decorated with banners and bunting so that nothing was missing for splendor and magnificence. On the scheduled day a great number of cardinals and bishops were present for the show along with almost all the city's nobility. The actors, who were picked from the whole student body, performed their parts so well that the entire crowd of spectators showed its approval by shouting and clapping.

But on the next day the Jesuits found fixed to the college doors a large sheet of paper with some verses to this effect:

> Let the Jesuits not console themselves with the people's applause.
> Soon they are to be expelled from Portugal, France, and Spain.

Nor are they to content themselves with the present pope
who will bring no assistance to them.

Many thought that these verses, so accurately predicting the future, were
composed by Cardinal Passionei. Surely they were written in the manner of
those demons who once gave responses from images. They were predicting to
the simple people the very events that they were setting into motion.

A letter gave another indication. There was a certain French priest by the
name of Clement who was an open Jansenist and was spreading that sect's
doctrine publicly in the city.[9] After a while he was ordered to leave for that reason. He wrote to his people in France that they were to proceed with fervor to
the accomplishment of their enterprise. They had nothing to fear from the
new pope. All access to him both in the papal palace and in the Congregation
of the Holy Office was blocked. There was no refuge left to the Jesuits.
Although the pontiff loved the Society very much, he is unable to benefit it
even if he should wish to. He will perhaps try to do something but it will be in
vain and to no effect. In this scenario the Jansenist was all too true a prophet.
His letter was returned from France to Rome and shown to many people
including myself.

Meanwhile Almada, seeing the pontiff's caution, was all the more fierce in
sounding the war cry against the Jesuits. Daily he drew to himself a larger
number of followers. For the most part, these were religious of different orders
and foreign priests. There was no Roman priest, as has been noted. On a certain fixed day, they came together in a predetermined house to discuss what
was needed to suppress the Society. Many proposals were made and opinions
[41] solicited. The execution of plans was left to Almada. None of this leaked
out to the public.

One thing was agreed upon at once: Every effort must be made to make
the Jesuits slip from the high esteem they had with the ordinary people. The
Jesuits had to be overwhelmed with libelous pamphlets spread through the
city. The old charges, no matter how false and though refuted a thousand
times, were to be published again and again. New calumnies are to be heaped
upon them. Lies must be told steadily, with conviction and firmness, zealously. Lies about matters in remoter places are not easily or so quickly discovered
and always stick a bit.

The gatherings of anti-Jesuit followers of Almada plotted the way of waging
war as the outcome showed. For after that time so many and such shameful
pamphlets aimed against the Society appeared, either newly written or
reprinted, that almost all of Europe was inundated with reproaches against
Jesuits. That foul outpouring spread to the distant Americas and to the Indies.

Next, there were some who in their desire to write up events in Rome spread pure fables each week to the disgrace of Jesuits. Others sent those tales to their friends, especially across the Alps. Others saw to it that they were reported in the *Lugano Magazine,* which then had wide circulation and popularity in Italy.

Then indeed the wicked would be especially exultant when they discovered some piece of truth on which they could build their monstrous lies. Let one situation serve as an example of the rest. In 1704, a medallion had been struck in honor of St. Francis Borgia. The medallion commemorated that famous earthquake which rocked the entire city and the fact that the saint's intercession was said to be powerful against earthquakes. The medallion bore the image of the saint and the inscription, "We will not fear while the earth is being shaken." It chanced that during those days a medallion of this type was found. There was no delay. They pretended that the medallion was recently struck by the Jesuits to show in bronze their steady and unshaken opposition to the king of Portugal. They brought the medallion around to their friends and to their enemies. They forced it upon whomever they met. They decried the strange pride, the marvelous rashness of men who, though they are so beleaguered, still dared to insult the king of Portugal in this way.

For a while the story gained some credence in Rome. To the great profit of the coin dealer, many medallions of the type were sold. But this man, since he was upright and a lover of justice, one day toward the end of his life emphatically declared in the presence of a large group of buyers that the die of that medal had been left to him by his father who had died forty years previously. To prove his statement, he showed the likeness of Borgia etched in bronze and [42] pressed out on paper with the date 1704. The obverse of the medallion had the same inscription, "We will not fear while the earth is being shaken," but the image was that of the duke de Uzeda, who was in those days the ambassador of the king of Spain to Clement XI. Thus the fraud was uncovered at Rome and the innocence of the Jesuits vindicated. But the calumny had been committed to writing and spread through other parts of the world. Perhaps even now in other places it remains fixed in men's minds and is believed with good faith.

Clement XIII's Attitude toward Jesuits

When the pontiff heard of these matters, he grieved for the wretched lot of the Jesuits and sometimes could not keep from weeping. But he never worked up the courage to check the effrontery of such an arrogant faction. He was not

Clement XIII (Rezzonico)

unaware of their hidden meetings which could have been scattered and dispelled by a single nod of his head. But he never gave the order. Rather he was swayed by Spinelli's advice. Spinelli kept harping away at the theme: Some things must be endured so that worse things do not follow. In this frame of mind, Clement never applied an effective remedy to the growing evil. He was always deterred from action for fear that he might exacerbate the king of Portugal. The uncontrolled fury and arrogance of Almada made him fear the more, for Almada kept threatening horrible things in the name of his king should there be any movement in favor of the Jesuits. The treacherous silence of the king himself added to the fear. Although he had received a letter from the pontiff announcing his election, he made no response even after several months so that he seemed to be doubting whether he believed that Clement XIII was duly elected and whether he wanted to revere him as the true successor of Peter.

I am quite reluctantly narrating such matters about the pontiff. He loved the Society very much. He gave me personally many excellent proofs of his benevolence. He seemed to be worn down by these events, to have been of faint heart, and to have been unwilling to check the growing storm against us in its rising. May I be permitted to say that he thought too humbly of himself and too highly of his advisers? If he had made determinations more on his own judgment than on the judgment of others, without a doubt he would have followed better counsels and would have resisted bravely the beginnings of the ills. For nothing less true could be said of him than that he was fearful by nature or ineffective in management. To the contrary, he had an enormous heart and when his pastoral office required it, he shirked no labor, no danger. This was proven by more than one test. But let us return to the track of the narrative.

In the midst of all this Cardinal Archinto, as stated above, had died. I will not pass over in silence that this important minister of the pontiff was considered no friend of the Jesuits. So all the more I am forced to praise in him a friendly trait. For in the beginning of his term of office, when *The Republic of Paraguay* [43] was being sold secretly, he ordered the seller to be sought out and expelled from the city. He sent all the copies of the book to us at the professed house.

Cardinal Torrigiani

Be that as it may, Cardinal Torrigiani succeeded Archinto.[10] He was a native Florentine, a man of proven goodness, a lover of the Society and more so of justice. He was a fast friend of his fellow citizen Ricci. Under his administration, the pontiff seemed to perk up somewhat and to be strengthened in the face of fear. At the same time the Jesuits' hopes were raised. The following was the first sign of this improvement in the Society's status. It happened that Torrigiani had received at Rome a letter full of lies from Giralamo Spinola, the pontiff's nuncio to the king of Spain.[11] In fact the letter had been written in Rome at those clandestine meetings. The letter contained the following urban events as if they were fresh and recent: Since the pontiff had learned of the Jesuits' wickedness, he forbade them to conduct any schools of literature. They were not to undertake the ministries of sacred preaching or confessions. They were not to come any longer to the papal palace. The Pope's two nephews who had been with the Jesuits in the Roman College were to be withdrawn and transferred to the Reverend Fathers of the Pious Schools. Accordingly, they had already changed their residence to the very famous Nazarene College. Ricci, the Father General of the Society, had been thrown into Castel Sant' Angelo and he was being put on trial by His Holiness' order.

The letter went on: The Companions seemed clearly dejected and dispirited by these things. They scurried here and there. Nowhere did they find help. Their friends grieved. Their supporters and the people generally hung suspended in wonder. The nuncio said innumerable copies of this Roman epistle were being spread about in Spain and were brought to religious houses by monks. Its author was not identified, but gradually unpopularity was being stirred up against the Jesuits. The letter alienated many. For who would not believe to be true things that were written with such assurance on Roman matters from that very city?

When he learned of these things, Torrigiani easily divined the source of these lies and where they were heading. Knowing well enough that the slanderers could not be kept from constantly trying similar ploys, he wrote in this vein to the nuncio in order to cut short any credence in such lies for the future: Those who wrote such things or who are about to write such are either envious men or have no conscience. For they are attacking with complete falsehoods and calumnies a very holy order, especially dear to the pontiff and most deserving of the Christian commonwealth.

This was the gist of the letter which Torrigiani signed by his own hand, and he sent the nuncio orders to distribute the letter around to all the bishops of Spain. He kept a copy at Rome and ordered that it be disseminated through the entire city. [44] What were the groans, what were the outcries of the Almada faction against Torrigiani! It was too great to be described in words. They made every place resound with their curses and threats. Almada was torn apart with pain and rage. The Jesuits, vindicated to a degree from infamy, enjoyed something of a respite.

Attempt on the Life of Joseph I

But at Lisbon, Carvalho was going along his own way (1759). He was bringing his plans to completion. It was the end of September when a blind rumor began to creep about at Rome. A wicked conspiracy of desperate men laid up the king of Portugal who was wounded by gun shots.[12] It was commonly thought he was going to die from his wounds. Nothing more convenient could have happened for the Jesuits, especially because the ambush was reportedly laid for the king for certain reasons that did not affect the Jesuits. Wiser heads, however, felt anxious because of Carvalho's character. They knew him to be fierce by nature, an accomplished fashioner of frauds. They had seen from his previous actions that he had planned the destruction of the

Society. They confidently foretold that the king would soon be better and the Jesuits would be, by hook or crook, implicated in this foul crime.

Their predictions did not prove false. Three months after the attempted murder of the king, an announcement was made at Rome that the king had miraculously recovered. The accursed murderers had been caught and thrown into prison. At the same time the Jesuits were put under house arrest and surrounded with armed guards. That fact so struck me that I thought we should go to extremes to avoid the threatening evil. Accordingly I tried to persuade Ricci to separate the provinces of Portugal from the body of the Society and to leave them to the governance of the visitor Saldanha as if they belonged elsewhere. He should ask the pontiff for the authority to do this if it were necessary. Otherwise the rest of the body cannot be saved, unless that member were amputated. That was certainly a radical plan, but perhaps necessary given the state of affairs. But if it had been adopted, Carvalho would not be sending more than a thousand Jesuits to Rome to Father General. But Timoni opposed the idea, taking it for certain that such a catastrophe would not ensue.

Meanwhile Carvalho hurried along the exaction of punishment for the attempted murder. The murder trial was completed less than a month after the accused were apprehended. They were subjected to the law's provision. The mind still shudders in recounting the inhumanity of the form of punishment. There was a huge scaffold erected in the largest square of the city. Under it was a pile of wood smeared with pitch and bitumen. A large number of cavalrymen and foot soldiers surrounded the scaffold to keep the crowd away. For the whole city streamed out to see the savage spectacle.

The first to come to view was Eleonora de Tavora. [45] She was a most respectable woman in her wealth, standing, and virtue. Up to this point she had been kept in a convent of consecrated virgins as if she were in legitimate custody. From the convent she was carried to the scaffold in a covered sedan chair. She was ordered to position herself on the block. The executioner cut her throat with a sharp sword. She is said to have accepted the deathblow with courageous heart and as befitted a noble and Christian matron.

There followed Eleonora in their turns: José de Mascarenhas, duke of Aveiro, Prefect of the Royal Residence; Eleonora's husband, Luis Marquis de Tavora, Chief Master of the Horse and once Regent of the Indies; then his son and brother, one of whom was a captain in the cavalry, the other a tribune of the archers; and finally his son-in-law, the Count de Atouguia. These five were easily the cream of the Portuguese nobility. Five other clients or servants of these drew up the rear of that unhappy procession.

As each one was led up on the scaffold, he was stripped, made to lie prone, and tied to a square cross. Then the bones in the feet and hands were broken with an iron pole. Finally, the executioner beat on their chests until they expired. Two of the servants, because they seemed more pernicious, were thrown into the flames alive and breathing. After this dreadful carnage, a fire was set under the scaffold and all the bodies were burned together. The ashes were thrown into the Tagus. Aveiro, a naturally fierce man and proud of his lineage and service, was wont to scorn Carvalho as beneath him. He did not cease howling as long as he was breathing, and he perished in a raving fit. The others in stubborn silence presented themselves to the executioner. This tragedy at Lisbon was acted out on 13 January (1759).

Nor was this the end of the savagery. All their property was confiscated. The Mascarenhas and Tavora mansions were razed to the ground. The coats of arms and statues of both families were taken down everywhere. Their names were erased from public inscriptions in order that the memory of their names, if it were possible, might not pass on to posterity. All of Europe rightly shuddered at the atrocity of this deed. But nonetheless Almada ordered the scene painted in vivid colors on a large canvas, thinking that his kinsman Carvalho had done something remarkable by defiling himself with the blood of such illustrious men.

The day before the execution, the printed court report began to be spread in Lisbon. The report supposedly proved the charge against the defendants. But the readers plainly saw that the document was too hastily put together. Many things were alleged to be clear, but were supported by no testimony, by no definite proof. No one confessed to a crime. No one was even questioned under torture. Concerning Eleonora de Tavora who was said to be [46] the spark of the conspiracy, the nuns asserted that during the whole month in which she was kept in their convent, no judge, no clerk, no investigator approached her.

Then, too, there were many things that had no likelihood. For the whole web of the plot was said to have been woven in this fashion: The duke of Aveiro was impelled by an implacable hatred for the king and he resolved to kill him in order to take over the kingdom. Accordingly he made an evil pact with the Tavoras and by great promises won their support and aid for the murder. Both families joined to themselves a picked band of assassins. They seized upon a period of the night when the king was returning to the city from his villa, riding in a carriage and with no escort. Divided into three groups they laid an ambush for him. The king, by God's favor, came out alive because the driver, as soon as he saw the gang of waylayers, turned around and drove the mules into headlong flight. The faithless men aimed their rifles at the fleeing king all the same and shot off some rounds of lead. From these the king received a serious wound in the arm.

Jesuits Implicated in Assassination Attempt

Doubtlessly the Jesuits were aware of this wicked conspiracy and were its fomenters. Three were named: Gabriel Malagrida, Jaô Alessandro Souza,[13] and Jaô de Matos.[14] This charge was based on what they called certain presumptions of the law which were said to be unassailable. The Jesuits had waged open war against the king over the change of territories in Paraguay. The king had expelled them from court and for that reason they were very angry. They had to hope for better conditions under a new reign. A few days before, Aveiro had begun to deal in a familiar and friendly fashion with them. Finally Eleonora de Tavora had made the Spiritual Exercises three years ago under Malagrida whom she revered as a saint. These, I say, were the irrefutable presumptions against the Jesuits and this a summary of their misdeeds.

Those knowledgeable in Portuguese affairs, when they read such stuff, scarcely dared to open their mouths as if they were overcome with terror. For it was a capital offense to utter even one unconsidered word. Yet they marveled at Carvalho's singular and incredible effrontery. He had no fears about selling openly these stories. He attached the name and prestige of a court to those so poorly contrived fictions. For what hope would Aveiro and his Tavora allies have of seizing the realm if they were supported by no troops, by no armed force whatever? If they wanted to kill the king, the men would scarcely have divided themselves into small bands given their number, their purpose, and their knowledge of fighting. They would not have used rifles at long range since their accuracy is always doubtful. Rather, at close range they would have accomplished their object with drawn swords [47] and would have easily overwhelmed with one rush the unaccompanied and unarmed king.

If they had dared to do anything against the king, they should be thought to have been stirred to it not from a hope of obtaining the throne, but from a desire of vindicating their honor. They did not want him killed, but moderately castigated. They had a reasonable hope that the king would bear the matter in silence and would forgive the injury because of their just grievance. In this confidence, even after the wounds of the king were made public, Aveiro and Tavora continued for three months to carry on their business publicly in the eyes of all and to go to court. If they had guilty knowledge of a conspiracy to murder, undoubtedly they would be grasping at flight for themselves and each would be looking out for his own welfare. Everyone saw that the private offense of Tavora did not pertain to the Jesuits and least of all could Malagrida be dragged into the affair. For three years now he was absent from Lisbon. Yet no one was surprised that the Jesuits were implicated in the alleged conspiracy since Carvalho had destined them for destruction on whatever charge he could find.

But whatever the judgment of men would finally be, Carvalho earnestly followed up on his beginnings. In order to give the conspiracy some appearance of truth, he ordered a search for arms on the same day that the conspirators were punished. He asserted that arms were stockpiled with the Jesuits. He sent a large number of agents to search carefully every corner of the Jesuits' houses. No arms were found. Some sort of pretext and cover-up had to be devised for the people. The Jesuits, as if they were caught in the blatant crime of treason, were confined to their houses. He ordered them kept there as if in prison. He stationed soldiers at the entrances who allowed no one to enter or to exit. He commanded that their property of every kind be administered by royal overseers, and he declared that the Jesuits' assets be seized until arrangements with the Supreme Pontiff had been completed. The royal treasury provided them with an allowance for daily living—a tostâo a day for each man.[15]

At the same time he recalled Malagrida from Setúbal to Lisbon. Malagrida was now in his third year of exile. At first Carvalho treated Malagrida gently, but a little later he ordered him dragged off to the jail for the worst offenders. To Malagrida he added de Matos and Alessandro. Although they were said to have been discovered in the same conspiracy, still they underwent no further punishment. We will see that only Malagrida was condemned to the severest penalty three years later, and then not on a charge of conspiracy or murder, but of falsified sanctity. This is a clear proof that the court report was obviously too hastily put together, as I said before.

When these things had been finally completed, the king very officiously answered the pontiff's first letter although he had to excuse the very tardy response. [48] He made no effort to hide his feelings towards the Jesuits. Due to their crime, he had experienced a supreme peril to his life. He claimed his entire realm was badly shaken. The same courier that brought the letter to the pope brought the court report to Almada. He in turn ordered their immediate translation into Italian, the publication of the sentence, and their dissemination through the whole city. He bragged that his kinsman Carvalho had concluded a case of such importance so quickly and so satisfactorily.

But at Rome men's critical faculties were sharper, their words freer, and there was no fear of Carvalho. It is remarkable how the measures were commonly scorned and derided. "Is this," they were saying, "Portuguese jurisprudence? Where are the accusers? Where are the witnesses? Where is there any compelling proof? Where is there an admission of crime, even if only made under torture?"

Since there was some rumor about the king's passion for the younger Marchioness de Tavora and since they saw that she was the only one of the Tavoras in such a general slaughter to be exempted from punishment, the views of all inclined to the position that the king, if some mishap had occurred, should think that he had brought it upon himself and should put up with it in silence. Almada fumed and fretted. He attributed this boldness of speech to the Jesuits alone as if they were inspiring these sentiments in the people and were supplying the very words. Whatever insults that he heard uttered against the King and his minister, he carefully collected and sent off to Carvalho as if they had originated with the Jesuits. He had no regard for truth or falsehood. Once when advised by a friend that he should write only what was certain and proven, he answered that he was writing everything since there were at Lisbon men of very sharp intellect who could sift through things and separate the true from the false.

Carvalho, however, took everything as truth. Accordingly, after the Portuguese Jesuits had been expelled, he thought the Roman Jesuits ought to be punished even more severely. He did not even hesitate to assert in a public document that a much more heinous crime had been committed by those who had stained the king's reputation with words than by those who had laid an ambush for his life. I do not know if he persuaded anyone of this, or even if he himself believed it.

Jesuits' Moral Teaching Attacked

Up to this point Carvalho had charged only three Jesuits with a part in the conspiracy. He could persuade no one that all Jesuits agreed upon it—even those who were farthest away on the distant shores of Asia or America. But he wanted all condemned and outlawed on that charge. He therefore fabricated a new and quite remarkable accusation which would embrace all. The accusation pertained to moral teaching. He asserted that writers of the Society approved tyrannicide. He falsely accused especially Busenbaum, a famous author among the Jesuits, of this pernicious doctrine.[16] From it there arose,

[49] he pretended, the most foul conspiracy. He concocted the accusation in many high-sounding words. He ordered Almada to have it translated immediately into Italian and to be distributed through the whole city. But the public laughed at it as the last attempt of a dangerously crazed man who wanted to save his bad case in any way he could. There were some who wittily commented that if Busenbaum were guilty of conspiracy, Busenbaum should be punished and the rest pardoned.

Perhaps Carvalho himself saw that his own writings had very little effect in stirring the public's feelings. Therefore he thought he had to use the authority of the Church, which was great everywhere, but especially in Portugal. With that in mind, he compelled all the bishops of the realm in the king's name to write and promulgate pastoral letters against the Jesuits. That, in the manner of sheep, they did not only promptly, but also with such severity of language that they seemed to be attacking some abominable sect of heretics and not a religious order. For they condemned not only their teaching, but also the Jesuits' life, morals, and institutions. Indeed in a way they were condemning themselves, for previously they had held the Jesuits in honor and esteem. They had been accustomed to use them for the ministry of all the sacraments, to praise and broadcast them as particularly suitable workers in tilling the field of Christ. Now they seemed to admit their ignorance and stupidity, for to that time they had seen nothing amiss in the Jesuits' teaching, morals, and institutions.

Of course the orders of Carvalho weighed heavily upon the bishops, nor was it permissible for anyone to resist. One bishop did resist: the Head of the Holy Inquisition, the king's brother, Antonio. He said he could not publish any writing abusive of the Jesuits. But his resistance did not go unpunished. Because of it the pious prince was removed from his office and relegated to a deserted monastery some distance from Lisbon. There he lived out his days in obscurity. And just by the by, Carvalho put in his place Paul Carvalho, his brother, without asking for a papal document of appointment, which is required. This was the official, of course, who afterwards, with the power invested in him as Supreme Inquisitor, condemned Malagrida for falsified sanctity.

Carvalho's purpose and effort were to despoil the Jesuits of their reputation and esteem with men as he had despoiled them of their property and liberty. Thus he hoped the proscription of such a famous order would be less distasteful to the people. Accordingly, in addition to Portuguese publications, he ordered libelous pamphlets to be printed at his expense at Rome, at Lugano, wherever he could. One after another he ordered them spread in order to crush the reputation of the Society. But the Jesuits had acquired too great a name for learning and virtue for [50] it to be erased by futile writings such as these. Friends of the Society rose up to its defense. Several saw to the publication of works by prominent authors which contained eulogies of the Society. By a clever fiction the works were said to have been printed in Fossombrone, Passionei's hometown. In a short time there was such a supply available that they almost equaled the hostile books in number and surpassed them in authority and weight.

I had thought this a surer and more expeditious way of countering the bad reports. If our superiors had adopted it, they would have been muzzling the mouths of our detractors so that they could scarce mutter a word. After the storm in Portugal was stirred up, many bishops of every nationality, first the Spanish, then the French, Germans, Belgians, Poles, and Italians sent letters of commendation of the Society to the pope. They earnestly requested that he not allow the order to be oppressed by the wickedness of the evil. They used the occasion to praise profusely the Jesuits' learning, their apostolic labors, and their morals.

The Pontiff's Response

To each the pontiff responded in this vein: he praised highly their zeal for the Society; he stated he shared their regard and professed that he held the order in no less esteem. My idea was to collect into one volume the letters of so many bishops, copies of which had been sent to us. They would be published with Benedict's letter to Saldanha as a preface. This would make the Catholic Church's judgment on the Society most evident. Their authority would balance the pastoral letters of the Portuguese bishops, which had been extorted by force and fear. Empty would be the libelous, anonymous pamphlets; empty the lies of the *Lugano Magazine* and other things of that sort. They would be mud in the presence of gold.

Ricci, however, would not approve my plan, for he thought the bishops would take offense if they saw in print what they had written to the pontiff in private. The expense of the publication may also have carried weight with Ricci. No concession was made to my exhortations, arguments, and pleas. Instead, these excellent testimonies to our innocence were put away in the Society's archives—for no practical use.

At this time the pontiff was considering filling the Sacred College of Cardinals with a new consistory. He was very much indebted to the Corsini family since he had received the cardinalate through their favor. The family was now asking that the pope add to the College of Cardinals the Dominican Giuseppe Orsi because of their frequent and significant service to the pontiff.[17] Clement was also on the point of adding one cardinal from the Jesuits. He was considering whom he should choose for the honor.

Occupied with the deliberation, [51] he consulted with Erba Odescalchi.[18] The pope was using Odescalchi as appointment secretary. He was an especially prudent man, friendly toward the Society, and already named a cardinal himself. But he held Spinelli in high esteem and suggested almost nothing to the pope which Spinelli did not approve. Odescalchi did not deny that the order which was so sorely afflicted at that time should receive a cardinalate both to ease their pain and as a bulwark and strength. But, he added, there is a danger that the king of Portugal will take an honor to the Society as an insult to himself. The king was so disposed that he took everything in the worse way. Would it not be more in accord with reality and safer to give the Society a cardinal who was a Jesuit in spirit and will, but not an actual member? When the pontiff asked how this might be done, Odescalchi then proposed Ganganelli.

Odescalchi had heard that Ganganelli was an exceptionally learned and outstanding theologian. Yet he was so devoted to the Jesuits that he could almost be said to be another Jesuit in the Conventuals' habit. He said that he had heard this more than once from Andreucci, his confessor, a well-known Jesuit, commended by his published works.[19] In this way the Jesuits would have a cardinal almost as if he were one of their own and the king would not be offended.

The suggestion pleased the pontiff especially since he knew the Conventual Franciscans got on well with the Jesuits. And so without further delay he assigned to the illustrious College of Cardinals, Lorenzo Ganganelli, even though Ganganelli was not previously known to him. Thus the French priest Clement had written correctly that all approaches to the papal palace were closed off and the pope, though most fond of the Society, would not afford it anything of significance for its honor or safety.

While these things were being transacted (1760), Almada could not bear the public murmurings and the open hostility of the city. So he went off to the suburban Grottaferrata, twelve miles from Rome. There he was passing restless days with a few of his followers, thinking of nothing but the Jesuits. Then a courier came from Lisbon with a letter from the king to the pontiff. The letter brought Almada back to the city immediately. In the letter, the king complained bitterly about the Jesuits, both the Portuguese and the Roman. He charged that the one group had conspired against his person with weapons, the other against his name and reputation with impudent words. He averred that both groups should be punished severely according to the nature of their fault.

Along with the letter the king sent a bill of petition from the Royal Procurator and the king recommended the bill to the pontiff. In it, the pope was petitioned for the faculty of inflicting capital punishment on clerics, even the ordained, who had been found to have attempted murder. In addition he petitioned that the faculty be given to a standing lay tribunal.

When Almada brought these documents to the pontiff, he responded that he would write a reply [52] to the king's letter. With regard to the privilege that was being requested, some consultation seemed necessary. Then Almada said that he did not wish to have any dealings with Cardinal Torrigiani who was hostile to his king. Therefore the Pontiff should give him some other cardinal with whom he could deal respectably. Any other prince at all would have rejected this shameless request with anger and the king of Portugal himself would have balked if perchance the papal nuncio had dared to ask something similar with regard to his prime minister. The pontiff, however, felt he was dealing with a madman, who might drag everything down. And so in order not, over a trivial matter, to lose the chance of winning some favor with the king, the pope judged that he should accede to the request and granted him Cardinal Calvalchini as an arbiter in the matter.

But Calvalchini thought the petition was most just in the part that dealt with an actual crime. But on similar matters that could be perpetrated in the future, he judged that more careful examination was needed, and he suspended judgement. Accordingly, a papal document was issued. In it, the Board of Conscience (that was the Portuguese for "tribunal") received the power to condemn to death clerics of any order whatsoever, who had conspired to the murder of King Joseph or who had abetted that crime.

The pope answered the king's letter in these words: the privilege petitioned by the Royal Procurator is being sent, but the standing tribunal which was still under discussion is not. The king may do what is necessary for the present case and he hoped that his prompt response pleased the king. The pope could not condemn enough the perfidy of those who dared to plot murder for such a good and outstanding king, and he willingly admitted that no suitable punishment could be found for such a crime. Yet he asked and begged for the love of Christ that the king not shed any priestly blood. With regard to the Portuguese Jesuits, even if some were enmeshed in the crime, the pope thought that since there are so many of them and since they are so scattered geographically, all Jesuits could not have been equal participants. Accordingly he asked that all of them not be considered as one. Rather he should spare the innocent. He would see about the Jesuits in Rome and if any were convicted of having harmed the king's reputation, they would not get off unpunished.

This, in brief, is what the pontiff wrote, fairly and wisely. Still Carvalho was gravely offended. He objected first of all that the pope begged that priests not receive capital punishment even if they were guilty of foul murder. Then he claimed that it was even more intolerable that the pope thought some Jesuits were innocent when the king of Portugal had declared all of them guilty. But these matters will be treated more appositely below.

Torrigiani Fails to Prevent Expulsion

To return to the thread of my argument, Torrigiani had added to the pontiff's letter, which was included with the document under the same cover, [53] his own letter to the nuncio Acciaiuoli. In it he made several suggestions about placating the disturbed Portuguese. Besides other things Torrigiani said that the pope would not refuse, if there were need, to send to Lisbon a Cardinal Legate *a latere,* who might investigate matters concerning the Jesuits and could make decisions with papal authority. Carvalho held even this against Torrigiani, as we shall see. So he joined this letter of his to the pope's and the copy of the document. They were put together under one cover and duly sealed. Torrigiani gave them to a trustworthy—so he thought—courier to take with all speed to Lisbon to the papal nuncio Acciaiuoli.

Almada, however, had sniffed out what was happening. Immediately after the pontiff's, he sent his own Portuguese courier, whom he held in readiness, with instructions to snatch from the papal courier's hands the letters whenever he got the chance and to bring them straight to Carvalho. He gave him a large sum of money for this. The situation turned out according to Almada's wishes. When both couriers were at Marseilles, the Roman courier was bribed. He feigned a chance fall and a dislocated arm. For this reason he could not go farther and gave the letters to the Portuguese courier. He, in turn, raced through the rest of the journey and handed the letters over to Carvalho.

For three whole days Carvalho had the materials in his possession. He himself proved that he had broken the seals and read the letters, for in his wanton impudence he broadcast things which he could not have known except from the documents. After the three days he ordered the packet to be delivered to

Acciaiuoli. When he wanted to bring the pontiff's letter to the king, he was unable to do so. For there was joined to the letter, as I said above, a document on inflicting capital punishment on clerics. Because, Carvalho asserted, a standing privilege such as was requested was being denied, the letter could not be presented to the king. Acciaiuoli, therefore, since he thought it outrageous that the papal seals were broken, delivered neither the document nor the letter to the king. Meanwhile the king, with Carvalho brooking no delay, issued a savage decree of proscription against the Jesuits.

It is worthwhile to learn what sort of decree it was. In the preamble, the king called the Institute of the Society holy, but the Jesuits were far too degenerate. He stated that the Society had been accepted in Portugal from its beginnings. It had obtained not only hospitality, but also wealth and the highest recognition from the generosity of the kings. In subsequent times all his predecessors, deceived by the false appearance of piety, favored the Jesuits, deemed them worthy of special favor, maintained them at court, and clearly preferred them to other religious orders. But the favors had a bad effect on Jesuits. They are made bold to try ever more atrocious things. And so in America they seized tyrannical control over many provinces. [54] Indeed if they were given time to strengthen their power, within ten years, all the kings of Europe with their joint forces would not be up to driving the Jesuits from their possessions.

Next, with incredible pertinacity, Jesuits waged open and continuous war in Paraguay against the king. They stirred up rebellion. They called peoples to arms. They supported the foul insurrection with their authority and leadership. In the end, they conspired against his person. They laid an ambush for him in an unholy attempt on his life. What is still worse, their coreligious have everywhere lashed out with calumnies against his honor and reputation.

These things the king said by way of a rambling introduction. Then he declared that all Jesuits to a man were manifest traitors, murderers, disturbers of the public peace, perjurers, calumniators. They are unholy, altogether corrupt, and absolutely incorrigible. Accordingly, he decreed that they be expelled from all territory under his jurisdiction, and that they be stripped of their natural citizenship rights. He forbade them use of water and fire. He proposed the death sentence for any who were found inside the boundaries of the Portuguese realm in whatever manner, in whatever religious garb they might be there. That same punishment was to be meted out to those who harbored any Jesuit under their roof or had any dealings at all with them. The younger Jesuits, because they were not yet introduced into the more hidden mysteries of the Society and were not yet immersed in the Jesuits' deadly teachings, could be, perhaps, judged guiltless. He gave them the opportunity to stay if the Cardinal Visitor released them from their vows and they took off the cassock of the Society.

The opinion of many is that if Carvalho had refrained from writing or if at least he had been more restrained, he could have won praise as a provident and honest minister even though he had done many harsh things. For there are some who are so disposed as to think that whatever kings decide upon is justly and well done. But because of his intemperance in writing, Carvalho shot himself, as the saying goes, in the foot. So he earned just about every-one's unfavorable judgment. We have read many of his writings which any reader would judge as incredible or very much exaggerated. To go no farther than the decree of the king (the biting style of which betrays that Carvalho conceived it and put it into writing), how is it that the Jesuits were so strong in America that within a space of ten years they would not be able to be over-come by even all the kings of Europe, and yet he himself, without the use of force, drove them all from their houses and put them on ships like cattle and deported them all the way to Italy? [55] How is it that all the previous kings with the exception of this Joseph and all the previous prime ministers with the exception of this Carvalho had been so dull and stupid that they were duped for so long and so basely by the Jesuits' pretence of piety? How is it that these two finally ripped the masks off the clever impostors? When Carvalho wrote stuff like this, he was mocking the whole human race. But although no one believed the words, still the king's edict of expulsion was carried out. [56]

BOOK III

Portugal, Part 3
Trial of Malagrida

There was great anticipation (1759)[1] on how Carvalho would go about executing the royal decree. The first idea that occurred was that a general exile on
a day preset for their departure would be declared for all the Jesuits. If that
were the only thing done, they would go off on the set date, each with his own
things, some here, some there as suited each. Thus it was done, as we shall
say below, in France. But Carvalho did not deem a worn path sufficiently worthy of himself. He was planning something unusual and kept people in sus-
pense for a long time. To be sure, nothing was more unusual and nothing
more against international law than that a thousand disturbers of one realm—
and those most criminal and guilty under the law—be deported and foisted
off on the kingdom of another prince, and left there to be maintained at that
other's expense. Carvalho certainly would not have dared this with any other
prince. Yet he decided to do this with the Supreme Pontiff to punish him, of
course, for his benevolence towards the Jesuits. And so he decreed that the
Jesuits be put on boats and sent to Rome to the pope.

Execution of Carvalho's Plan for the Jesuits

In this way the Roman Jesuits would also be punished since they would be
forced to provide essentials for the Companions. For he set aside not one cent
for the sustenance of the exiles. He was not unaware of the fact that the pope
had cannons at Civitavecchia. If these, as many wanted done, were turned on
the ships, they would be forced to sail away from there and return to Portugal.
But Carvalho was confident that the pope would act not for the majesty of his
kingdom but for the common charity of the faithful. Clement's well-known
kindness and goodness increased Carvalho's expectations.

Once he adopted this mode of procedure, Carvalho ordered it to be observed everywhere, both in Portugal and in America as well as in the parts of Africa and Asia that were subject to the king. The military was to seize suddenly the houses of the Jesuits. The Jesuits were to be rousted immediately from their residences so that they could not take anything with them and then put on boats. He put in charge of these matters men whom he trusted, who seemingly would exercise no mercy. The ferocity of the agents in Brazil was such [57] that they crammed hundreds of Jesuits into the holds of ships and did not allow them, during the long voyage of several months duration, to come on deck and take fresh air. The wretched men pined away, worn out by the excessive heat and thirst, especially in the tropical zone. Some perished right there. Yet a savage soldier kept watch night and day at the hatch and would allow no one to come out, even for a moment. When finally, after the long ocean voyage, they sailed into the Tagus, they shut the ships' portholes so that no one could look in or anyone be seen. And so as long as they rode at anchor, the Jesuits were forced to endure, in addition to the closeness of quarters and the foul air, another kind of torment: darkness.

In this manner up to 1,200 Jesuits came to the Papal States by various conveyances. The main reason why there were not more was that Carvalho thought that major superiors as well as treasurers of the colleges and court confessors were to be kept in jail. Secondly, among the missionaries there was an admixture of Italians, Germans, Poles, and Belgians. He sensed that exile would be a blessing for them, not a punishment, and so he shut up all the foreigners in dreadful underground cells. These jails had recently been built on the shores of the Tagus. There the Jesuits wasted away with the filth, the thirst, and the darkness of the damp prison. Finally, the biggest reason was that most of the younger members were lacking. For the visitor Saldanha had used a faculty, which the pontiff in general had not given, to release men from their vows and to offer freely letters of legitimate dismissal.

With incredible firmness very many rejected this concession. They were not moved to defection by blandishments of every sort nor by extravagant promises. Nor did hunger and thirst, by which they were wasted and pinched, break what the authorities called their stubbornness. In the end at the urging of the older Fathers, they accepted the letters of dismissal and, taking off the Society's cassock, they returned to their parents' homes. And so not even one Jesuit was to be seen in the whole realm of Portugal. The landed property of the Society, on the basis of the Padroado as they call it, was transferred to the royal treasury. The furniture was put up for auction and sold cheaply. The buildings of the colleges were put to different uses. The body of Francis Xavier which was the object of much public devotion in Goa, was handed over to the Dominicans. But let us look at some things closer to home.

Jesuits' Reception at Civitavecchia

The first to put in at Civitavecchia were 133 priests. The ship's captain had previously brought them to Genoa with the idea that they would be carried from there to Rome on another boat. The people of Genoa generously supplied them with food and other essentials [58] and showed marks of respect to the Jesuits who were in their port. But in order not to violate international law, they forbade the Jesuits to disembark.

Their reception at Civitavecchia was scarcely different from the welcome given the early confessors of the Christian faith. Like them, the Jesuits were marked and scarred by the hands of tyrants. All were wasted away with a shocking leanness and covered with filth. Yet in their faces they showed a certain happiness, which was an indication of their innocence and purity. The city poured out to meet them when they came ashore. The pitiable lineup elicited many tears. Once off the ship, they went straight to the church on bare feet in the manner of suppliants to give thanks to our Savior God. For by His constant help, they had survived so many dangers of the stormy sea and had escaped unharmed the hands of the fierce Carvalho.

The exiles stayed at Civitavecchia a bit longer than was necessary since we had not yet decided where they were to go or how they would get there. During this whole time, they were very kindly fed and refreshed at the expense of the pontiff. That infuriated Almada all the more as if the pope thought he should embrace with special favor rebels against the king of Portugal and men condemned by a public court. Accordingly the pontiff, in order not to further irritate this insane man who always interpreted things for the worse, thereafter stopped kindnesses of this sort though the crowds of exiles were steadily increasing.

Timoni's Providence

The General had entrusted to Timoni the whole planning for the Portuguese. Timoni was a remarkably wise man and experienced; but, in my judgment, he made unsatisfactory decisions. The first group of exiles, about whom I have spoken, he brought to Tusculum in carriages sent from the city. He directed that they be put up in the large villa of the Roman College. The second group which soon followed, he wanted located at the villa at Castel Gondolfo where the General and his curial officials take their leisure. As group after group arrived, he rented two large houses in the city. He set them up in the manner of colleges and fitted them out with appropriate furniture and all the household wares. In those houses he crowded almost 600 Jesuits.

Each of the new colleges had its own Portuguese rector. There were in their number professors of the sciences and scholastics who were studying philosophy and theology. There they had the same lifestyle as anywhere else in our order. There was the same daily order, the same strictness of discipline. The Roman people stood in awe of this, and confessed that only Jesuits could have done such things. And the project was no less expensive than it was marvelous. [59] There was an immense amount spent to establish the two colleges so quickly. Food for so many guests was costly at Rome. It was not clear with what confidence Timoni had imposed upon the General this burden when he did not have the resources. But the good man, as he had believed the Jesuits would never be expelled from Portugal, so now he was in hopes that they would very soon be recalled to their old condition and privileges, and he braced himself and some of the Companions with that hope.

Some of Ours did not approve of Timoni's provisions. Many were displeased that in a city of such biting wit, there were visible the loathsome figures of the exiles which gave a topic of conversation to the prattling crowd and a cause of laughter to our enemies. They did not go about in twos as we do, but in fifteens and twenties. They wore enormous, wide-brimmed hats. They put spectacles on their noses. They frequented the busier streets of the city and very many were swarthy and unseemly in complexion. Many Italians would have preferred that the Portuguese be divided up into small groups and distributed through the colleges and villas of the province and made subject to Italian rectors in the Italian way. Others wished that if rather large colleges had to be built for the Portuguese only, then they be erected far from the city in the towns of Emilia or Piceno where sustenance was readily available and prices cheaper. Many could not approve of the fact that for the sake of foreigners, Father General and the foremost Fathers of the order were depriving the youth of the Roman College of their needed recreation at Tusculum.

To tell the truth, what worried me was that if we were to continue in this fashion, we would be reduced to beggary. I felt that that was the very thing Carvalho wanted. And so I was requesting that Jesuits at least be allowed thereafter to accept stipends for masses. I showed that that would be no inconsiderable relief of our need. But I was never able to obtain this permission. Timoni kept saying it was an inviolable law that the members of the Society not accept the usual stipend for masses. It was wrong to violate this law. He acted as if the law of common life were not also sacred and much more important and would no doubt collapse among us if we were reduced to extreme need.

In the midst of this Timoni died, worn out more by a broken spirit than by disease. He clearly was an excellent man, endowed with many virtues. Because of these virtues he was advanced to the highest offices in the order, all the way to Vicar General. Perhaps he might have been picked for General if he were not a Greek. He had a great gentleness, much patience, a remarkable evenness and balance in adversity as well as in prosperity. He was marvelously charitable towards all and so generous that he gave the appearance of largess. For when he had the money, [60] he readily gave what each one needed. He spent an enormous sum of money for the needs of the Companions, but he himself was content with little, or rather with insufficient and old things. It was never clear where he got so much money. Among so many laudable things, there was this one defect in him: he deferred a bit too much to others' opinions and trusted his own judgment too little.

Ricci's Expedients

After the death of Timoni, Ricci, who was accustomed to following that man's advice, did not think the policy with regard to the governance of the Portuguese should be changed. Perhaps the vain hope of an early return to Portugal was deluding Ricci too; or he continued the policy because in the beginning many were coming to the aid of their friends, and ample financial help was given, especially by Spain and Poland. But when that generosity gradually decreased, Ricci thought up various ways of collecting money. First, the alms that used to be liberally dispensed to the poor, especially to the Capuchins, he ordered to be devoted to feeding the Portuguese. Next in financial matters he practiced a wise frugality, to which he was prone by nature and training. He curtailed all expenses that were not absolutely necessary. He even cut back some on our daily board. But how little was that which was taken from a plain and very moderate table? Finally, he imposed a certain tax on all the colleges of Italy to be paid at equal intervals through the year. But the payment was difficult and slow in coming partly because the colleges had their own financial problems and were not able to pay and partly because some princes would not allow money to be withdrawn from their realms and sent to Rome.

Since he was in these straits, Ricci set aside some moneymaking properties, destined for pious uses, to feeding the Portuguese. He sold some very valuable gifts from princes, especially paintings, which were kept uselessly in the house. He also disposed of the churches' sacred vessels. From the professed house alone, enough engraved silver was melted down that 26,000 gold pieces were realized. The Roman people grumbled since they saw such a treasure being destroyed and the magnificence of that church diminished.

When, however, not even in this way were resources sufficient to meet the burden, Ricci finally came, willy-nilly, to the position he should have taken in the beginning: the Portuguese priests could accept the usual stipend for masses. When that was done, there was a steady income and the pinch of daily provision was greatly relieved.

Things then went more smoothly, especially since the number of the Portuguese was lessened in many areas. For in a short time more than a hundred died either of old age or from the weight of their struggles. And bishops took a large number for their use in conducting seminaries and in administering parishes. Then Ricci, following better advice, [61] suppressed the two recently founded colleges in the city. One house was rented in Trastevere to accommodate 150 elderly men. To another group of the same number, he granted the permanent use of the villa at Castel Gondolfo, but he ordered that the Tusculum property be returned to the Roman College. Some of those Portuguese who were forced to leave either Tusculum or Rome, he distributed through the colleges of Umbria and Piceno, where there was plentiful food. Others he sent to the colleges of Emilia, Ferrara, and Bologna. He had to give some a certain amount of money. For mass stipends were not everywhere readily available, and some colleges were too poor to support these new guests. Yearly he sent money here and there, drawing it from donations of the faithful and from the surplus of the Roman College.

As things were going along in this way, it happened that the king of Naples cut off the income of the Roman College. Very soon new exiles would be arriving: Spaniards, Neapolitans, Sicilians, Parmensians. The Roman College could scarcely sustain its own with its resources, let alone help others. Then Ricci, with every other avenue closed, implored the pontiff's help. The pope pitied the lot of the Portuguese who alone had no pension provided by the king. So that the poor wretches not be forced to roam the region and to beg their food door to door, the pontiff collected up to four hundred of them into his palace at Urbania. He ordered that 12,000 gold pieces a year be paid out from his treasury to sustain them. But the outlay exceeded 12,000 gold pieces in subsequent years. Now the latest furies of Almada recall the narrative to himself.

Almada and Tensions between Portugal and Rome

The Portuguese king, as was said, rejected the papal document that conceded a faculty to the royal Portuguese tribunal, but one limited to the present situation. Almada insisted on a permanent faculty such as the king wanted. In order to bind the king to himself by a new favor, the pope wrote a response according to the king's wishes. And in order not to offend Almada again, he ordered that the document of concession be handed over to Almada for editing and transmission to Lisbon. Almada, looking closely at each word, wanted some things changed. They were changed. Again he found something he wanted taken out. It was taken out. When he was still not satisfied, he asked that the document be sent to Lisbon before it was officially signed. There the king and his council would review it. Meanwhile they were to await the king's response. That too was conceded—so great was the pontiff's humoring of that most undeserving man.

But while the answer was awaited, suddenly a new seed of discord between the king and pontiff was sown. Almada brought to the pope a letter of the king in which he nominated as the new bishop of Bahia a certain Manoel de Sant' Inez. [62] He said the see was empty since the bishop of that city, de Mattos, resigned voluntarily. The pontiff was aware that de Mattos, because he had refused to condemn the Jesuits unheard, was forced from his see, deprived of his property, and driven to beggary. So the pope requested to see the document of abdication which should have been attached to the king's letter. Almada answered that it would be coming soon, but it pleased the king to announce the new bishop's name as quickly as possible. But the pontiff said that could not be done before he had seen the document of abdication. He ordered that meanwhile the apostolic letter, which they call a bull, be held up.

To that Almada complained loudly. The majesty of his king was being injured. He was claiming that a simple statement of the king carried more weight than any document, however much that document may be sworn to. Or could what the most faithful king clearly and plainly affirmed be called into question? The pontiff's ministers replied that it could not be called into question that the laws prescribed and custom confirmed that a bishop's document of abdication, signed by his own hand, was to be placed in the minutes of the Consistorial Congregation and be kept in its archives.

While these things were being tossed back and forth and nothing was being resolved, three couriers on one day came to Almada. The city was astonished and on edge with anticipation as to where the situation was heading. Almada immediately collected a number of his scribes. He shut himself up indoors with them and did not emerge for three whole days. After the three days, he asked for an audience with the pope. When that was delayed a bit, he asked that delays be cut short. He had a weighty matter to treat in his king's name. The pontiff rightly marveled at such haste. But he anticipated only something dire, judging from the steps taken. He set a date for the audience—the day after tomorrow.

But the day before the audience, a letter came from Spain with the news that Cardinal Acciaiuoli, who was the papal ambassador at Lisbon, was expelled from Portugal in great disgrace. One could then understand why there was such haste. Carvalho, of course, since he had inflicted such an injury on the pope, was trying to make himself into the plaintiff rather than stand as the accused. He was demanding that the pontiff make amends for the injuries which he contended were heaped upon the king. He had sent a letter to that effect to Almada, a letter filled with complaints and accusations. The king ordered Almada that unless he received prompt satisfaction, suitable to the gravity of the offenses, he was to leave the city immediately. And Almada, when he had seen to it that many copies of the accusations were made, was hastening to bring one to the pontiff before he could learn about Acciaiuoli's expulsion. [63] He was not, however, successful in this. For the pontiff heard the unconfirmed rumor about Acciaiuoli. But he thought he should wait to look into the matter and put off the interview with Almada again. What that mad man then planned will have to be told presently. Now I will briefly explain why the cardinal and papal ambassador was so undeservedly expelled.

Filippo Acciaiuoli, a noble Florentine, was nuncio of the Apostolic See in Portugal. For a long time he was in great favor, both with the king and with Carvalho. He not only won favor because of his excellent mental gifts, but also because some of his kinsmen from the Acciaiuoli family had taken up residence in Lisbon and made Portugal their homeland. The favor remained during Carvalho's first measures against the Jesuits. Acciaiuoli either approved of

them or hid his displeasure. But after the conspiracy was made public, he saw
that many innocent parties were being accused. He could not approve that in
any way. The king then began to suspect him of favoring the Jesuits more than
was right. Thereafter his meetings with the king were rarer and more difficult
to arrange.

In the midst of this Acciaiuoli was made a cardinal. It is customary everywhere for kings to place the red hat on a new cardinal's head. But this honor
the king refused for some reason in Acciaiuoli's case. Afterwards, when
Carvalho had intercepted by trickery Torrigiani's letter to him, Acciaiuoli was
considered an open enemy of the king. The king could, to be sure, by one letter, have brought about his removal from office and recall to Rome. But
Carvalho did not want him recalled, but expelled with disgrace. He was waiting for the occasion to inflict that injustice.

The occasion was not far distant. It happened that the king's daughter, the
princess of Brazil, as was expected, was marrying the king's brother Peter with
the pope's indult for consanguinity. On the day of the marriage, all the ambassadors to the king, except the pontifical nuncio, were informed through mes-
sages sent by the king's minister Da Cunha about the happy and auspicious
event. Acciaiuoli was pained that he was the only one passed over. He asked that
a similar notice of the wedding be sent to him, but he did not get his wish.
When, therefore, the other ambassadors lit up their houses at night with candles
to show their joy, he deemed that he should not light any tapers of rejoicing.

But that was the very thing Carvalho wanted. Six days passed. A letter from
Da Cunha was brought to Acciaiuoli. In it, the king expressed his decision
that Acciaiuoli was to leave Lisbon immediately for the sake of public peace
and out of consideration of Acciaiuoli's life and reputation. Within four days
he was to leave Portugal entirely. [64] It was a Sunday and the cardinal by
chance had gone into the residence chapel to offer mass. He was not shaken
by the sentence and asked only for the time to say mass. It was denied. He
asked that at least he be allowed to attend mass before his departure. Not even
that was granted. They answered that public safety required his immediate
departure. A group of soldiers stood in front of the door. They would
undoubtedly do violence to the archbishop, cardinal, and what is more, pontifical ambassador if he were to delay at all.

Acciaiuoli took off his priestly vestments and put on a travelling coat. He
first sailed across the Tagus in a swift sailing craft and then was put into a carriage that had been prepared for him. In it he was carried off to the borders of

the kingdom on a trip that took four days. Thirty soldiers crowded around the carriage. In appearance, they were there as an honor guard; but in fact, they made his departure like that of a prisoner.

The route was through Estremoz and other fortified towns. Nowhere was he greeted—as is the custom for cardinals—with cannon shots. In this fashion Carvalho scorned the dignity of the papal ambassador and cardinal. He wanted to take his vengeance for whatever zeal Acciaiuoli had shown for the unjust oppression of the Jesuits, or more accurately, for their innocence. But now let us return to Almada.

When he learned that the pontiff had put off the day for his audience, the man became incensed and could not stop himself from going to extremes. He immediately sent around to each individual ambassador of a foreign prince a thick volume of papers. Simultaneously, he had an edict posted at St. Anthony (which is the Portuguese church). The gist of the edict was this: The ambassador of the most faithful king can no longer decently stay at Rome, where no regard for his dignity is had, where the chief minister of the pontiff wages open war with his king, and where, finally, no satisfaction is offered to the king for so many injuries from the Jesuits. Having said this by way of preface, he announced his imminent departure and informed all Portuguese about his leaving. They should all come at a stated hour to his house where all formal ties with the Roman court shall be declared broken.

When the edict was reported to the pontiff, he saw that Almada was trampling upon him with such words, and not only that, but also he was, in a way, usurping a prince's right. For it is the peculiar right of a prince to post edicts in public. But he kept his anger inside due to the intervention of Cardinal Neri Corsini, who, since he was protector of Portugal, happened to be bringing to the pontiff the king's letter announcing the marriage. Due to the efforts of this peacemaker and to the pope's natural mildness, the affair might have been patched up if Almada had not provoked the pope's anger with a new and worse act of effrontery. [65]

For Almada thought that the pontiff was not appeased by the intervention of Corsini, but terrified at the threat of his departure. So he ordered a new edict to be posted in the same place, according to which he cancelled his announced departure. He said he did so because the Holy Father recognized the justice of his requests and had entrusted the handling of Portuguese affairs to Cardinal Corsini alone, and left Torrigiani out altogether.

The pontiff, however, did not brook this audacity coupled with a most bold-faced lie. He openly proclaimed that he wished to hear nothing about

Portuguese affairs until Almada had left not only Rome, but also the papal domains. The wretched man was caught off guard by this unexpected pronouncement. Although he wanted nothing less than to leave and was threatening departure only with a view to getting his way, he was forced to pack up his things quickly and to leave.

He was more fortunate than Acciaiuoli in that there was no Carvalho in charge at Rome and international law took precedence over the desire for personal vengeance. So he was allowed to go freely and respectably, not in the fashion of a prisoner. The pontiff had soldiers and attendants who could have conducted him to the borders, a thing which many wanted done, and thus pay Almada back tit for tat. He went off sad and sorrowing. He had done not a single good thing at Rome. He was missed by no one save the wicked haters of Jesuits. Along with him, all the Portuguese were forced to leave. Since many had been inhabitants of Rome for some time, this caused some considerable trouble, but they went off in various directions.

Accusations against Acciaiuoli, Torrigiani, and the Jesuits

And now the whole city was reading that large volume which Carvalho had sent from Lisbon. Almada had ordered it to be transcribed in several copies, and he had distributed them to the kings' ambassadors. The volume was full of accusations against Acciaiuoli, Torrigiani, and the Jesuits. And even now there were some who said that Carvalho would have served his interests and reputation better if he had put nothing into writing, or if he had at least written more temperately and moderately. There were many falsehoods in that volume, many inept things that detracted from the writer's credibility and made his bad case worse. To give an example, Acciaiuoli was accused of arrogance since he had requested that the royal wedding be announced to him in writing when that courtesy had been extended to none of the ambassadors. Yet there is extant at Rome a copy of the note with which Da Cunha had advised all the royal ambassadors of the wedding with the exception of Acciaiuoli.

They claimed that Acciaiuoli was whisked off so abruptly in order that he not suffer anything untoward from the angry mob. For the people had taken amiss the fact that Acciaiuoli had not lit candles, and, considering the omission contempt for the king, the incensed rabble was on the point of rioting. [66] Without a doubt they would attack Acciaiuoli with stones or with some other kind of weapon unless he were snatched from imminent danger by military intervention. But that was a pure and obvious lie. For during the three days of festival they had kept candles burning. Acciaiuoli, however, wrote that all was calm in the vicinity of his house and not one single voice of protest was heard. But before he was led off, another six days had passed so that the incident was hardly remembered. As he was leaving, a guard of soldiers was said to have been added for his protection. But why were not a number of days set down before his having to depart, which is the most obvious manner of imposing exile? Why was he escorted all the way to the border of the kingdom? Why were the honors customarily afforded cardinals denied to him? Thus people were discussing the matter. They concluded that Acciaiuoli was exiled in such an undignified manner because he did not agree at all with Carvalho's unjust harassment of the Jesuits.

Torrigiani received no better treatment. He was accused of waging open and relentless war with the most faithful king. Why was that? First of all because he wrote a letter to the Spanish nuncio, as we said above, in which he called those men criminal and hateful who were spreading so many lies about the Jesuits. But by what other name was he to chide them? We read that Henry the Great [2] used a similar expression when he spoke in the Paris Parlement on recalling the Society to France. "I have noted," he said, "that those most opposed to the Jesuits are either Calvinists or wicked priests of both clergies." Secondly, Torrigiani was attacked because he ordered that those who were secretly peddling libelous pamphlets against the Jesuits at Rome, be sought out, and he punished one of them with exile. Also, Torrigiani had written to Acciaiuoli, telling him to admonish in a friendly manner Cardinals Saldanha and Atalaja because what they had decided to do against the Jesuits displeased the pontiff and seemingly the measures ought to be abrogated.

And these charges, even if they were true indications of a hostile spirit, were being falsely attributed to Torrigiani. For it was Archinto, as we said before, who exiled the secret seller of the pamphlets. Archinto and not Torrigiani had written the letter to Acciaiuoli. The other proofs of his waging war carried the same weight. For because the pope, in keeping with his native gentleness, requested in the letter mentioned above that priests' blood not be spilled, Torrigiani was accused of approving the murder attempted by the Jesuits or of thinking it ought not be appeased by capital punishment. Because the pontiff had recommended that the king not consider all Jesuits as one and the same, but should separate the innocent from the guilty, Torrigiani was said to have insulted the king who had declared that no one in the Jesuits' ranks was innocent. [67] Because, finally, Torrigiani had proposed the sending of a Cardinal Legate *a latere* to investigate and judge the Jesuits' situation, he was again accused of hostility towards the king. Supposedly Torrigiani thought there was no justice, no judicial power in Portugal so that judges and executioners had to be brought in from elsewhere. But those who read these charges stood in amazement at Carvalho's impudence, for he seemed to be freely admitting that he opened the seals and read the letters sent to the apostolic nuncio by courier. That is a violation of public trust and of the sacred rights of ambassadors. Next, they considered the accusations ridiculous. Clearly no one saw any war waged with the most faithful king.

Carvalho was, in fact, looking only at the Jesuits. He claimed that they had done most serious harm to the majesty of the most faithful king by means of their calumnies. Such harm was even graver than that inflicted by those who had conspired to murder him. He was complaining that up to now they had gotten off scot-free. Nor was he accusing this or that Jesuit of such an outrage, but, to use his words, "the whole government of the Society." It is hard to grasp what he meant by that. For how had Carvalho learned of Jesuits' conversations had in Rome? From Almada's letters, of course, as was said above. But Almada indiscriminately gathered whatever he heard was said, true or false, and sent these remarks on to Carvalho without any distinction.

Again I ask, how did Almada know Jesuits spoke against the king? From the reports, to be sure, of his henchmen who were all enemies of the Jesuits. Torrigiani was correct when he said these were either wicked or spiteful. They were people who made a pact among themselves, as shown above, to lie and to overwhelm the Jesuits with complete calumnies. Excellent witnesses, indeed, and worthy of being those on whose sole testimony the case seems to have been conducted!

I will not deny that I heard many, both Jesuits and non-Jesuits from every rank, age, and sex, revile Carvalho with their curses. But all spared the name of the king. Nay more, they were acknowledging that he was by nature an excellent and most just prince, nor would he have allowed such things if he was not misled by the wicked artifices of Carvalho. But Carvalho, as if he himself were king, called his critics the king's critics. And since he could not attack all because of their infinite number, he was persecuting only the Jesuits because these alone he had harmed, these alone he feared.

But at the end, I wish to make a liberal concession. Granted, if you wish, granted, I say, that some Jesuits at Rome spoke somewhat less prudently against the most faithful king in that trying ordeal of their Companions, still there should have been an allowance made for their pain, not punishment meted out. For what law is so inhuman as to forbid one being whipped [68] to groan, to shout out, to whine? Or what is the moderation of grief when one suffers a true and wrenching pain? But enough on these matters.

The Aftermath of Almada

With Almada gone, the city seemed to return to its usual peace and quiet. The Jesuits were especially heartened and renewed. It was very much in their interest that that troublesome man be as far away as possible. Only his follow- ers and henchmen were grieving—most of them paltry parasites, all of them enemies of the Society. Deprived of such a patron, they saw the way to further harassing Jesuits was cut off and they were afraid that they might have to pay for the illegalities that they had gotten away with to this point.

And in truth the pontiff, who up to that very day had put up with many misdeeds out of respect for the king of Portugal whose name and authority Almada brought up every other word, was now freed of that concern and ordered strict investigation of the worst offenders and appropriate punish- ment. The first to be thrown into prison was Nicola Pagliarini, the printer who was bought by Portuguese money and who provided Almada with the press and the expertise to print the libelous pamphlets against the Jesuits. The case was tried by the most honest of judges; by unanimous verdict Pagliarini was condemned to the galleys. But the pontiff lessened the sentence. He did so either out of his innate kindness, or as the rumor had it, from the intercession of his nephew Ludovico Rezzonico who was then at Rome, or in the hope of winning over the king of Portugal. The pontiff imposed only this on Pagliarini: that he not set foot outside of Rome. Even that provision Pagliarini scorned. For with the help of friends, he sneaked off to Naples and from there went by sea to Lisbon. There he enjoyed Carvalho's good graces as one who had done signal service to Portugal. Not only was he enhanced with honor and rewards, but also, to remove the disgrace of condemnation to the galleys, he was enrolled into the Portuguese nobility.

Pagliarini's case was scarcely finished when Florio was imprisoned in Castel Sant' Angelo. He had an otherwise good reputation, but he had added, as we said above, material to the letter of visitation appointing Cardinal Saldanha and signed them. The charge against him was never revealed, but in his own conscience, he thought he should be condemned to death. For in the dead of night while he was sleeping, he was awakened by some unusual noise (festive torches were being prepared, ones that are burned by custom on certain days through the year). He thought the hangmen were coming and that he was being carried off to punishment. He was seized with such terror that he grew stiff with fear and on the next day he breathed his last.

Through that same time many others, partly from the ranks of foreign priests, partly from religious orders, were driven into exile. They were condemned not by any formal judicial procedure, but by public rumor of having disturbed the peace of state by distributing seditious pamphlets or by spreading tales. [69] Among them were two Piedmontese priests, De Gros and Capriata.[3] They were raising a hue and cry about the moral teaching of the Jesuits. They could be said to be the trumpeters of the Jansenist sect. Some of the Dominicans were rather vociferous. Dinelli was especially so.[4] He was a learned man and a fine Latinist. But he was equally bold and arrogant. He appealed in vain to the good faith of his powerful patrons that he not be expelled. He employed intercessors with the pope in vain. And yet this vindication of the Society was brought about—to give each his due credit—by the work of Boxadors.[5] He was Master General of the Dominicans and is now a cardinal. Being noble and moderate, he worked for peace and concord between the Dominicans and Jesuits, and allowed none of his men to rail against us too freely. Finally, to mention no others, there was a certain Piarist, Natali by name, who dared to treat theological matters that were beyond his training.[6] Accused of perverse doctrine, he was ordered to go into exile.

Because of the severity of these expulsions, there was such terror instilled, especially in hostile religious, that all fell silent for the moment. For it is the gravest kind of punishment for most religious to be exiled from Rome. For there they foster their hopes of improving their station. There are certain spurs to their ambition there which they cannot find elsewhere. For this reason it is all the more apparent that if these measures had been taken from the beginning, the insolent faction could have been checked at its origins and certainly it would not have had so many and such great successes. I urged this course often, but in vain, upon Cardinal Rezzonico.

Not only, as I said, did the enemies fall silent, but also many in a sudden conversion came over to the Jesuits' side. They may have been sincere in this or may have been adjusting to the tenor of the times. The sudden change in the Dominican Mamachi caused particular surprise.[7] He was a man of remarkable learning and famous for several works of genius. But he was a Greek by nationality and up to this point had taken the lead among the Jesuits' enemies. When he saw that Almada, the pillar of the faction, had been expelled and that the pontiff was intent upon checking the sedition, he reversed his sails to avoid the contrary wind and the threatening storm. He attached himself to the supporters of the Society, so much so that he was to be considered as most friendly. A certain Piarist did not take kindly to this reversal and published a pamphlet in which he called Mamachi a theologian driven by the wind. And he did not hesitate to reproach Mamachi for his "Greek faith." And this charge was not without merit. For in the next pontificate, when a strong wind blew from Spain, Mamachi changed sides once again and rejoined [70] the Jesuits' enemies. He seemed to be a timeserver and changed his loyalty with the change of fortune as often as needed.

Meanwhile some of the troublemakers had been exiled. Others, gripped by fear, were keeping quiet. Then the pontiff thought of choosing some Jesuit for the Sacred College of Cardinals. He thought that this compensation for its injuries was owed to the order that had been so buffeted and bruised. The papal courtiers, following Spinelli's advice, deterred him from doing this. Although the pontiff was now suspicious of Spinelli and showed him less favor, still Spinelli, while seeming to do something else, was able to suggest his wishes and views through some of his representatives. Some pointed to the quick renewal of a pact with the Portuguese king provided no new causes for anger arose. But if the pontiff had shown himself in any way more kindly disposed to the Jesuits, no hope for reconciliation was left. The pope was attracted by that hope and terrified by the additional threat. Once again he was deceived by the appearance of justice and dropped the entire consideration. But now the story directs me to close the whole tragedy of the Portuguese persecution with the final act.

Trial of Malagrida

Malagrida was finishing his third year (1761) of imprisonment in the royal prison of Lisbon and his case was still not decided. Everyone was surprised that the punishment of this helpless Jesuit was delayed so long. For he was alleged to be, on the basis of his public acts, the principal author and architect of the conspiracy against the king. Yet the other conspirators, though easily the principal people of the realm with regard to wealth and nobility, within the space of a month were apprehended, charged, condemned, and as we have seen, shamefully and cruelly slaughtered.

But another wonderment replaced the one over the delay. When it was announced at Rome that Malagrida had had the ultimate punishment inflicted upon him, it was not for treason, not for conspiracy against the king, but

Gabriel Malagrida, S.J.

on a charge either of heresy or of feigned holiness. That so struck the minds of men that those who up to that point had doubts were now convinced of Malagrida's evident innocence, and they remarked that his innocence was confirmed by the testimony of Carvalho himself. But because the deed was the height of Carvalho's wickedness, the matter should be reviewed a bit more closely.

Carvalho had decided in his mind to put Malagrida to death. At first he accused him of starting the conspiracy against the king. On the strength of this charge he ordered Malagrida to be dragged off to the royal prison. But he understood well enough that he could persuade no one that such a man could have initiated the plot. For he had been absent from Lisbon for three whole years. He had no dealings the whole of that time with any of the conspirators. He had no correspondence with them. So Carvalho decided to hang another charge upon him—one that could more readily be believed and would brand the Society [71] with an equal or even greater mark of disgrace. Also it had to be a crime punishable by death. And so he accused him of feigned sanctity. He ordered Malagrida to be transferred to the jail of the Holy Inquisition as an impious sycophant who was seeking the reputation of sanctity by fake miracles and by a false appearance of supernatural visions. Carvalho handed him over for punishment to his brother Paul, who, as we said above, was head of the tribunal.

Paul shared his brother's schemes and was lured by the hope of the cardinalate to go even beyond what was needed for the punishment. For the investigation was secret as is the custom of that tribunal. In it, Paul declared Malagrida not only a pretender to holiness, but also impure, heretical, and stiff-necked in his heresy. Since that was a capital offense, the secular judges to whom he had been handed over deemed that the law's provisions should be observed. It is established custom in Portugal that those whom the Holy Inquisitors have declared heretical receive their punishment with great public fanfare. They call it the *"auto-da-fe."* They observed, therefore, the formalities of custom and law.

Tributes to Malagrida

Gabriel Malagrida, a very well known man because of his achievements and a saint in the opinion of all, was covered with a conical cap (called a *carocha*) to disgrace him. He was dressed in a ridiculous manner and surrounded by a crowd of attendants. A gloomy line of penitents preceded him. The executioner followed. The crowded throngs of people looked on in horror. He was led to his platform of death. It had been erected in a large square. There they broke his neck and killed him. The body was burned and the ashes thrown into the Tagus River.

This most respectable Italian gentleman received this reward for his services. As a youth he came to Portugal and went from there to the Indians of Maranhão. He brought those barbarians to the faith. He had given himself completely to developing the growth of holiness in these recent Christians. For more than forty years he toiled with unremitting labor. He had spread far and wide the reign of Christ and, at the same time, the reign of his king. If he was not truly a saint, it is difficult to comprehend how he could have acquired the reputation for holiness and have maintained it for so long. This was his reputation not only with the credulous and simple Indians, who venerated him almost as a man dropped down from heaven, but also with the nobles at Lisbon, with the very perceptive court, and what is more, with his fellow, keen-sighted Jesuits.

Although even slight faults are easily noted in common life, the Jesuits nonetheless affirmed that they never saw any in Malagrida. He never departed in the least from religious observance. Although he was a foreigner (and that can usually be an odious term), still the people preferred him to their own native Portuguese and declared him a truly saintly man.

In the royal palace the estimation was similar or even greater. Once, when he returned from America to Lisbon, [72] the man who was then prince of Brazil and now King Joseph, went out to the ship to meet him. He did not think it out of place to kiss his hand as a sign of respect. King John V thought so highly of Malagrida that at the end of his life, he wanted to make the Spiritual Exercises under Malagrida's direction, to lay before him matters of conscience, and to breathe his last as Malagrida assisted him with the last rites. When John's death was announced at Rome, Pope Benedict spoke kindly of Malagrida. In an allocution in which he informed the Sacred College of Cardinals about the death, Benedict did not hesitate to affirm that the king, even if he had strayed in his human weakness, still had departed with excellent hope for a better life since he entrusted himself at the end of his life to such a holy man and had expired in his arms. The speech is in print, and there could be no clearer testimony to Malagrida's holiness.

What shall I say now about Queen Marianna of Austria, John's wife? She was a woman of remarkable piety and her biography, as I said, has been published. She so wanted Malagrida to attend to her in her last illness and to assist her that she wrote to him in America for that one reason and asked with humble prayers that he hasten his return to Europe. For she thought her dying day was imminent. And in truth he got on a boat immediately and returned. In their first conversation, he spoke rather freely and openly with the sick queen concerning her approaching death. The courtiers, not wanting such frankness, then excluded him for being too outspoken and kept him away from the queen. And so it happened that she passed away without seeing again the priest whom she had hoped for so much and whom she was expecting each hour. Thus, of course, even when matters are of the greatest importance, poor princes are deceived.

I pass over now the veneration of the people for Malagrida. I pass over the miraculous and preternatural things that were told about him. I ask this: Is it credible that when the highest and the lowest in all of Portugal felt so clearly and so constantly that Malagrida was a saint, that Carvalho alone saw in him fraud and pretence? I would believe Carvalho made nothing of the difference between true and faked holiness provided he did away with the person he so hated. Maybe he wanted him killed in disgrace for the very reason that he thought him holier than the rest of the Jesuits. In this way he would mark all Jesuits with disgrace by the punishment of one. With this mentality, I think he would choose the Apostle of the Indies, Francis Xavier, for punishment if he were alive. He definitely left unpunished the two other Jesuits, de Mattos and Alessandro, whom he had declared guilty of conspiracy. Of course they were less holy. [73]

As usual for him, Carvalho did not look out enough for his own good and made the mistake of publishing the charges against Malagrida. He wanted to defame the Society, but he merely revealed Malagrida's innocence and his own disgrace. The records of the trial were published at Rome. The trial took place at Lisbon before the Sacred Tribunal. All who read the court record exclaimed that Malagrida had been unjustly condemned. The innocence of the man came shining through those records so much that the Society's more perceptive enemies saw to their immediate suppression and it became impossible to find copies or to purchase them at any price. But let us present a sample of the record.

To begin with, no charge was brought against Malagrida for anything done outside of the prison of the Holy Inquisition. So he ought not to have been put there in the first place. But once shut up in prison, he is said to have written two books tainted with heresy. One was on the future coming of the

Antichrist, the other on the life of St. Ann. If he really wrote these books, he should have been called mad rather than heretical, and in fact he was out of his mind. Let a few examples illustrate this.

He was claiming that Ann had married with no other design than to preserve more completely her virginity, as if she had not borne children. The Virgin Mary, when carried in Ann's womb, sometimes wept, and when she did, so did all the angels in heaven. Mary was accustomed to speak with her mother from the womb and to have uttered these very words, "Rejoice, Ann, my mother; behold you will conceive" (for Mary had not yet been conceived when she was saying this), "and you will bear a daughter who will be called Mother of God." Because of this utterance eight whole days were spent in heaven in games and dances. Ann was an abbess in some monastery at Jerusalem. She had a sister named Baptistina who went daily to the fish market to purchase fish for the monastery. At Ann's death there was disagreement among the Three Divine Persons as to the honor and status she should have in heaven. The Virgin Mary had a spell and almost passed out at the greeting of the angel. For that reason, the dancing which the angels carry on in heaven was interrupted and reassumed more joyfully after her ascent.

These and other statements of the sort, which would be long and tedious to note one by one, were, in the judgment of the inquisitors, so many heresies. But in a kinder interpretation, they were mere ravings of a madman who deserved the treatment of Christian charity, not punishment. It was not very surprising that a man of his age, when suddenly snatched from his religious house and clapped into prison, was disturbed by the unexpected turn of events and could be shaken from his mental powers. Certainly [74] the judges suspected he was silly and the court proceedings testify to that. But because he seemed to answer questions appropriately, they judged him to be sane. As if, of course, a madman is incapable of answering questions; or when there is question of a man's life, a hesitation is to be put aside for such a trivial cause!

The second part of the proceedings ascribed two crimes to Malagrida. These were mutually inconsistent and could not be put together. The first was that while in prison, he had made a pretence to holiness. He had heavenly visions and made many predictions to his companions as if they were derived from heaven. He wanted to appear to be inspired completely by the Divine Spirit and to be truly holy. The second charge was that his companions frequently saw him performing certain obscene and shameful acts by which they were mightily offended. But if anyone is so immodest and so bold as to do such shameful things openly before the eyes of all, he certainly does not want to be considered and called a saint. Or he would be absolutely mad if he sought the reputation and glory of holiness despite such behavior.

If Carvalho had adverted to this inconsistency, he never would have allowed the charge of immodesty to be put into the proceedings, especially since crimes of that sort do not pertain to the jurisdiction of the Holy Inquisition. But he was carried away by his zeal to defame the Society. So he wanted that charge added, but by so doing, he made Malagrida's innocence the clearer and did away with all credibility for his judicial procedures. Accordingly, his friends at Rome rightly saw to suppression of the court records. They cannot be read without some reproach of the Portuguese, for they show the great ignorance of the judges and even greater injustice.

But there was no tribunal in Portugal so holy that it was not controlled by the will of Carvalho. Even the Holy Inquisition, as was said, was headed by his brother Paul. Unless he saw to it that Malagrida should be condemned some-how, he would never obtain the cardinalate. And for such a deserving deed, he was in fact chosen for that august rank. But he never received the insignia of a cardinal, for he died the day they arrived at Lisbon.

At the end let me not omit that this same courier who brought to Rome the judicial proceedings concerning Malagrida also carried a rather extended account of his death. A certain Capuchin named Norbert,[8] about whom fur-ther mention will have to be made below, had composed it at Carvalho's bid-ding. He was now calling himself Abbé Platel (for he had removed the Capuchins' cowl) and was living at Lisbon as a client of Carvalho. In the account Platel claimed he was an eyewitness of the whole tragedy and that Malagrida had died steadfast in his heresy with no sign of repentance. [75] But this most vile man, who gained renown by pure lies, impressed no one.

But let this be the end of Portuguese matters. We have treated them rather extensively both because many events took place at Rome before our very eyes and because the destruction of the whole Society started there. Now we must treat events in France. [76]

BOOK IV

France

Already some things had begun to be stirred in France which seemed to shake the Society's fortunes. In the space of one year, 1762, the French, who are given to prompt action, forced the Society out of their entire realm. Out of so many colleges and houses which the Society possessed for almost two hundred years throughout its five provinces in that large nation, not one was left. The beginnings of this ruin, its progress and outcome, the series of calamities that came in between, I intend to tie together in one narrative. I will leave for others' investigation the true and more secret causes which up to now no one has clearly expounded. I hold this for certain: The causes put down in the public records were not the true ones or at least not the more important ones.

It is not an unfounded suspicion that Carvalho communicated his designs to special members of the Paris Parlement and to the duke de Choiseul who was then the prime minister of the king and a hidden supporter of the Society's enemies. These enemies were secretly stirred up by Portugal and together spun a web for the Society's destruction. As I consider the dignity of these officials, I find such a plot incredible. But this is certainly more credible: The sect of the Jansenists had the greatest role in these events. The Jansenists seized the opportunity to avenge with one blow all the setbacks they had received from the Jesuits. With the Jesuits out of the way, the Jansenists hoped all would be easier for them thereafter. But I leave these things for the middle of the narrative.

Lavalette's Scheme Brings Financial Disaster

The first stage of the catastrophe is clear. There was a Jesuit named Lavalette,[1] a man of very great intelligence and acumen in business transactions. But he was too independent and careless about laws and rules. He was carrying on business transactions for Martinique, an island mission in North America. He was openly engaged in profitable trade on the pretense of building up the mission. A bitter war was raging between the kings of France and England and the English preyed upon all sea traffic. Consequently many French traders who had business dealings in those islands [77] were suffering daily losses and were forced to return to France. Lavalette bought their plantations cheaply and transferred them to the mission's program. But he did not pay the French traders with ready cash, but promised that remittance would be made in France from several funds and that payment would be made by two bankers in Marseilles.

To these men Lavalette was going to send ships from the mission loaded with American goods, and at the same time, he would give to the creditors letters of credit, which each could redeem for the agreed amount. This kind of business transaction was useful for both parties, and of itself honest and just. But the laws of the Church forbid it to a religious. For a while the scheme worked well. The foreign goods were sold dear at Marseilles. From the money returned, the creditors were paid off. Each one was getting what he wanted. But a major snag occurred when English pirates intercepted some of these merchant ships. Those who set the value of the cargo at the smallest say that it exceeded two million French livres. The two Marseilles bankers were pressed by the holders of the letters of credit, but were without money and destitute of hope. They had put all their hope on those ships. When they were unable to pay, they were declared bankrupt. And while they were thus ruined they also brought down other banking people along with them inasmuch as they had close mutual ties. There was general unpopularity for the Jesuits who were accused of having brought these losses upon the poor wretches.

But the Marseilles bankers did not lose their heads. Quite rightly they thought these ships had been captured. Their cargoes were still the responsibility of Lavalette, but the misfortune should not be deemed a fraud on his part. They appealed to the protection of the laws before the city's magistrates. These examined the matter closely and at the end decreed that the superior of the Martinique mission, who was profiting from the trade, must repair the damages. By common agreement, this was a most just judgment. The Jesuits were able and indeed were obliged to come up with the money demanded. They could use the extensive estates which they had on the island. If they could not pay it all, they should at least pay part. Meanwhile they should soothe the pain of the creditors, build up their hopes, and have a concern for their own good name and reputation. If they had done that, the mouths of their revilers would have been shut and the dispute settled with little fuss and minimal damage to the Society.

But when the magistrates' decision was announced, the Fathers made an ill-considered response. I do not know on what they based their hopes, but they contended that it was a private concern of Lavalette and legal action should be taken against him. For if any Jesuit rashly loads himself down with debt, [78] that debt does not seem to be the Society's responsibility. It is remarkable how that response irritated the whole business community of France. The Jesuits certainly put themselves in a terrible bind.

It was to be expected and very much to be feared that the merchants and bankers would appeal from the officials of Marseilles to the Paris Parlement.[2] There were already, as we indicated above, those who were ill-disposed to the Society in that body. They were waiting for just such an opportunity to overwhelm the Society. Thinking that this was the time and occasion, they happily waded in. In order, however, not to seem ill-informed, they first ordered that the Society's rules be handed over and they commissioned some censors of their appointment to review the rules. The censors reported that the Society's laws provide that no contract can be made without the General's authorization. Not only was the businessmen's and bankers' case upheld, but also the Father General was sentenced to make good the losses. That sentence meant that Ricci owed to men with whom he never had any dealings not less than one and one-half million French livres.

News of this sentence shocked and troubled Ricci. He had few resources and he had just about drained them all in support of the Portuguese. He turned in every direction, but he could not see how he could find such a large amount of money. His pain was all the more justified since it was not his fault that things were in such a strait. Scarcely had he heard what sort of business Lavalette was conducting in Martinique when he severely reprimanded him. He ordered him to stop his enterprise, to relinquish the management of the mission, and to return immediately to France. Not content with that, he gave another letter to the superior of the mission with orders that he remove Lavalette immediately from Martinique and insist on his prompt return. But by the worst of luck the letter had been lost in the long voyage and had not arrived at Martinique. But still to prevent even worse things which he sensed were threatening from France, he determined to try everything to pay the debt.

It chanced that at that time Martinique had passed over to the hands of the English. The Society had a lot of resources on that island. Ricci ordered an experienced and prudent Jesuit by the name of Forestier to go from Rome to

London.[3] He gave him instructions to pay off Lavalette's accounts by sale of Martinique properties or by borrowing on them. [79] It is unknown to me what success Forestier's expedition had. But whatever happened to him was in vain, for the Paris Parlement was making judgments on things other than Lavalette's merchandise and the Marseilles bankers' losses.

Paris Parlement Plots Expulsion of Jesuits

One thing was being aimed at: Expulsion of the Society from France as it had recently been expelled from Portugal. The leading members of Parlement were concocting this scheme. At Rome Passionei had already predicted it. Cardinal Spinelli treated of the matter in a steady correspondence with the duke de Choiseul. That may be the reason why, as he neared death, Spinelli ordered that all his correspondence be burned in his presence while he looked on. The Parlement was only seeking some semblance of right which might cloak over the violent oppression. This was found, you might be surprised to learn, in our very Constitutions.

The censors whom I mentioned went through and scrutinized the laws and rules of the Society. They reported that they found some provisions which were contrary to France's laws and which could not be harmonized with them. It was especially troublesome that Jesuits are bidden to obey their superior in a blind sort of way, with no examination of the reasons why the superior was prompted to give the command. They asserted that there was everything to be feared from such a blind obedience. For whatever the superior orders, whether it is right or wrong, must be done with no hesitation. The rule, however, added the exception, "Unless the superior has ordered something forbidden by divine law which would clearly be a sin." If the censors had not passed over in silence this very important exception, there was nothing which they would have to fear in the blind obedience of Jesuits. For people ought to obey their kings in a similar way. Soldiers ought to obey their officers like this, and all the more so, religious ought to obey their superiors. For religious are pursuing the perfection of obedience and seek eternal rewards from it.

Next the censors accused the very structure of the Society's governance. They maintained that that structure did not fit French ways. That is due to the fact that the supreme power belongs to the General of the order, who resides in Rome. His power is unlimited. He makes final decisions as he wishes, in both the Society's business and for its men. He has individual Jesuits subject to him like bought slaves. He can almost trample them under foot. No tyrant can be imagined who could dominate so haughtily, so freely.

To these objections, they add some truly remarkable contentions. If anyone believes them, I cannot but marvel at his simplicity. They claimed that in all the royal courts, besides confessors, there are hidden Jesuits who [80] have pronounced a vow of obedience to the Society's General. They are to inform him of all secrets they learn of and they are to obey with complete submission whatever he commands. Thus all princes are in a certain way at risk to the Father General of the Society.

While the appointed censors of our laws and Institute were reporting these things, others were used to review the moral teaching of the Society. These demonstrated that there was no crime, no fierce and despicable outrage that did not find a champion among the authors of the Society. They spoke of probabilism as if it were a most execrable beast, while in fact not only many Jesuits, but also many other professors were always supporters of that view. From it, as if from a poisoned fountain, seditions, assassinations, thefts, every kind of dishonesty, and every monstrous crime sprang up spontaneously. They tried to show that all such things were approved in the teaching of the Jesuits. They asserted the teaching on tyrannicide was common and quite acceptable to Jesuit authors. To show this they cited Busenbaum who makes no mention at all of what we call tyrannicide. They had gathered all these passages into a large volume in which the countless errors, allegedly excerpted from Jesuits' works, are systematically reviewed.[4] When these accusations were laid out in the Parlement, although a large number of members were in favor of the Society, still their opponents were in the majority and two decrees of the Parlement were made. You would not know which of the two was the worse.

First, a copy of our Constitutions was condemned to the flames. With that copy, works of thirty-two authors of the Society, and those generally from the famous writers, were to be burned in public by the hand of the executioner. Secondly, the French have an appeal procedure which they call *comme d'abus.* This they used against the Apostolic Constitution of Paul III, who had first approved the Institute. They were now saying that that Institute was impious and they appealed against all the other constitutions of the supreme pontiffs who had confirmed the same Institute, praised it, and loaded it with favors and privileges.

This is something that will rightly astound you still more. While the reviewers made such harsh judgments on the Institute and maintained that it should not be tolerated in France, they still were praising Jesuits as good, honest, learned men and admitted they were estimable except for the fact that they belonged to the Society and observed its practices. The reviewers' position was that they can be good men and called such who pursue bad regulations and not the opposite, that is, that regulations are to be called good when they are pursued by good men.

These first steps indicated where the Paris Parlement was heading unless it were checked by the king's authority. The king did check the impetus [81] a bit by his decree that abrogated the Parlement's two resolutions and ordered that this decree of his be placed in the Parlement's minutes. At the same time, he sent a letter forbidding Parlement to treat further anything concerning the Jesuits. He wished to investigate the entire matter on his own. The response to this order was couched in humble language, but with a consistent firmness: Parlement cannot obey without failing in its duty and cannot desist from the action it had initiated against the Jesuits. There was question of the welfare of France. There was question of the safety and well-being of the king to which it resolutely wished to look. Yet the king insisted and sent a new letter demanding Parlement's submission to the prince's authority. The members then put aside their contumacy and grew quiet. They recorded the royal decree in the minutes and ceased attacking the Jesuits.

But the king, to avoid the appearance of arbitrariness and to give a legal face to the matter, handed over the Jesuits' case for judgment to the French clergy, who happened to be meeting at Paris at that time. But at Rome the pontiff, as he ought to have been, was greatly irritated when he learned what the Paris Parlement had done. It had acted against not only the Institute of St. Ignatius, but also against the sanctions, actions, and decrees of the Apostolic See. This was a daring and new thing, something previously unheard of among Catholics. The pope thought he ought not gloss over his indignation at the deed.

Clement XIII, French Clergy, and Jesuits React

He called a meeting of the cardinals and delivered an address on the matter. It was full of dignity and strength. The pope was pained, he was particularly horrified that a secular, profane body had called the institute of a religious order impious when the Council of Trent and the Supreme Pontiffs have called it pious, holy, and praiseworthy. At the end of the discourse, by the power entrusted to him by Christ, the pontiff rescinded, revoked, indicted, and declared utterly void that decree of the Paris Parlement. Taking that stance showed great priestly courage and a praiseworthy sense of duty, but the rest of his conduct was not consistent with it. When he was about to publish the address and make known his view, a thing which all good men were asking him to do, he grew afraid that things might get worse in France. At the urging of some too timid cardinals, he ordered the speech put up in the archives of Castel Sant' Angelo.

Meanwhile the French Jesuits, when they saw their situation was critical, were looking out for themselves and their affairs as far as this could be done. Twenty-seven older Fathers gathered at Paris and signed a document in which they declared their condemnation of the doctrine of tyrannicide. They bound themselves by strict vow to never allow any of their men to teach the doctrine in writing or orally. That move was right and wise, but done in vain. For although their accusers had thrown up this doctrine to the Jesuits, [82] they were still aware of the fact that the doctrine had been forbidden in the Society from the time of Henry the Great. It was excluded under obedience. Nor was it treated by any Jesuit after that time or touched upon in conversation, except in passing.

The step that was not sufficiently thought out, not to say, that was foolish, was the following. In that same document the French Fathers professed that they embraced the four main positions in which the Gallican clergy dissent from the Roman See.[5] This declaration did nothing for them in France since it was late, and greatly displeased the pope at Rome and cast a great cloud over their reputation. For up to this point, the Jesuits were the only French clerics never to have approved those articles. They had preferred to refrain from treating such matters rather than to add their vote to a doctrine that was little consonant with papal power. They forfeited their reputation for signal reverence for the Apostolic See by this unsolicited, unnecessary, and unprofitable declaration.

Others, more cautiously and in a way better suited to the circumstances, took up the written rebuttal and refutation of charges brought against the Society. Cerutti made an excellent defense and vindication of the Institute of the Society and its laws.[6] He was a young man of outstanding talent and a very skilled writer. He was Piedmontese by birth and perhaps my account will return to him below.

To that collection of errors that I spoke of above, a clear, written response was made. It was shown that if Jesuits had mistakenly taught lax propositions condemned by the Church, that was not a fault peculiar to them, but a common one of writers from every order. No error was found in writers of the

Society, the exemplar of which had not preceded in others. The accusers were challenged to produce even one Jesuit who, after the Supreme Pontiff had taken a position, had taught something contrary to that papal teaching. Of course, no such could be found.

Responses in Writing

To this written response could be added the fact that recently the Dominican Daniele Concina in his *Christian Theology* had eloquently expounded and proposed the doctrine of tyrannicide.[7] Yet no one protested against him or his order for this. There was a certain hidden defender of the Society, a witty fellow, who took this serious matter as a joke. When he saw, on the one hand, that in Portugal the Institute of the Society was called pious and holy, but the Jesuits were expelled because they allegedly had departed from their rule; and, on the other hand, the Jesuits in France were called respectable and honest, but nonetheless deserving of exile because they scrupulously observe an impious Institute, he proposed the following solution: To reconcile and balance things, let the French Jesuits go to Portugal, [83] and let the Portuguese go to France. With only their locales changed, the Jesuits would be pleasing and acceptable to both peoples, nor would there be any reason in the future why they should be expelled.[8]

There was great anticipation in France as to what the select investigators from the clergy would decide on the question of the Jesuits. The king had submitted three things for their scrutiny, the Institute, the power of the General, and the Jesuits' teaching. Six archbishops were named to examine the questions, those of Sens, Paris, Narbonne, Embrun, Auch, and Bordeaux; and there were an equal number of bishops, those of Langres, Valence, Chalons, Bayeux, Nouan, and St. Papoul. They were all knowledgeable in secular and ecclesiastical law. They were morally irreproachable and the most dignified of France's hierarchy. In addition they used very learned men as advisors, both theologians and lawyers.

After a careful study, they gathered at Cardinal Luynes' house and each brought with him his opinion in writing. This was agreed upon by all: Nothing could be holier, more prudent, or more useful for the public good than the Institute of the Society. The General possesses no power that is contrary to the laws of France. The doctrine of the Jesuits is orthodox and conforms to that which is generally handed down in Catholic schools. Nothing is found in that teaching that could threaten the safety of kings or the peace of kingdoms. Individuals added to these comments an unsolicited testimony to the excellent lives and morals of the Jesuits.

Luynes collected the ballots. Carrying them with him and accompanied by a train of bishops, he went to the king. When he first approached the king, Luynes remarked, "You have in these pages, my king, the view of the French clergy on the Jesuits. They commend the cause of the Jesuits to you with no less zeal than they do the cause of the Catholic religion to which the Society is closely linked." This was clearly a magnificent eulogy, and I, for my part, do not know if any other order can boast of such in its annals. The king seemed to be greatly pleased by Luynes' address. When the king saw his confessor Desmaretz, he congratulated him on the clergy's complimentary judgment on the Society. He bade Desmaretz's fellow Jesuits to be of good heart.[9] Next he told the royal family. Their grief was turned into incredible joy. The queen, a very holy woman and very fond of the Society, the Dauphin, his wife and his unmarried sisters, the king's daughters, leapt for joy. They shared a very great enthusiasm for the Society.

The Jesuits, relieved now of their fear, were congratulating themselves on the happy outcome of the business [84] and accepting with gratitude the congratulations of their friends. But their situation was not made better thereby.

Choiseul, the king's prime minister, was secretly in agreement, as I said before, with the Paris Parlement and its designs. He was powerful in the royal court in all matters, and was equally estranged from the Society and from Rome, where he had been the king's ambassador. Members of Parlement were clearly accustomed to resist the king's wishes openly and to treat his commands with a certain contempt. Now the support of the king's minister added to their confidence. They were irked rather severely by the clergy's declaration. So they began not only to continue the hostile investigations into the Society, but also brought over to their side the parlements of Toulouse and Rennes. These followed the example of Paris and published decrees that were very similar to its. They contradicted the Apostolic Constitutions with the same sort of name-calling.

Louis XV's Plan Fails

The king, on advisement again, vetoed all these transactions, ordered the parlements to abstain from such detractions, and said he was the sole and supreme judge of the Jesuits. He truly wanted them to be safe and unharmed. But he thought he had to concede something to so many members who were pressing so stubbornly and with such unanimity for the ruin of the Society. So he sought a middle road which, as he thought, could displease no one. The Parlement members seemed to him to be not so much against the Jesuits as against the name of Rome, for he felt the French did not take rule by foreigners easily. What if, he was proposing, the Jesuits had their own head in France, and were ruled by him without consultation of Rome? Power would then be transferred to a native son and he would be subject to the laws of France. Such a person certainly would have less unpopularity and would not provide any cause for suspicion and dangers which were now being alleged.

What more did Louis do? He ordered a swift courier to be sent off immediately to Rome to his protector. At that time it was Rochechouard, bishop of Laon, and later a cardinal.[10] He instructed him to treat with Father General on the matter of establishing a vicar-general for France. Such an official would direct the provinces of the realm by his own absolute authority. The Father General would be involved in this fashion: He would choose whichever Frenchman he wanted for his vicar. After six years, he would choose a successor to him, and at that fixed interval through the ensuing years, would substitute other vicars. Thus he would maintain his supreme authority over the Society, but no one could be annoyed with the Jesuits in France.[11] Rochechouard faithfully did his king's bidding. Ricci was surprised and troubled by this proposal. He dared not make a snap decision on such an important matter. Nor in truth could he. He asked time for consultation, and a very brief space was granted to him. [85] He summoned his assistants and asked what they thought should be done. They all decided to approach the Supreme Pontiff and to submit the proposal to his decision.

A matter of the greatest importance was at stake. There was grave danger on either side. If the request were not granted, the destruction of the Society in France seemed certain. But if the concession were made to the king of France, it would surely have to be granted to other kings too. What sort of body would the Society be then, when it does not cohere to its other members or to its head? Several Societies of Jesus would result, not the one Society that Ignatius wanted subject to one superior. Finally, the whole framework of this building, constructed once with such great skill, would have none of its stability if the connecting links were undone. Who could vouch for what sort of men Jesuits would be when separated from the rest of the body and freed of ties to Rome? What if they were to grow slack? What if they were to slip gradually from the observance of a rather strict discipline to a more lax kind of life? Would it not be preferable to have no Jesuits rather than bad ones?

The Jesuits discussed these matters privately among themselves. Ricci brought the question to the pope. He weighed the entire matter and at the end thought that the king's request should be flatly turned down. He uttered the famous saying, "Let them be as they are, or let them not be." With that the negotiations were quite quickly broken off and terminated. I know some criticize the remark, thinking that if the concession of a vicar-general had been granted to the king, the Society could have been preserved from complete shipwreck in France. But nothing at the time showed that a radical destruction was in the offing. To the contrary, the idea of a vicar-general raised fears that the Society could be split into parts and that would be the next worst thing to its destruction. It is silly to evaluate deliberations from events. Men would often change their deliberations if they had the power to foretell the future.

Paris Parlement Issues Decree of Proscription

This response was brought to France. The king, who should have expected no less, ceased his efforts to protect the Society. He left its lot in the hands of the Paris Parlement. That body acted as if all bars had been broken. It burst out and let loose a pent-up hatred for Jesuits with such force that nothing of theirs, not even their name, was left in France. It would be a long task to relate what sort of decree of proscription the Parlement made and with what violent language it was composed.[12] It contained more than thirty pages. I will summarize its contents.

It rehashed at length and in a fine literary style the three charges that I have been speaking about: Charges against the Institute and laws of the Society, against the moral teaching of the Jesuits, and against the powers of the General. It scorned the judgment of the clergy, and inveighed against the power of the General. [86] The Parlement charged that whatever ills had afflicted France through the past two centuries were derived from those sources. The decree enacted that a Society, which called itself "of Jesus" in order to subvert all human and divine law, was no longer to be tolerated in France.

After that proem, the decree laid down the following prescriptions on what the Parlement wanted done with the Jesuits and their affairs. Since the self-styled Jesuits had attached themselves to an impious and execrable Institute, they were all to be considered freed from their vows and, in fact, were free. They were to change their garb. Within eight days, they were to leave their houses and colleges. Each one was to go home or to seek a refuge somewhere else. They were not to observe the laws of the Society. They were not to obey

Father General or any other superior of the Society. They were not to live in community. All their permanent property was confiscated. Movable goods were to be auctioned off. From the proceeds, part was to be set aside for pensions so that they could have a decent living. The rest was to be spent on establishing schools for youth, maintaining public teachers, and undertaking some pious works. I note, in passing, that not even a thought was given to paying Lavalette's debts.[13]

It would be permissible, however, according to the Parlement's prescriptions, for the Jesuits to dwell where they preferred within the boundaries of the realm. Also they could be appointed to positions in the public lycées, to parishes, and to professorships provided they pronounced an oath of fidelity to the king and they abjured all the opinions that had been crammed into that collection of errors that I have described.

This was the gist of the Paris decree. Other parlements of the realm issued decrees that were very similar. For the Paris Parlement was, as it were, the head of the rest. It claimed an authority over the others as if they were parts of a body subject to it as head. But the king considered all this ratified. I do not know his state of mind. He may have acted at Choiseul's prompting, or out of a desire for peace, or because he felt the great power of the opposing faction could not be broken without much violence and public disturbance. He even sent away from the court the archbishop of Paris, Christopher Beaumont, a very impressive and holy man.[14] Because he courageously stood up for the rights of the Society and the Church, he was exiled to some distant corner of the realm far from the court.

Who can narrate what a great change in the situation followed shortly thereafter? The well-attended colleges, the pulpits of the churches, the sodalities of the fervent fell silent in a moment. The cassock of St. Ignatius, which inspired veneration everywhere in France and honor in the court for those who wore it, within a few days ceased to be seen at all. That enemies exulted with joy who [87] doubts? Especially in the ranks of the Jansenists! But some good men bemoaned the fact that innocence was overwhelmed by the wickedness of the evil as if all judicial procedure were suspended. Then some missed their old friends and advisors, others their favorite teachers, still others their well-tested and proven moral guides.

Bishops especially grieved the loss of suitable training for youth and of qualified helpers in sacramental ministry. They were looking in vain for replacements elsewhere. Meanwhile the majority of the companions returned to the homes where they were born and reared. City officials willingly summoned many, especially from the more learned, back to their homes, and put them in charge of educating their youth. The Dauphin himself and leading courtiers undertook the pensioning of some. Some, however, especially from the elderly, had no place to go whether because of lack of relatives or because of the hard-heartedness of those relatives they did have. These were forced to seek shelter in public hospitals. To speak of no other, Yves André, that very learned man who wrote a very well known book entitled *On the Beautiful,* was absolutely destitute and died in a paupers' hospital in Caen.[15]

But though scattered in this way, Jesuits were trying to keep the Institute of the Society as much as they were allowed and were tendering their obedience to superiors. If any of the young members wanted to be released from the obligation of the vows, the Fathers Provincial readily gave them letters of dismissal by a faculty granted to them by Father General. The rest conducted themselves in France as other Jesuits would do in England or in Holland. These, although they wore secular garb and did not live in community but separately in their friends' houses, still all had regard for their provincial and gave obedience to Father General.

Jesuits Choose Exile over Breaking Their Vows

The Paris Parlement easily found this out and thought it was not to be tolerated at all. And so in order to destroy completely the remnants of the dispersed Society, it ordered that a certain oath be proposed to individual Jesuits. The Parlement was certain that none of the Jesuits would subscribe to the oath's contents. The formula of the oath called God as witness that each Jesuit in his conscience revile, curse, and judge as most wicked the Institute of the Society. Further, each will have nothing to do with the superiors of that order and will explicitly exclude obedience to Father General. Who would not think that such an oath would cause the swearer scruples? With this one step taken and with its gradual application through the provinces, the Parlement destroyed what little was left of the shaken and broken Society. For the Jesuits did not consider the sanctity of their vows [88] less than the comforts of their homeland. But they outspokenly repudiated the impiety of the proposed oath. They preferred voluntary exile to infidelity to their vows to God. Many went to Avignon, others to Lorraine since King Stanislaus was in power there. He not only protected Jesuits with his patronage, but he also obtained from his son-in-law, the king of France, leave to permit the Jesuits to stay there permanently and undisturbed. Some, further, sailed to Martinique or Canada. These two areas in America had recently come into the power of the English. They would be better off among the Protestant English than among the Catholic French. There were also not a few of the young men who migrated to Italy, to Germany, to Belgium, and even to Poland. They sought refuge in the colleges of the Society, ready for every vicissitude, provided they could live their lives among the Companions.

No one, indeed, as far as I know, from that large number of Companions swore that impious oath out of fear of exile, except for one. He, least of all, should have committed such a sacrilege. I am speaking of Cerutti, the Piedmontese, who had recently written a highly lauded vindication of the Society and its Institute. He was in the vigor of his youth, though of humble origin, but very talented and good looking. He was caught up by the allurements of Paris: The applause of men of letters and the friendship of aristocrats. So that he would not have to leave these things, he did not hesitate to swear the oath as prescribed. This was sheer madness, for the judges, despite his oath, condemned him to exile since he convicted himself of lying by his defense of the Society's Institute and his current repudiation of it. He was stripped of the pension the Dauphin had given for his use. Hated by all good men and marked with public infamy, the poor wretch betook himself to Holland.

Clement XIII's New Constitution Brings Hope of Survival

When news of these events came from France to Rome, Pope Clement, as if he were better able to mourn such a great catastrophe of the Society than to repair it, decided that at least the holiness of the Institute, so undeservedly assailed, ought to be compensated and somehow vindicated. Therefore he issued a new constitution in which he reviewed the many great benefits that had flowed from the Society's ministry for the Christian commonwealth.[16] He expressed his feelings concerning the order and he eloquently stated what he wished would be the feelings of all followers of Christ. Finally, he confirmed and glowingly praised the Institute of Ignatius which had already been approved by other pontiffs. [89]

He sent that constitution to all the bishops of the Church. The document, so timely in its composition and promulgation, was no little comfort to the Jesuits. It prompted many of the bishops to intercede anew for the Society with the king of France. For they were not despairing of the Society's restoration in their sees. The king himself gave some grounds for the hope, for he was not at all, it was clear, against the Society. Consequently, if any Jesuits were to return secretly to France, he would not consider them criminals.

The Dauphin, the heir of the realm, very much raised hopes, for he had up to now openly criticized the parlements' actions. Accordingly, if he were to assume the power, he would surely revoke those measures. And finally the entire royal family earnestly and particularly favored the Jesuits and constantly pleaded their cause. But by bad luck it happened that the royal Dauphin, that fine prince, who was almost a twin to St. Louis in his outstanding piety and prudence, passed away at that time though he was still in the prime of l ife (1764). All of France, if you except only the enemies of the Jesuits, mourned with sincere grief this bitter misfortune. Marie-Josèphe of Saxony, the Dauphin's wife and a woman endowed with every physical and intellectual gift, added to the grief of the royal household and the realm when she followed her husband shortly thereafter. The Jesuits became greatly dispirited since they were deprived by these happenstances of powerful patrons.

But suddenly a new ray of hope for better things flashed forth. Choiseul, who played the leading role in the court, was reported to be in secret agreement with the Paris Parlement. By order of the king, he was dismissed from office and forced not only to leave the court, but also to depart from the city. When the parlements of the realm then persisted in frequent resistance to the king's commands and cloaked their inflexibility with words of compliance, the king endured the mockery no longer and dissolved the parlements. He ordered some of the members to be exiled to the outskirts of the kingdom. He put in charge of the courts equally learned men, but ones who were more compliant. This edict of royal power terrified all of France since it was unprecedented. It brought about a big change. No one opened his mouth against it. The decree was obeyed. An irony of fortune occurred at that time. It happened that certain Jesuits, returning to Paris, met with some Parlement members who were being sent away. With a happy shout the Jesuits wished them a pleasant and prosperous journey.

Meanwhile in this state of affairs the next step seemed to be the abrogation of the Parlement's old decrees against the Jesuits. Many bishops were earnestly working for this with the king, especially the archbishop of Paris, Beaumont. For the king admired him for his holiness and prudence. He had taken the bishop into his confidence [90] and used his advice on everything. The chancellor, Maupeou, who carried great weight with the king, thought the abrogation should be made.[17] The king's daughter, Marie-Louise,[18] humbly requested the king to take this step. She, by a nowadays rare example of piety, valued the cross of Christ more than royal garb and preferred to follow the footsteps of St. Theresa among the virgins consecrated to God. The king, besieged by such powerful petitions, was just about making up his mind to restore the Jesuits. But while he delayed and put off the day, the king of Spain intervened.

Spain Demands Total Expulsion by France

It might be truer to say the hidden power of God intervened, by which all human affairs are guided. But in a moment the entire hope evaporated. For King Charles of Spain, who had expelled the Society from his realms, had sniffed out the plans of King Louis. So he immediately sent Count Aranda to deter the king from that idea.[19] Aranda reminded him of the Family Compact that the Bourbon princes had entered upon. He began to demand that there be no place at all in France for Jesuits, not even in Lorraine where some had remained under the protection of King Stanislaus. To drive the Jesuits out would have been against his word while Stanislaus was alive. But since he had died the year before, Charles, with unbelievable insistence, demanded the expulsion as a matter of the highest importance. Louis was not to appear to violate the Family Compact, nor was he to make an enemy of his neighboring king. Not only did Louis then not take back the Jesuits into France, but he also ordered them to leave the colleges of Lorraine. How he finally expelled even those in Avignon will be told more appropriately elsewhere in my work.

I would like to add here a little appendix. From this one thing, brother, you will understand how dangerous those times were for us at Rome and what snares were being laid for me personally. Before I narrate the story, I want you to know and be assured of this: Although I am accustomed to write a lot as time and situation require and have often made bold to engage in controversy with private individuals for the defense of the Society, still I have never dared to rail at nations or princes even in the slightest. I have always greatly feared the very name of prince, let alone that I should want to upbraid princes too irreverently. I am timid by nature and most fearful of the powerful. Have the patience now to hear how an unjust detractor has made me pay the price for my writing.

Defense of Cordara against False Charges

When the Paris decrees were most strident against the Jesuits, it happened that lightning came down from a cloudy sky and struck the coat of arms of the king of France, which had been attached to the ambassador's door. The papal coat of arms, however, which was next to it, was untouched. A certain clever man, rather than a prudent one (the type abounds in Rome) looked upon the event as material for mocking [91] the French king. And so he wrote some Latin verses that were insulting to his name. These immediately began to spread through the city.

I knew nothing about these things, nor had I heard anything even about the lightning bolt. I can swear to this. Yet at a large gathering of nobles, there was a person who shamelessly asserted that I had made those verses. He passed that off as something that he had personal and firsthand knowledge of. There was by chance one of my friends present at that meeting (it was Ludovico Valenti, now a cardinal).[20] Although he said nothing to the speaker who was so positive, still the next day he met with me and most kindly warned me about the matter.

I was utterly dumbfounded. I felt that some most undeserved charge was being too easily heaped upon my head. I did not, however, panic. I thanked my friend profusely for the revelation. I went off right away to Cardinal Colonna, the one they called Sciarra and who serves, as we say, as protector of the kingdom of France.[21] I was on good terms with him. When he, as is his wont, began to joke, I interrupted him and explained about the libelous verses that were falsely attributed to me. I was prepared to swear an oath about my innocence if he wished. Then he said seriously, "There is no need for an oath. When a good and noble man such as I know you to be, gives testimony about himself, he is more credible than a sworn witness." He added, "You should know, however, that you have been delated to Count d'Aubeterre on this charge." (D'Aubeterre was then the ambassador of the king of France.)[22] "He was very angry," he continued, "with you and discussed the matter with me. I took the opportunity to soothe the man's ire and I kept him from taking any steps against you. But now you should be of good heart. I will make it my business that he correct this mistaken judgment about you and recognize the calumny." After saying this, he turned the conversation to other topics. Finally, he sent me off free from every fear and greatly relieved in mind. With such ploys as this, our enemies were attacking. [92]

BOOK V

Spain and Naples—Two Sicilies

We turn from events in France to those in Spain. We undertake to trace as briefly as possible the most shocking calamity of the Society which led finally to its ultimate ruin. But the story must go back a little farther. In the year the Society was proscribed in Portugal (1759), Charles, king of Naples, was summoned to ascend the throne of Spain when his brother, King Ferdinand of Spain, died without offspring. Since it was very important for us to have a favorable prince at this difficult time, Ricci hastened to Naples to pay his respects and to wish the new king good luck.

Jesuits' Situation after Charles Becomes King of Spain

The king received Ricci kindly and with royal and Spanish dignity. Although the king was sparing in words, he answered Ricci's commendation of the sorely tried Society in such a way that there seemed no cause for fear. Nor was there indeed any reason to fear that the king was hostile. For to begin with, he inherited a love of the Society from his father, Philip V, and from his grandfather, Louis XIV. In addition he kept two Jesuits at court: Ildebrando, the confessor of his wife the queen, and Barba, the tutor of his children. And now upon Charles' departure for Spain, he left a third Jesuit, François Cardell by name, as the language teacher of his young son, the new king of Naples.[1]

In the Paraguay business which had so incensed the court of Lisbon against the Jesuits, he was on the Society's side. For he learned from the secret correspondence of Ensenada, the prime minister of the king of Spain, that the exchange of land was not to Spain's advantage.[2] If the Jesuits had not wanted the exchange made, he, as heir to the kingdom of Spain, was glad and content. What about the fact that he had recently bestowed a signal honor on the Jesuits of the Roman College? For the Jesuits had extensive land holdings in the kingdom of Naples. Since they were non-residents, they were paying over a long period a heavy tax, which they call the *valimento*. Scarcely was Charles asked to relieve them of this burden when he did so with a rare display of generosity. For all these reasons we had no doubts that everything would be well for us in Spain under the new king. [93]

Queen Amalia from Saxony, a woman of remarkable piety and no less prudence, raised these hopes even higher. From her infancy, she had been imbued with great love for the Society. If she had lived longer, she could have counteracted all our adversaries' machinations, no matter how cleverly contrived. Such was her favor and influence with the king. But reasons for fear were not lacking.

Before Charles set sail for Spain, he disinherited Philip, his oldest son. The doctors said he was an incurable imbecile. Charles renounced the throne of the Two Sicilies and gave orders that Ferdinand, his third son, be hailed king of Naples in the usual manner. Since he was too young to assume the responsibility of ruling, Charles gave him eight guardians, men picked from the nobility, by whose authority and consensus the state was to be administered. But one in the group of eight was dominant and swayed the judgment of all: Bernardo Tanucci. He was carrying on a frequent and familiar correspondence with Charles. He reported to his colleagues that whatever he wanted decided was affirmed by Charles' authority. Whether they liked it or not, they were forced to go along with Tanucci's views.

Tanucci was a newcomer to public service. He was born of humble parentage in the country town of Chiusi.[3] When he came to Naples from Etruria, he got the chance to insinuate himself into the king's favor. He so succeeded in this that Charles often fled the cares of government to enjoy the hunt and left the entire burden of ruling with Tanucci. Tanucci had a thorough grasp of civil law, which he had long taught at Pisa. He had a great gift for management. His character was upright. He had absolute loyalty to the king and an incredible capacity for work. Remarkably tenacious of the right, he gave no quarter to favoritism or to bribes. He turned down every gift, no matter how great or how freely offered.

But either because he was unduly zealous for the king's prerogatives out of preconceived notions or because he was envious of Rome's preeminence over other cities of the world, he was notably hostile to the Roman Curia. He tried in any way he could to reduce the power of the Supreme Pontiff. He was heard to say in informal conversation, that the pope's pallium had to be shortened a bit. He had an especial antipathy for Cardinal Torrigiani. He undertook many measures to do Torrigiani harm and issued rather unjust decrees that were contrary to our ancestors' usage and ordinary procedure. But it is not appropriate to list them here.

As to the Jesuits, if he did not love them, at least he seemed to hold them in esteem beyond other religious orders. He had brought matters of conscience to one of these [94] and he was in the habit of making his confession to him. But if the interests of the kingdom demanded it, if harm was to be inflicted upon the pope or Torrigiani, he would not hesitate to harry and destroy whatever Jesuit interests were in the way. Such a man Charles put in charge of conducting affairs. When he had sailed to Spain from Naples, he continued consultation with Tanucci by letter.

Other causes for fear came up shortly after these events. Queen Amalia, a little after she had come to Madrid, lost her confessor Ildebrando, who passed away. She was determined to have a Jesuit for a confessor. Since she had heard that among the Jesuits at Naples Savastano enjoyed a great reputation for learning and prudence, she wrote him a letter in her own hand, which was full of kindness and regard. In it she asked that he not be unwilling to come to Spain. She wished to entrust to him the direction of her conscience. She sent the letter by courier. Savastano set out without delay. He had just arrived at Genoa and was preparing to set sail from there. But an unexpected messenger from the court arrived first. Savastano was to go no farther, for the queen had died from a sudden illness.

Nothing more disastrous than that loss could have happened to the Society in Spain. For it was clear that at court Count Aranda, the duke of Alba, Campomañes,[4] and other powerful figures were undertaking many measures against us. There was not the slightest doubt that at Rome Passionei, Spinelli, Marefoschi,[5] and other leaders of the opposing faction were in accord with the Spanish ministers. If Queen Amalia were alive, all their attempts would be blunted. When I heard the news of her death, I all but shivered and could not hide the panic that seized my mind. For the little verses that I have mentioned elsewhere had not slipped my mind. It was hardly a coincidence that they proclaimed that the Society would be expelled from Spain. I sensed that the prediction was all too true and the fates were conspiring against us.

It happened that a little later the king's confessor also died. He was a very good man, a Franciscan of the Strict Observance. He was a simple man, not at all used to court intrigues. While a successor was being sought by order of the king, Manuel de Roda,[6] who was then conducting the business of the Spanish embassy under Cardinal Portacarrero,[7] saw to it that another Franciscan be chosen. This nominee was living in the monastery which they call Forty Saints and was a friend of de Roda. He was a Spaniard by birth and very much different from his predecessor. He was clever, subtle, and most important of all, hostile toward the Jesuits.

De Roda and the Cause of Palafox

When the new confessor came to Madrid and became the guide of conscience for the king, he persuaded the king, first of all, to seek the beatification of [95] Venerable Juan de Palafox, bishop of Osma.[8] It is uncertain whether he did this out of civic pride (Osma was his hometown) or for hatred of the Jesuits. Surely, if Palafox were enhanced with the dignity of sainthood, then his letters would acquire more weight for vilifying the Society. He is said to have written these letters to Innocent X and all the reproaches against our good name contained in them would seem then to be confirmed with pontifical authority.

For this reason Jesuits were eager to divert and to delay the cause of Palafox. On whether this was sufficiently prudent, I will not take a stand. But I, for my part, would have preferred that the Jesuits had no part in Palafox's cause. It was notably deficient in itself and would not have met with success. Very learned men from various orders were handling it with mature judgment. Finally, the Jesuits knew the pope wanted to put an end to it and many of the more prudent men saw this very fact. Yet some of the more fervent, impelled by love of the Society, openly and plainly impugned the holiness of Palafox both orally and in writing. The only thing gained from the attack was that they provoked the king of Spain. The more zealously the king backed the cause with his recommendations, the more open and firm were the objections that he heard the Jesuits were raising. Although many on the commission judged that Palafox was not sufficiently deserving of public cult, still the Jesuits were said to be the only ones blocking and thwarting the beatification. The King was convinced of it. I think that this was the first and chief reason why King Charles was alienated from the Jesuits.

Then it was most unfortunate that at that time Portacarrero finished his days. He was an especially upright man and very friendly towards the Society. He was replaced on the Spanish delegation by the Manuel de Roda whom I mentioned. De Roda was indescribably clever, self-possessed, and very good at deception. He came from a poor background, but was promoted in the court due to the Jesuits' efforts. Outwardly he showed himself their friend. He often visited the professed house. In turn, he entertained certain Jesuits of his nationality at his home. But secretly he was contriving measures against the Society. He had a close friendship and frequent contact with Marefoschi, the secretary of the Congregation for the Propagation of the Faith. He had handed himself over completely to the faction of our foes. He had gone over to the other side with the South American Vazquez, the General of the Augustinians, who had formerly been a friend of the Society, but who was subsequently alienated by some offense.[9]

Now, therefore, that de Roda was a royal official, he carried on a frequent [96] correspondence with the court at Madrid. He lost no opportunity for influencing the king against the Jesuits and against the Roman Curia. To mention some of the more noteworthy cases, the king very much wanted Marefoschi to be elected to the College of Cardinals. He never got his wish. He asked that Lermio and Diomede Carafa, two bishops who were devoted to him, be promoted. On behalf of Carafa, he had written twice in his own hand. He received a rebuff. When de Roda reported to the court on these matters, he threw the blame on the Jesuits, who considered those they knew to be well-disposed to the king to be their enemies and the Jesuits tried to abase such. De Roda added that the pontiff, Torrigiani, and the Rezzonicos were all on the Jesuits' side. One little word of Ricci carries more weight than any number of recommendations and requests from the king. Marefoschi and Vazquez wrote in the same vein. Even Cardinal Orsini, a thing which will surprise you, wrote the same sort of thing not out of hatred for us, but from eagerness to make a mark for himself.[10] His letter carried all the more weight and authority because he boasted he was a Tertiary of the Society,[11] because he went to Ricci, the General of the Society, for confession, and because he was on very friendly terms with several Jesuits, but especially with me.

Charles Opposes Jesuits and Roman Curia

It is easy to imagine how the king took all this. Afterwards, he seemed to be in open opposition not only to the Jesuits but to the Roman Curia. His former regard for the pontiff slackened a lot. Let these two situations be the proof that I submit. It was an old and common desire of the faithful that the Sacred Heart of Jesus, inflamed with such great love for men, might be honored with special piety among Christians. Letters of petition for this feast were sent by various bishops, but especially by the Spanish ones. The pontiff yielded to so many requests and decreed that the Heart of Jesus was to be honored henceforward with its own liturgy. The king, however, forbade that this pontifical decree be received in Spain because the request was said to have been granted to the special requests of the Jesuits.

But that was relatively insignificant. The second proof was this. An Italian version of Mésenguy's catechism began to be circulated in the city.[12] It was a pernicious work which Benedict XIV had previously condemned for being infected with the poison of Jansenism. It was widely read and praised. The harmful virus was spreading unchecked. There were some cardinals in the Holy Office who said the work was condemned because of the Jesuits' ill will and not for its just deserts. In this state of affairs, in order not to fail in his duty, the pontiff decided to have the book censored again. He thought that he should avoid using the Congregation of the Holy Office. So he gave the task to twelve theologians chosen from every religious order. Only the Jesuits were excluded. [97]

After a careful study, the view of all the theologians, with the exception of one Franciscan of the Strict Observance, was that the catechism of Mésenguy clearly reeked of pure Jansenism and ought to be kept out of the hands of the faithful. Consequently, the pontiff condemned the work again and sent the letter of condemnation to all the bishops of the Church. There was question here of the dogma of the Christian faith. Up to this point no Catholic had denied to the supreme pontiff the power of declaring dogma. Yet King Charles did not allow this letter of the pope to be promulgated in Spain. He even ordered that the copy posted on the doors of the Holy Inquisition be torn down, and he expelled from Madrid Manuel Quintana, the Supreme Inquisitor. For Quintana had obeyed the pope without the king's knowledge and had ordered the letter posted.

In addition, Charles decreed that thereafter no papal letter of any kind, whether addressed to the bishops or to a private individual, was to be received unless the king had been informed beforehand and had given his approval. Thus the prince, otherwise an excellent man, had changed his attitude in dealing with Rome and was influenced by the views of his courtiers. However, in this matter, there are some who think he followed not the advice of his courtiers, but only the urgings of Tanucci.

With the king so disposed, we had everything to fear in Spain. Only one thing was lacking. Someone more ruthless was needed to put the final touch to the preparations. He was not long in coming. For the king's new confessor, to return the favor to his friend, saw to it that de Roda was summoned to the court and established as one of the close advisors of the king. With de Roda's help, the confessor easily influenced the king's thinking and led him where he willed.

No one at Rome doubted that de Roda had been recalled to hasten the destruction of the Jesuits. Before he set out for Spain, they say he was asked why the Spanish did not follow the example of the French and Portuguese and crucify the Jesuits. He answered that the time was not yet ripe. They had to wait until the "little old lady" closes her eyes in death. By that term, he wanted Elizabeth Farnese understood. She was the king's mother and nearly eighty years old. As long as she was alive, de Roda had no hope that the expulsion could be pulled off.

These matters were being openly discussed at Rome. If the Society's superiors had paid heed, had made a correct appraisal, and had reacted vigorously, they would have turned the threatening storm aside or maybe would have even avoided it altogether. But they dismissed such reports as vulgar gossip. The king's well-known integrity and innocent conscience removed any worries. Charles was a prince who never acted rashly or capriciously. He was used to doing all according to the laws. They could not dream that he would wish to condemn the innocent unheard [98] or to drive them into exile. His actions tended to lessen the fears. For, scarce had he come back to Spain when he sent Cevallio to Paraguay. Cevallio was a proven and trustworthy man who was ordered to look closely into Jesuit affairs. After a long and careful investigation, Cevallio made a report on the Jesuits that prompted the king to send sixty other Jesuits to Paraguay at the royal expense. Who would think, in the light of so recent a favor, that the king was alienated from the Jesuits? Add to this the fact that Jesuits had recently quelled an uprising in Quito. When the king was informed of this, he wrote a very kind letter to the provincial in which he praised the peacemakers for their services and directed that they receive his thanks.

Mounting Danger to Jesuits

Since many similar reports from the Companions were arriving at Rome, our superiors were not alarmed. But not even these good men were reflecting that nothing is more changeable than the favor of princes. Just like other mortals, princes can be deceived, and more than others, they are subject to circumvention. For many of them are guided only by the advice of their ministers. Nor were superiors taking into account the fact that at the court of Madrid, there were two men, de Roda and the king's confessor, who were wielding great power with the king and who were closely allied in their desire to secretly contrive the ruin of the Society.

There were those at Rome who were in agreement with these two. They had a like hatred for us. They were equally clever. They kept supplying material for the conflagration and daily added new firebrands. Although Azpuru, a man of long-standing probity and a friend of the Jesuits, had succeeded de Roda in the embassy, still there remained Marefoschi, Vazquez, Nicola Azara, and perhaps others taken into the same pact.[13] They were acting in concert and sending many false reports to Spain. In letters full of hate, they were pressing for the destruction of the Society. Our superiors made little of these reports or even held them in contempt. As if they were sure of events in Spain, they slept on, wrapped in a certain fatal lethargy, though the danger was pressing.

Meanwhile (1767), things at Madrid were being done in the utmost silence. Indeed the papal nuncio, Lazaro Pallavicini, although he kept a close watch on movements at court, had never detected a thing.[14] Yet after the Queen Mother had died, there were some indications of the rising storm. For certain parties had secretly introduced into Spain the French book [by Cerutti (see p. 81)] that had defended the Society's reputation. A strict judicial inquiry was made into the matter, and those who were responsible were punished according to the laws. Although that action was not unjust, still it raised [99] great wonderment in Spain, where, a short time before, books libelous toward the Society were condemned by a public court, and were, as we said above, burned by the hand of the executioner.

Also, when one of the Jesuits had set out on a journey to Rome to conduct the business of his province, royal agents ordered him to stop at the border. They did a thorough job of searching him, going through all his bags. Then they made him retrace his steps. No one understood the drift of such an unusual occurrence, but grave suspicions were stirred. Clearly these events showed the attitude in the court about the Jesuits had changed. Many took fright because of the sudden about-face in treatment.

Up to now a great pillar of support and a bulwark for the Jesuits was the Marquis Gregorio Squillace.[15] He enjoyed great authority and favor with the king, and looked out for the Society. But the common people of Madrid suddenly rose up in rebellion. They terrified the king with this memorable uprising and forced him with their threats and mad shouting to expel Squillace. Once that was done, the king was without a faithful minister and the Jesuits without their powerful and almost only patron. There was no further delay for the king's edict which was to expel the Society from Spain.[16]

The edict was totally unexpected by the Jesuits. The first rumblings of it so surprised the leading Fathers of the order that they were astonished by its novelty, speechless, and paralyzed in their confusion. They seemed to have been struck by a lightning bolt. They were not unaware that after the Spanish Jesuits received such a lot, because of the Family Compact, those of Naples, the Sicilies, and Parma would follow suit. By these steps the entire Society was hastening to its destruction. Many accused Pallavicini of stupidity or even of perfidy. Of stupidity if he had not seen that such a momentous thing was being set in motion right under his nose; of perfidy if he thought he should keep the movement a secret. Later, however, it was learned that he was free from all blame.

The pontiff was seriously wounded by this unexpected message. He immediately wrote a letter of complaint on the matter to the king. He admonished him paternally about his mistake. He asked the king through the love of Christ and through whatever is sacred everywhere to want to correct his error. Let the king reflect what evils will ensue if these men are driven away. Jesuits were devoting themselves to the salvation of so many souls, to such helpful labors and ministries. They had up to now kept especially the Indians faithful to Christianity after their conversion from paganism. Let the king consider that someday he will have to give an account of those Indians to Christ, the King of Kings. If any Jesuits had merited punishment, let the king inflict it upon them by his royal power. But the order, founded by a Spaniard, St. Ignatius, was blameless. [100] It had performed countless services for the Christian commonwealth, especially for Spain. Let the king not expel it from his realms. Let him act in accord with his native fairness, in accord with his old respect for the Apostolic See. Finally, let the king make a sacrifice of this decree to him, the pope, his most loving father, who has already been overwhelmed more than enough by the setbacks of the times, and who asks the favor not so much for the Jesuits as for the king's salvation and glory. Though Clement wrote these things with the bitterest pangs of pain, I do not think the king read them. Certainly, the letter availed nothing at all. The edict of the king was no sooner issued than it began to be enacted.

Enactment of Charles' Edict

On one and the same night, at midnight, both in Madrid and in the other cities of Spain, soldiers suddenly surrounded the houses and colleges of the Society. They woke the Jesuits up. They announced their exile in the king's name. They put them all in wagons and transported them to the nearest ports. From there they were to be transferred to Italy and to the pontiff.

At the same time the king's orders were sent to the remoter parts of Spanish America, to Peru, to Mexico, to Quito, to Chile, to New Granada, to Paraguay, to all the ocean islands. Each of the governors was to carry out the same measures upon the Jesuits in his province. Carvalho was the model for implementing the order. The Spaniards were not ashamed to follow the footsteps and trail of that man. Care was especially taken that the announcement of exile catch the Jesuits unawares and completely unsuspecting. All were gathered into one place. The king's edict was read publicly. Each was permitted to keep his personal possessions and bring them along, but not, however, manuscripts, books, or money. They were forced to depart immediately.

Great was the amazement of people when religious, who were generally thought to be the most serviceable of all, were being suddenly whisked away for no known reason. The Indians in Paraguay were especially amazed when the sixty extra Jesuits who had barely set foot on their land were put back into ships and deported far away along with the other Jesuits. They grieved to have the Fathers, who were their sustainers and directors, torn from their breasts and embraces. A great and pitiable disaster for religion ensued when no pastor of souls was left there, when no minister of the sacraments was left. The losses were too great to be adequately described in words. But nothing was so important that it would take precedence over gratifying the hatred conceived for the Jesuits. I wish to note in passing that though the Jesuits allegedly had assumed a tyranny over those regions and had Paraguay as almost their own kingdom, still [101] they freely surrendered to a handful of soldiers when they had barely heard the king's command, and they allowed themselves to be led off from their "kingdom" to wherever their captors were to lead them. Let us now see what sort of edict the king issued.

It was addressed to the prince of Asturia, the heir of the kingdom, and bore the title of pragmatic sanction.[17] As is his wont, the king said first that he prefers nothing more than the happiness of his subjects. Next, because it was beneficial for himself, his descendants, and the entire nation of Spaniards, he forbade the Jesuits, as public enemies, the use of fire and water. He condemned them wherever they were under his jurisdiction, whether in Europe or in the New World, to perpetual exile and he ordered them deported from Spanish soil. He laid down the death penalty for anyone of them who would dare to return under any pretext whatsoever, in any costume whatsoever. He transferred the property of the Society to the royal treasury. He entrusted the churches to the bishops. The services performed by custom or by law by the Jesuits for divine worship or for the needs of their neighbors he ordered to be paid for thereafter at the king's expense. For individual Jesuits he directed that a certain amount of money be paid out annually in order that they could sustain life in exile. But this was done on condition that if any written defense of them appeared, they would be deprived of the pension.

The condition appeared to many to be too unfair. For who ever forbade the accused his natural right of self-defense? What would happen if some spiteful outsider were to write a defense for the very purpose of depriving the Jesuits of their pension? But the following was even more remarkable. The king kept saying that there were many and grave reasons for demanding the exile, but they were shut up in the safety of his heart and he would reveal none of them.

Those who were driven into exile came to approximately five thousand. It was certainly unprecedented and something unknown to that day to deprive such a throng of people of the rights of their native land, to strip them of their property, to send them off into exile from their common fatherland, and to do this with one act of the will and for no known cause. But it was easy to see why the king's ministers wanted the matter so arranged. They saw that people generally did not approve the reasons which the Portuguese and French proffered, and they did not have any more acceptable causes to offer.

Speculations on Charles' Reasons for the Edict

Since, however, just and grave reasons for the exile were alleged and the fact that there were seemed likely, the minds of all concentrated on figuring them out. People managed to come up with a few in their speculations. Some thought up one explanation, others another. Many, influenced by the grave appearance of things and measuring the crime by the severity of the punishment, thought the Jesuits were guilty of treason. There had been an uprising at Madrid about which I spoke above. [102] The Jesuits were suspected of having goaded the people into taking up arms. But that was incredible and no one with any sense could believe it. The king had not ordered that any one Jesuit be punished above the rest. Rather, he maintained the same attitude towards all of them. Further, it was especially to the Jesuits' interest that Squillace, a very honest man and much attached to the Society, not be removed from office and deported from Spain.

Some were more inclined to think that the courtiers themselves stirred up the riot with a view to removing Squillace and thus becoming able to overwhelm the Jesuits without any opposition. Some were claiming that the king was shown a forged letter of Ricci which alluded to a disgrace concerning the king himself and to a plot for regicide.[18] I do not find that incredible. For what will one not dare to do when he has determined to ruin the innocent? I am the more inclined to believe this because they say that to this day King Charles is most inimical to Jesuits, cannot bear to hear their name, and very much fears their hidden plots against him.

These views do not come so much from the truth of the matter, but from some probability. Stories were spread as each one's opinion led him; and the guesses varied. I, to speak my mind openly, think that the king had shut up in his heart no other reason than the one I reported a short time before with regard to events at Rome. Letters were being written from Rome to the court at Madrid that had the result of inflaming the King against the Jesuits, against the pope, and against the papal household and chief minister. The letters said that at Rome the king of Spain counted for nothing. The Jesuits, especially the leading men of the order (they called them the "Sanhedrin"),[19] were waging a stubborn and open war with the king of Spain. They immediately blocked what they knew was pleasing to the king. They opposed all his wishes. The pontiff deferred more to the Jesuits than to king of Spain. Honors and holy orders were being distributed to the Jesuits' followers and backers. Those whom the king recommended were being neglected.

When these and other things of the same type were constantly dinned into the ears of the king, who would be surprised that a prince who was very jealous of his dignity grew angry at last and pondered expelling the Jesuits and sending them to the pontiff? Kings are touchy by nature and nothing is more intolerable for a potentate than to be scorned. I think these were the only causes for inflicting the exile; truer causes are sought in vain and are never to be found. Because, however, the reports made to the king were not true, or even if they were true, the offenses were too trivial to merit such a stiff penalty, the ministers thought the causes of the exile were to be covered over with a cunning silence. Thus it was left to each and everyone [103] to impute the gravest of outrages to the Jesuits, but no one could disprove the edict's unfairness.

Changing Attitudes toward Jesuits

However that matter stood, it is remarkable how easily the wills and judgments of men were bent to the caprice of the prince. The Spanish bishops, who had so earnestly and so flatteringly commended the Society to the pope when it was harried in Portugal, issued pastoral letters shortly after the edict's promulgation, which were full of reproaches against the Society. The order which they praised to the skies when they were free to speak, they now loaded down with open-ended charges when they were to conform like slaves.

A great change in attitudes was also seen at Rome after the receipt of the king's edict. Azpuru, the king's ambassador, was, as I said, a very good man and friendly toward the Society. He had been our frequent visitor; he suddenly ceased to be seen with us. Zelada, who had risen to various offices due to the special help of the Jesuits, used to visit the leaders of the order almost daily. But since he was born of a Spanish father, he not only suddenly deserted us, but also, which was a graver matter, went over to the side of the Master General of the Augustinians.[20] Another case was that of prince of Piombino, Cajetan Boncompagni. He was a man of outstanding piety and nurtured from boyhood among Jesuits. He had an especial love for Jesuits and had set aside one of his carriages for the daily use of Father General. His house could be called the common inn of the Companions. But because he was prefect of the royal household and was knighted by the king, he suddenly broke off all contact with the Jesuits and would see no Jesuit after that.

Doria Pamphili added something further to this avoidance simply on the grounds of his being one of the Magnates of Spain.[21] Up to this time he used to deal most familiarly with us. After the edict, he not only stopped coming to visit us, but also would not grant an interview to his very dear uncle, Fabrizio Carafa. Anyone who had any reason to have regard for the court at Madrid, nobles, commoners, religious as well as laypeople, immediately withdrew from all contact with the Jesuits. Indeed they began to avoid Jesuits as if they were afflicted with the plague.

Let one story serve as an example: The Spanish Trinitarians, whose motherhouse is in Rome, professed themselves so devoted to the Society that they would follow no other theological opinions than those of Jesuits. Recently, when one of their family, Simon de Rojas, was beatified, they commissioned me to write his life. They also wanted me to put my name on the title page. But after the Society's expulsion from Spain, when they were celebrating the new blessed's feast in their church, the Trinitarians [104] very rudely turned away from the altar some Spanish Jesuits who had come to the church to worship. So fickle is the support of men and, when the wind changes, friends defect to the opposite side.

Dispersal of Spanish Jesuits

Meanwhile King Charles had ordered that the Jesuits be put on ships and transported to Civitavecchia to be left to the pope's jurisdiction. But the pope already had enough and more than enough exiles from Portugal. He foresaw that if he were to admit the Spanish Jesuits, those of Naples, the Sicilies, and Parma would surely follow. He accordingly thought they had to be rejected and prohibited from landing. Therefore it happened that those who arrived first were forced to ride at anchor just outside the port. In the end they sailed to Corsica, with the good graces of the Genoese. For the Genoese interests on that island were unsettled due to civil war and they exercised almost no control because of the islanders' unbridled stubbornness. When asked in the name of the Catholic king to admit the guests, they readily agreed to it. Accordingly, one group of Jesuits after another was carried to Corsica in various ships and then they were distributed through the towns of the region. You would scarcely believe how affectionately, how hospitably, how honorably the townspeople received them. They helped them with shelter, food, and all the necessities of life. Because of such kindness shown them, the Jesuits, though in great poverty, were content enough with their lot.

But they were not to be quiet very long. For the French had meanwhile come to the aid of the Genoese. After many and various wranglings, the war was finally brought to an end and the rebels forced to surrender. Then the French commander annexed the island for the king of France. When that was done, not only the Spanish Jesuits, but also the Italians, who had two colleges at Bastia and Ajaccio, were forced to leave Corsica and to seek some other place of refuge. They were all carried by boat to Genoa. The Italians quite easily found places to stay on the mainland. But the Spaniards, who had no place to go, called upon the good faith and mercy of the pope, the common parent of all Christians. They were granted their request to be admitted into the papal jurisdiction. After a short trip through the territory of Parma and Modena, they came to Bologna. Several stopped there. Ferrara received many as did Ravenna. Others were distributed among the towns of Emilia, Forli, Imola, Cesena, Faenza, and Rimini. These areas abounded in crops and they vied with one another to receive the Jesuits who brought Spanish gold with them. The more Jesuits they received, the more they asked to be assigned to them. [105]

Orderly Conduct of Jesuits in Exile

It is of interest now to know how the exiles were governed. The number and names of the provinces were retained as before. A house in each city was rented for the use of the Companions. In the house, the distinguished and the lowly dwelt side by side. There were just about as many colleges of the Society as there were houses. Each had its rector who watched out for the others and enforced the observance of the rules. If any of the younger members asked for dismissal, it was readily granted. If any had committed some grave offense, they were sent away, even against their will. The pensions of individuals were contributed to a common fund from which all were sustained with like food and clothing. Each of the rectors reported to his provincial, and the provincials brought their business to him whom we call the Assistant for Spain. He, in turn, consulted with Father General on matters of common concern. You would say that the Spanish Society had not at all been destroyed, but only transferred to Italy.

That situation, which was a marvel to many and ought to have been an example for all, displeased our enemies. At their prodding Azpuru sent one of his men with a scribe and witnesses to Father General. The agent was told to inform the General that it was the king's will that there be no further vestige of the Spanish provinces. Not even the names were to be retained, but the body that was called the Spanish Assistancy was to be considered completely destroyed. To fulfill this command, Ricci was to erase the name of the Assistancy from public records. The provinces which were formerly called Toledo, Aragon, Baetica were to be named thereafter for some saint of the Society.[22] But concerning the form of governance, he suggested no great change in order that the religious not be left unchecked outlaws. One can judge how closely our enemies looked into our affairs from the fact that they pored over the more intricate details of the Institute in order to take offense at even the finer provisions. But at the same time it is apparent that they were not yet thinking of the total suppression of the Society. They had not yet conceived the hope of bringing that about.

Jesuit Optimism in Spite of Disasters

The Jesuits, on the other hand, though weighed down with so many disasters, were predicting a happy outcome for themselves and moved forward with a sure hope. The Society, they were saying, is under the protection of God. Up to now, God wanted things to be strained and destructive so that we, having been stripped of every human safeguard, might look to Him alone and place all our hope in Him. Without a doubt, Jesuits would, within a short time and with a great increase in honor, return to Portugal, France, and Spain. Should there be need, miracles to effect this will not be lacking. Many were speaking in this vein. If anyone were to have doubts, they found fault with him as being too little spiritual. [106]

Signs from God were alleged to bolster this confidence. Such, of course, is the last refuge of the wretched in lamentable and dire straits. Retz,[23] the Father General of the Society, was said to have received signs from God in his prayer. The Society appeared to be on the point of extinction, but was then recalled, in a sudden reversal of fortune, to its original stature and splendor. Although only one lay brother, who was the silliest of people, testified to this sign, it was considered a proven fact and was spread through all of Italy for the comfort of the Companions.

Besides this sign, Francis Xavier was said to have appeared to a certain pious nobleman in Sicily who was very ill. The man's health was restored and he predicted that the lot of the Society was to turn for the better. The same prediction was made at Rome by Aloysius Gonzaga to one of the novices. The novice was very near death, but Aloysius cured him in a second. These stories were written up and put into print. From such publications many picked up their spirits to hope for the best.

But the Spanish Jesuits had such sure and favorable premonitions of a better lot that it seemed sinful not to believe them. There was a famous author, Idiaquez,[24] who was a nobleman, enjoyed the reputation of prudence, and was well known in all of Spain for the positions he had filled. He recounted that, besides other signs from heaven, the Blessed Virgin showed herself to a certain pious youth who was in ecstasy. She openly announced that the Jesuits would be recalled to Spain within a short time. He was asserting that the vision was well authenticated. Jesuits placed such faith in his words that many, as if time were growing short, hastened from Bologna, Ravenna, and Ferrara to the Virgin's house at Loreto, for fear that if they waited any longer, the trip back to Spain would preclude their visit.

The same conviction gripped many at Rome to such an extent, indeed, that some were making bets on it and were predicting the date of the Spaniards' return. I saw someone who made a wager on the matter and who paid out twenty pounds of chocolate when he lost. Thus even grave men, when they want something a lot, are often deceived by their hope and determination.

Jesuits Exiled from Naples and the Sicilies

While the Spaniards were awaiting their certain return to their homeland, the Neapolitans and Sicilians considered it certain that they were not to be driven from their homes. Some nuns, who were said to have divine visitations and to speak with heavenly inspiration, had clearly predicted their safety. Tanucci,

R.P. FRANCISCUS RETZ PRAGENSIS
PRÆPOSITUS GENER ALIS SOC. IESU XV.
Electus in Congregatione Generali XVI die 30
Novembris 1730.

Breithart sculp. Prag.

Francis Retz, S.J.

the master of the kingdom, was deliberately nurturing and fostering their sense of security. He uttered not a word that betrayed hidden designs against the Jesuits. To the contrary, he answered inquiries with favorable words. He wanted to swoop down upon them unprepared and prevent them from sending anything out of the kingdom in anticipation. But anyone with sense [107] foresaw that, given the close ties of the kings, the whirlwind unleashed in Spain would erupt sooner or later in Naples. But the Jesuits put their trust in the comforting prophecies and thought they were beyond any risk of danger.

But suddenly soldiers roused them from their sleep. On one night, troops surrounded all the Society's colleges both in Naples and in the two Sicilies.[25] They made a proclamation of exile for the companions. For Tanucci had decided to follow the examples of Portugal and Spain. Although he was able by a simple nod of his head to effect their departure from the kingdom of Naples to the Papal States on a fixed date, he still preferred to use force. Here is something for you to marvel at. There were exactly eight companions stationed at the college at Sora. Several of them were feeble old men, barely sustaining life because of their illnesses. Yet he sent four hundred armed soldiers as if to storm a citadel. There were seven houses of the Society at Naples and about twenty-four in the other cities of the kingdom. All of them were left empty in a moment. The companions were first brought to Puzzuoli, some by carriage, some by boat. Then, put on a ship of larger draft, they were carried to Terracina, which is the border between the Papal States and Naples. There they were herded ashore like brute beasts. For Tanucci was a remarkable scorner of the pope's majesty and thought the insult ought to be inflicted upon the pontiff.

The Sicilian companions were led off and transported in a similar way except for the fact they were treated a bit more humanely. This treatment was due to Marquis Fogliani, the administrator of the kingdom of Sicily.[26] He was a very just man and most friendly toward the Society. Because the king of Sicily has some sort of jurisdiction over the island of Malta, the Grand Master of the Knights was forced finally to send away the few Jesuits who lived there.

They say that King Ferdinand, an excellent youth, when asked to sign the edict for the Jesuits' exile, was very reluctant. "What have these religious," he was remarking, "done to deserve such a serious penalty? They have taught me the rudiments of reading and religion. In many ways they serve well and generously the nobility, the common people, every rank of citizen. I have heard nothing reproachful about them, as I have about so many others." Tanucci got nowhere with his exhortations and entreaties. The king resisted to the point that his confessor Bishop Latilla intervened. The bishop told him that his father, King Charles, wanted the expulsion and he instilled in Ferdinand a scruple about not obeying his father. Finally then, although most unwillingly, he put his name to the decree. Those who tell the story add that the next day Latilla was stricken by a sudden attack of apoplexy. [108]

Whatever the truth of that may be, when the Jesuits were scarcely exiled, Tanucci confiscated for the royal treasury all their property that was on Neapolitan soil, including the land which belonged to the Roman College. He gave the houses over to others to live in. He sold the furniture at auction. He melted down the sacred vessels and silver statues of Ignatius and the other saints of the Society. He turned all the consecrated treasures to cash. He even ordered that the venerable symbol of the Society, the very name of Jesus, be erased and destroyed wherever it was found sculpted in bronze or marble. He seemed to want and to be trying for this, that no trace of the Jesuits would remain and that not even a memory of them would pass on to posterity.

To distract all public displeasure from himself, he issued a document in which he tried to place some semblance of justice upon these unjust acts of violence. He was claiming that the Neapolitan and Sicilian Jesuits were justly deported to the Papal States because the pope ought not to have repulsed the Spanish Jesuits after he had admitted the Portuguese. By rejecting these he had inflicted an injury upon the king of Spain. He justified the confiscation of whatever property the Jesuits had in the kingdom on the grounds that once the owners were expelled, the property belonged to no one and rightly devolved to the royal treasury.

Jesuit Life in Rome

But at Rome there was someone who wrote a counter document to Tanucci's, in which the author showed the two confiscations were quite illegal. He made an especially good case for the property of the Roman College. Tanucci was forced by the weight of the argument to back down somewhat and to direct that the matter be decided in the Council of St. Clare. Although the judges decided that the property had been illegally confiscated and decreed that it should be returned to the Roman College, that was, as far as I know, never done. But let us now return for a bit to our exiles.

As was stated, these were cast ashore, unfamiliar with the roads, and stripped of every human resource. Yet due to the kindness of the inhabitants, they found sure and respectable housing, a comfort in their trouble. The Neapolitans, since they had arrived first, went off to various closer towns in

Lazio and the Roman Campagna. Many settled down in Terracina to be closer to their friends and relatives. Others settled at Priverno, Sezze, Cori, Anagni, Frosinone, Segni, and Ferentino. The majority went to Velletri since it was a larger city. Some went all the way to Aricia, a town subject to Prince Chigi and bordering on Albano. The provinces they call Castro and the Patrimony received the Sicilians. They were distributed to the various houses in Viterbo, Monteplascone, Tarquinia, Toscania, Bagnoregio, Valentano, and Ronciglione. The people received them not only with kindness but with great joy. [109] They all led the religious life as much as their difficulties allowed. All applied themselves to helping their neighbor insofar as they were permitted. Some, however, it must be acknowledged, went too far in their fervor. While applying themselves unstintingly to these works, they stirred up unpopularity for themselves with other religious. Even in good works those sayings are to be observed: "Nothing in excess" and "Whatever your pursuit, no matter how praiseworthy in itself, it must be tempered with modesty."

After the Society had been expelled from both Sicilies, people at Rome pretty much avoided us and almost a solitude settled in. Visitors are frequent in the city, from all over the world and particularly from the kingdom of Naples. Suddenly, all contact with Jesuits was forbidden to those travelers. Further, many of the Roman nobles possessed towns and entitlements in that kingdom as benefices. Access to these people was no longer open to Jesuits, nor were the nobles permitted to approach the Jesuits.

Cardinal Orsini, as ambassador of the king and wanting to do Tanucci a favor, watched over the situation with close attention. He sent each of the nobles a note which threatened the ire of the king if they did not obey his words. Orsini and the ambassadors demanded a severity such as was never employed even between hostile nations in time of war. A Jesuit was not allowed to visit his brother or father. Orsini did not allow anyone to enter their churches or even to go to confession to a Jesuit. He reached such a peak of severity that, not to mention anything more serious, he forbade Marcantonio Colonna, the pope's vicar who otherwise had full episcopal powers in the city, to enter the Jesuits' churches.[27] If he were to disobey, then all the Colonnas' properties in the kingdom of Naples would be confiscated.

Meanwhile hidden observers kept careful and constant watch at our doors to see who went in, who came out, and where we would go outside our house. They reported to Orsini and Azpuru. Occasionally under the cloak of business to be done, they sneaked people into the houses to investigate what was going on inside and to find out, feigning friendship, what our deep feelings were. To be sure, night and day we were surrounded by informers. As in just about any group, there are those who are incautious and leak information, so some readily allowed to get out certain things which ought to have remained secret.

None of this particularly troubled me, but I did miss seeing and conversing with my friends such as Tiberio Ruffi, Giuseppe de Sangro, Ignazio Boncompagni, Scipione Borghese, Antonio Simone, [110] the Cardinals Pirelli and Perrelli, and Prince Doria Pamphili. Henceforward I had to be wary of Orsini whom I had previously found to be most friendly. Nor could I visit Cardinal York with whom I had been very intimate.[28] To tell the truth, I found these disruptions very hard to take. For I took great pleasure in these friendships and I valued my friends above every human consideration. There were, however, some noble houses in the city to which Orsini's decrees did not pertain. The fewer there were of them, the more earnestly and fervently I cultivated their friendship. [111]

BOOK VI

Parma; Election of Clement XIV

All were absolutely convinced that after the banning of the Spanish and Neapolitan Jesuits, banning of the Parmensian Jesuits would surely follow. For Ferdinand, the duke of Parma, was a Bourbon. Although he had not up to this time shown himself opposed to the Society, nonetheless he was so bound and intertwined with the rest of the Bourbon princes that he would, according to the Family Compact, do whatever they wanted. His uncle, King Charles of Spain, doubtlessly wanted the Society expelled from Parma. Du Tillot,[1] who was not so much the prince's minister as his guide and director, openly and honestly stated that of his own accord he would initiate nothing concerning the Jesuits. But if the King of Spain were to command, as was to be expected, something against the Jesuits, he would then not hesitate to carry out the order.

The Jesuits' Situation in Parma

Some of Ours, however, still put their faith in prophecies made by some little women who were said to be divinely inspired. Ours thought that we would never be moved from the place. It has been noted that with the graver Fathers, the more they were generally perceived as observant and experienced in the things of God, the more stubbornly they clung to this optimistic view and grew a bit angry with others, as if they were of faint heart and weaker faith. The pious credulity of a certain Father reached the point that he was not afraid to say openly that even if exile had already been proclaimed and horse-drawn wagons had come and the Companions were placed upon them, they would still not go into exile. For the horses, to be sure, would not move a step forward due to a divinely sent stupor. Such was the great reliance on omens and prophecies. Whether the horses would in truth move was soon found out. But to show the circumstances surrounding the implementation of the exile, we must begin at an earlier point.

Du Tillot had long been the prime minister of the duke who at that time was Philip, the brother of the king of Spain. He was a Frenchman and enough of a revolutionary to start a movement away from traditional laws and institutions. For he attacked the liberty of the Church and its long-standing immunity. Pope Clement took these measures most gravely as very bad precedents, especially in a principality which the Farnese family held [113] as a feudal possession from the supreme pontiff. He considered Parma as still a fief of the Apostolic See and subject to it. He knew well enough that his duty was to see to it that the Church, entrusted to him by Christ and God, nowhere receive any harm. After he had put up with many things in silence, at length he raised his voice to avoid the appearance of approving misdeeds by his saying nothing. He warned his erring son in a paternal fashion, and he was eager to call him back to the right track. He proposed certain things to be done that were fair and good. He did not at all refuse to bend certain rules for Philip's sake, to surrender some of his own rights, and, as far as he could, to make concessions to an otherwise excellent prince. But du Tillot was demanding more than could be justly granted. He stubbornly insisted upon his way and was rejecting all conditions of agreement, no matter how just they were. He continued to abuse the sacred rights of the Church not a whit less.

While these things were going on, Philip happened to come to Alessandria. The marriage of his daughter Ludovica provided the occasion. She was engaged to Charles, the prince of the Asturias, and had been sent to Spain. While he was staying there, Philip was joined by his sister Maria Antonia, the wife of the duke of Savoy and the duke himself, Vittorio Amedeo (for these two had come for a visit from Turin). He spent some days there in pleasant diversions. But he suddenly fell ill, and though vigorous in age and strength, within a few days, he died.[2] Many interpreted Philip's death as a punishment from God in payment for the violated rights of the Church and the disrespect shown the authority of the Supreme Pontiff. Of course, such people were unaware of the fact that the outrages belonged not to the prince, but to his minister who sorely abused the prince's confidence and trust.

Du Tillot Challenges the Pope

Philip's son Ferdinand succeeded him. He was a youth of the highest endowments, but still a boy. He was not yet capable, because of his youth, of taking the reins of government, though he assumed the legal position. That increased the more the power of du Tillot. His opposition to the Church was in no way lessened. The pontiff, in order not to fail himself and his duty, again treated of a concord and proposed new terms. He was not heard. The pope pressed with entreaties and admonitions. He sometimes leveled threats. He did not budge du Tillot a bit. When, therefore, all proved in vain, the pope finally took steps that the evil would grow no bigger. He assumed his priestly role and used a weapon in the pontiff's arsenal. He promulgated an apostolic document in which he reviewed certain decrees of Parma against the laws of the Church.[3] He declared that whoever made these decrees, ordered them, or saw to their formulation had incurred the punishments established by law. Therefore, he pronounced them bound by anathemas and condemned to the solemn penalties.

The pope acted correctly and properly if one looks only to law and usual procedure, for many examples [114] of such coercive measures occur in the annals of the Church. Nothing forbids the pontiff's excommunicating anyone in the flock of Christ who is recalcitrant. But according to the tenor of the times, it occurred to many that the pope acted without due caution. Perhaps Clement did not consider sufficiently the character of the kings' ministers, the tight bond between them, and their obsession with their sinister plots. Nor did he reflect sufficiently on the fact that while the resources of the duke of Parma were small, he was related by blood to very powerful princes. These would undoubtedly come to aid his cause at the prompting of the ministers.

There were, to be sure, some who remarked that when similar decrees were made at Naples, Madrid, Venice, and Vienna, the pope passed them over in silence. These also should have been passed over. The most the pope could have done was to advise all the faithful in a public letter that in many places initiatives were being taken against the rights of the Church. Because of the difficulty of the times, he puts up with the abuses patiently, but does not approve of them by his silence, and does not want them ratified and confirmed nor ought such conduct be an example. All see that laws sanctioned either by the authority of supreme pontiffs or general councils are in effect as well as the punishments laid down for violators. If Clement had done only this much, they would say that he would be fulfilling his duty and no prince would be offended and the misdeeds would not pass into ordinary procedure. But Clement preferred to take a shorter route and brought the important issue to an almost ruinous extreme. For the royal ministers clamored that not only Parma but the whole Bourbon family had been gravely insulted by the pope's actions and each stirred up his king to avenge the common injury.

The ambassadors, therefore, of the kings of Spain, France, and Naples approached the pontiff in a group. They declared to him in measured terms that if he wanted to placate the offended princes, he must recall his document and declare it null and void. One may see in this demand how the times had changed, how much the fervor of religion had cooled, and how reverence for the pontiff had become a thing of the past. Formerly if the pontiff had inflicted an anathema upon anyone, no matter who he was, he had no doubts that what was bound on earth was bound in heaven. Accordingly, he humbly begged to be absolved, and provided he was again received into the body of the faithful, he did not refuse to do the penance imposed. No one considered religion shameful for himself.

Indignant Bourbons Act to Expel Jesuits from Parma

Now these three Catholic princes acted as if they were provoked by an injustice because a kinsman of theirs had become entangled in ecclesiastical penalties. From the pope they ask not for absolution, but in a menacing fashion demand satisfaction. Because in his document the pontiff had called the Duchy of Parma his own, they demanded that these words too be taken back [115] and stricken as if the Roman pontiff had never had any right to that domain or no longer had it. They were demanding two things which they knew could not be conceded. But they were asking for them for the very reason that they be denied and they would take offense at the rejection and make it grounds for graver measures. For that had been the agreement among the clever royal ministers. The pope did, in fact, deny both demands.

Because of this, the king of France, as if he had received the opportunity to get reparation for an injury, sent troops into Avignon. He drove out the papal troops and officers, deposed the magistrates, and occupied that large and very old patrimony of the Roman Church. At the same time the king of Naples invaded the Duchy of Benevento and, snatching it from the pope's dominion, claimed it for his own. Clement was little moved by these seizures. If the vengeance taken were to keep itself within these bounds, he would console himself with the awareness that he acted justly and holily. But as I shall state shortly, the indignation of the kings went beyond his expectations.

Meanwhile the Jesuits of Parma, whom the general public thought so wise and clever, were resting secure in their reliance on predictions and forecasts. Carnival time had rolled around again during those days. The Jesuits directed that stage shows be given for the people in their famous College of the Nobles. They peacefully passed the time amid the usual recreations. They acted as if they were sailing on a tranquil sea and no storm clouds were gathering. But suddenly soldiers with rifles and fixed bayonets surrounded their houses, not only at Parma, but also as Piacenza, Busseto, and Fidenza (which town they more usually call Borgo San Donnino).[4] The entire armed forces of Parma were involved. At one and the same moment the companions were informed that they had to leave, taking their possessions with them. A large number of wagons were on hand. The horses, contrary to the prophecies, moved forward well enough. The Companions were welcomed very warmly in the territory of Modena, which lay on their route. A short journey from there brought them to Bologna.

Who would not think that this last expulsion would completely satisfy the King of Spain? Who would not say that his anger with the Jesuits was spent? Yet it was not. He wanted the entire Society eliminated all over the world. He fixed that objective deeply in his mind as if all the prestige of his kingdom hinged on that one thing and it was the sum of all important matters. Therefore he first brought over to his side the king of France on the basis of the Family Compact. Next, he added his son, the king of Naples. Through common petitioners at Rome he ordered that the pope be questioned in his own name and in the names of those kings concerning the suppression of the Society.

Nevertheless, the pontiff was waiting. [116] For he did not see how the suppression pertained to the king's complaint about the Parma business. He smiled to himself at the forwardness of the petition. How could he be led to suppress the order which he had recently approved, confirmed, and praised once again by an Apostolic Constitution? The ambassadors of the kings, however, were pressing matters. If the pope were to do that one thing, they promised, the rest would be easy and every difference would be reconciled. He delayed his response and thought time was needed for further deliberation on a matter of such grave consequence.

Tanucci Threatens Rome

But Tanucci saw that the pontiff was very fond of the Society and could scarcely be moved with requests. Accordingly, he decided that force had to be employed. To this end he began to make some claims on the Duchy of Castro, and as he had invaded Benevento, he was said to be thinking of invading Castro too and was readying soldiers and arms. But that show of force did not greatly move Clement. When the rumor was spreading that six divisions of foot soldiers with the complementary number of cavalry units would soon be arriving, he said that force ought not be repelled by force. If the troops have come up to the city gates, he will open them of his own accord. He announced that he would go out to meet the armed soldiers unarmed himself, carrying only a cross before him. Such was the man's reliance on religion, or such the constancy of his mind and heart.

You would scarcely believe, brother, how rattled I was by this state of affairs. I passed days and nights in acute mental distress. The duchy they call Castro is not large in area, but extends almost to the very walls of the city of Rome. Yet it is sufficiently wide to cover all the consular roads that lead to the interior of Italy. Thus it cuts off every exit from the city. Accordingly, if the Neapolitan forces seized that region and blocked the roads with pickets, the Roman people would be thrown into great difficulties. Add the fact that French troops were said to be coming from Corsica to the Neapolitans' aid.

Cardinal de Bernis, the new ambassador of the king of France, was eloquently protesting that his sovereign was acting not on his own initiative, but at the prodding of the king of Spain, and solely from, he was claiming, an adherence to the Family Compact.[5] But no one had any doubts that on the score of that same adherence, he would join forces with the Neapolitans and pursue the common objective of the family with their joint forces. What was to be expected if the Roman people, dissipated through leisure and luxury, were to see armed men approaching, bent on using extreme violence upon them? Would they favor so much the name of the Jesuits? Would they want to submit their own safety to the trial for the Jesuits' sake and patiently put up with the destruction [117] of their large city along the lines of the unforgettable example of Charles the Bourbon?[6] Add to this the fact that many from the riffraff at Rome stood ready for any crime. For a small sum of money they could be incited to break into our houses and they would not be afraid to slaughter us to a man.

These were the reasons for fear common to all the Jesuits. But I had some peculiar to myself. For any works defending the Society that had appeared up to that time with any bite to them were being attributed to me. This was done out of some prejudice or other, as if there were no one else at Rome who knew how or wanted to write in that vein. Thus many were assigning to me in their guesswork the tract written to counter Tanucci's document although its author could not be learned for certain. Hence there was an enormous dislike for me among the Society's enemies. I could have no doubts that, given the occasion, they had me marked down for punishment. Therefore when soldiers were said to be advancing to the Duchy of Castro, constant worry and concern engulfed me. The panic came to the point that for a while I looked about for a way to flee. I was thinking that I might slip away to Tuscany or to Piedmont before the way out was shut off. I saw what would happen from a long way off and judged the danger should be met in timely fashion.

Sudden Death of Clement XIII Eases Tension

But such are the vicissitudes of human life that the same day, 2 February 1769, suddenly brought an end to my discomfort and simultaneously freed other Jesuits from fear and the city from imminent danger. For on that day, the feast of the Purification, Pope Clement in the morning had conducted the services of that feast and had distributed the blessed candles. After dinner, as was his daily custom, he went to some church or other. He scarcely had gone to bed that night when he succumbed to a sudden seizure and heart attack.

He was clearly an outstanding pope, comparable with the best if he had lived in better times or at least if he had relied more on his own counsels rather than those of others. For in addition to remarkable piety and a marvelous modesty despite his lofty station, he had a keen intellect. His judgment was the soundest. His strength of mind was up to the most difficult of tasks. But he thought too humbly of himself. He very often made decisions on the basis of what others urged upon him, not on what he wanted or felt. But what is worst is that he judged others according to his own mind-set: if anyone put up a front of piety, he could scarcely suspect there lay beneath the facade fraud and treachery. Indeed, if he had not at the outset given himself to the direction of Cardinal Spinelli, [118] there are some who think he would have looked out better both for his own dignity, and the concerns of the Society. For by the time he began to follow the advice of that man of great integrity, Torrigiani, things had reached such a state of collapse that they could not be restored. Efforts to do so actually did harm, for they inflamed the more the wrath of the princes. But at the death of Clement, which came so unexpectedly to the city and world, the angry feelings of the princes seemed to subside and the Roman people were freed from a great fear. For after these events, Tanucci ordered the troops he set aside for the invasion of Roman territory to keep to their quarters. It was as if he wanted it understood that his quarrel was not with the Supreme Pontiff as such, but personally with Rezzonico and Torrigiani. For my part, though I grieved the loss of a pontiff who was marvelously kind to me, still I felt relieved from a great fear.

Clement XIV (Ganganelli)

Election of Ganganelli as Clement XIV

Now people's, especially the Jesuits', concern was who would be elected to take Rezzonico's place. Friends of the Society desired a favorable person, foes wanted an adversary. As each one's inclinations moved him, he called for this or that cardinal to be advanced to the supreme honor. I am not ashamed to say that I was leaning toward one whom the Jesuits wanted least of all. At this point, brother, bear with my recounting what happened to me. In the evening of that same day, Cardinal Vitaliano Borromeo, as was his custom, came to see me.[7] He spoke openly and at length concerning the election of the new pope. "I see," he remarked, "that the election will be difficult and stormy. I certainly am unable to judge which member of the Sacred College is to be preferred. For I have traveled to distant lands on delegations and have been absent from Rome so long that I am little acquainted with my colleagues. But you," he added, "whom would you vote for?"

I answered that I was not troubling myself very much on the matter; but at all events I felt certain that he would be pontiff whom God, who directs all in secret, has chosen and judged to be best for either renewing the Church or for punishing and correcting it. But Borromeo was still undecided and pressed me anew and urged me, though I was reluctant, to freely express my opinion. Then I said that Ganganelli seemed preferable to the others and most suitable for the times.

Borromeo was dumbfounded that I was proposing a cardinal who was generally considered anti-Jesuit. I answered that for the very reason that he was considered anti-Jesuit, I would want him advanced before the others. Rezzonico, to be sure, stirred hatred for himself and for us through his obvious benevolence toward us and inflamed the wrath of princes to our ruin. Ganganelli would not be suspected of excessive zeal for the Society and accordingly [119] can benefit us. Furthermore, he is, as most monks are, a very astute man, who can easily sniff out sly tricks. He is not readily deceived and ensnared by trickery. Finally, he is an upright member of a religious order and ought to be reckoned a God-fearing man. Given the sort of man he is, even if hostile in other respects, there seems no need to fear injury from him. To these observations, Borromeo, a clever man if ever there was one, had nothing to rejoin. But I, over and above these things, thought Ganganelli was hostile to the Society only in appearance, and not in fact. Although it is not easy to persuade many Jesuits of this, I even now hold it as certain. I will undertake the proving of this subsequently if the heavens approve.

Now we must discuss his election. I know that fantastic tales are circulated about that election. They are so ingrained in men's minds, especially the laity's, that they cannot be uprooted. They say that Ganganelli was elected by the money and efforts of the king of Spain and that the pontificate was pledged to him on the condition that he suppress the Society. This is not true and can be asserted only with the greatest rashness. I will put down in writing some of the more secret transactions which went on in the election. My sources, reliable ones, I think, are the Cardinals Gianfrancesco Albani, Borromeo, Bonaccorsi,[8] Veterani,[9] Bufalini,[10] Serbelloni,[11] and Fantuzzi.[12]

After the customary nine-day period of mourning for the deceased pontiff, the cardinals retired to the rooms of the Vatican palace. They were many in number, but very few who could be prudently elected. The transmontanes had to be excluded. The younger cardinals too, and the elderly who were infirm and close to the grave were excluded. Finally, they were to be excluded who seemed less worthy of the high honor because of some defect either of nature or of mind. What is more, there had to be excluded ten very prominent cardinals because the Bourbon princes had stated, while Clement was still living, their opposition to them as being friendly towards Jesuits. The princes plainly and openly declared they would have nothing to do with these ten. One was not allowed to even consider them. For what would be the danger to elect a pope whom so many Catholic princes would hold suspect as being ill-disposed toward them? All things weighed, the choice was reduced to two: Stoppani[13] and Fantuzzi, the former from Milan, the latter from Ravenna.

Both were highly regarded for their integrity and prudence. Not all, however, praised Stoppani without reservation. Many distrusted a bit his hidden and subtle thoughts. Some even showed themselves openly opposed to him. Almost all [120] the enthusiasm swung toward Fantuzzi as he was a more open and more learned man. But he manifestly rejected the honor, either naturally shrinking from the cares of that office or fearing the very serious ills which he saw threatening at that time. He would not allow himself even to be discussed. He refused with such insistence that he threatened extreme measures unless they desisted. It did not seem good to confer the benefit on one so unwilling. With the views of the Fathers changing daily in this fashion, and their minds wavering, the election dragged out without issue.

Meanwhile Ganganelli, although he was in the lowest rank of the cardinals and was hindered by an unfavorable report, still received two votes each day, though the casters were unknown. The other cardinals so disapproved these votes that they were indignant that there were in their gathering those who would secretly support such a man. The greatest opponent was Castelli,[14] a man most esteemed for his learning and holiness. Those who were neutral followed his authority and were motivated by only the Church's advantage.

The election was dragged out almost to three months without any success, nor could they find any way out of their disagreements. When Ganganelli by chance was asked whether he would want to add his vote to Stoppani's supporters, he answered, "Absolutely not; for if he were pope, he would surely suppress the Jesuits." He said this so quickly and decisively that he seemed to have spoken his mind. The remark spread through the conclave and influenced the thoughts and feelings of many. Ganganelli's reputation improved with very many. A sudden change of heart on Castelli's part was added to this and ended the matter.

For, as was said above, Castelli was the stoutest opponent of Ganganelli. Suddenly he was changed almost into another man. He called a meeting of his followers. He said, "I have often asked God to be present at this most important business and to be gracious to the Sacred Conclave. I especially prayed that He show me His divine will. Now as I look around, it is perfectly clear that no one in this state of affairs is preferable to Ganganelli." This speech stirred all tremendously. As it was less expected, so it penetrated the deeper into their minds, especially because many had already begun to grow weary at the long delay caused by the impasse. And so those who were present readily concurred with Castelli's view.

The leaders of the factions met towards nightfall. On Castelli's motion, de Solis,[15] representing the king of Spain, and de Bernis, representing the king of France, freely and most gladly agreed upon Ganganelli. They preferred none other. And Pozzobonelli,[16] who was the spokesman [121] of the Emperor did not object at all to joining their ranks. There was some worry about Rezzonico. Nothing could be carried in the face of his opposition, for he led the numerous faction of his uncle Clement. But hardly was he asked about Ganganelli, when he said, "Since, indeed, you deem him worthy, I will not stand in the way of his election as pope. I only ask that Fantuzzi be sounded out first."

What he asked for was fair and could not be reasonably denied. But there were in the group those who were displeased that the business which was just about wrapped up should be prolonged further. Whether it happened by chance or whether somebody's initiative was at work, Fantuzzi conveniently came on the scene. When he learned that he was the topic of discussion, he first modestly asked the Fathers to stop annoying him. He did not want to be made pope nor to be put in the limelight. As he repeated his remarks, he gradually grew so heated with anger that he seemed on the verge of a fit of fury. Accordingly, minds again turned toward Ganganelli and there was agreement on his election. It was deep into the night and many cardinals had gone to bed. Nevertheless they decided that some should go around immediately to the rooms, inform their colleagues of the agreement, and ask for their concurrence. For there was danger in delay. No one opposed except Orsini, who objected in vain and cried out that Ganganelli was a masked Jesuit. The rest, however, scoffed at this.

Then in a group several went to the room of Ganganelli. They first kissed his hands as a sign of respect for the newly elected pontiff. Then on the following morning (for there was no time for further consultation or for stopping the election), they duly cast their votes and elected him pontiff for the well-being and happiness of the Christian commonwealth.

The cardinals whom I have named above narrated to me these events as I have recounted them. Of these, Gianfrancesco Albani was one who played an active part in those proceedings. He added this at the end: "We could not make a good man, such as we wanted, pope; we did not want to make a bad one. We made a doubtful man, but no one better could be elected." It may be that the king of Spain chose Ganganelli beforehand. It may be that the king received the announcement very happily. That is quite believable. For if other indications had been lacking, Ganganelli had taken up the promotion of Palafox's cause and strenuously advocated his beatification. But a simple, bald account of events shows how false are the charges of some who attribute Ganganelli's pontificate to the wealth and power of the king of Spain and who rashly fabricate some prearrangement, linking the suppression of the Society with his election.

As to what sort of man Clement XIV was in fact (for Ganganelli took this name for himself), [122] the judgments of men are so various and contradictory that it can scarcely be defined for certain. If you listen to Jesuits and their supporters, there never was a worse pope. If you listen to the Society's enemies, there was never a better one. The former malign his reputation excessively, the latter extol it inordinately. Each one judges as his personal feelings prompt him. To state openly what I feel, I think he was more unfortunate than evil. I will never praise him to the skies, but on the other hand, I will do my best to defend him against unfair detractors. What he determined for the Society, I know for certain that he did, not willingly, but from necessity and most reluctantly. But there will be a more suitable place for speaking of the matter elsewhere in the work.

Cordara's Flight of Fancy

Now, brother, before I go further, allow me to submit to your hearing a certain dream of mine, which even now gives me pleasure. At the time the cardinals were discussing the election of the new pope, Emperor Joseph, a very important prince, suddenly came to Rome. After he had seen the major sights of the city, he conceived the desire of seeing also the inner rooms of the Vatican palace where the cardinals were being confined. I believe he wished to see the Sacred College face to face and to greet them. There was doubt whether he might be permitted to enter. For the regulations forbid that anyone at all be admitted within that enclosure. But after discussion, it was decided that Caesar was not held by these laws. And so on an arranged date, he was present with his brother Leopold, the grand duke of Tuscany. He was not only admitted, but also received with great honor and met by all the Fathers. He received a complete tour.

While he was there, I was saying quietly to myself, "What if the cardinals, tired by such a long disagreement, were suddenly inspired by the Holy Spirit to acclaim Joseph as pontiff? Why could they not do that? He is a widower and although still a young man, recoils from a new marriage. He has great piety and prudence. It did not seem believable that he would want to reject the papal tiara joined to the imperial dignity. What reverence would there be then for the Apostolic See? With such a man as pontiff, one who has more than a hundred thousand men under arms, the Tanuccis, the de Rodas, the Carvalhos would henceforth be scarcely so insulting as they were toward Rezzonico. This, finally, would be an instant remedy for all the ills threatening the Society." Thus I deluded myself with an empty thought and I took delight in the foolish error to the extent that I communicated it to some of my Companions. But that flight of fancy, as far as I know, occurred to no one except to me. Certainly the cardinals preferred Ganganelli.

Clement XIV Begins His Pontificate

Since he had heard that nothing had harmed the Jesuits as much as the well-attested kindness of his predecessor, Ganganelli [123] decided from the outset of his pontificate that he should lean in the other direction. He showed himself so hostile that he would not allow an audience to Father General. His intention was excellent—to conciliate more easily the king of Spain and at least to bring about fairer conditions. But it was perhaps a less prudent policy, for it certainly failed of success. For pretence avails nought in that all-seeing city where there were some who saw into his mind however veiled over he kept it. These, of course, were writing frequently to the court at Madrid. The king should not let himself be fooled. The pontiff's enmity with the Jesuits is feigned. He is acting shrewdly to drag out the time, to find meanwhile some honorable way of reconciling the parties, and ultimately to preserve the Jesuits from harm. Let the king therefore persist in demanding the suppression of the order firmly and explicitly and reject all other terms. These admonitions made such an impression on the court at Madrid that when the pontiff proposed various measures to avoid the suppression, the king answered with only one word: suppression. He finally wrenched it from the pontiff willy-nilly. Thus the Supreme Pontiff ought never to have left the royal track of truth and sincerity. Ganganelli learned from his experience that the duplicity and sham of the political craft were a false and vain support. But let us run through the entire course of the deed.

In the midst of all this, Almada, that awful madman, resurfaced. As we said, the previous pontiff expelled him from the city and he had traversed several areas of Italy. He was expelled from every one of them because of his intemperateness or else he was held up for ridicule. Back in the city, he had resumed looking after the affairs of the Portuguese embassy. He did so all the more arrogantly since he saw that the power of the Rezzonicos and Torrigiani had been reduced. He was confident he would enjoy favor with the new pontiff who he thought was hostile to the Jesuits. Up to this point the king of Portugal, who had been lodging many serious complaints with the pope against the Jesuits, had not yet made mention of suppressing the Society. But now, when he had heard that that very thing was being demanded by the Bourbon kings, he instructed Almada to join their ambassadors and to urge the same request in the name of his king too.

But the Bourbon ambassadors, the Cardinals de Bernis and Orsini (the former of whom looked after the affairs of the king of France, and the latter those of the king of Naples), and Azpuru, bishop of Valencia (who was serving as the Spanish ambassador), repulsed Almada's efforts to insert himself into their meetings. They stated that they were acting in consort according to the Family Compact with which the king of Portugal had nothing to do. Almada accordingly [124] was forced to continue on his own, apart from the others.

The Bourbon ambassadors, approaching the pontiff together, asked, each in the name of his king, that the pope by his apostolic authority completely suppress and wipe out the Society of Jesus, which had been dispersed and proscribed in so many lands, and condemned by public opinion everywhere.

At this point Ganganelli could reveal his true sentiments—a thing which Rezzonico could not do without the greatest danger. With almost one word he could have ended the matter with the Society preserved. What if he had answered freely, openly that he would accede to the kings' will insofar as this was possible, but that he was unable and unwilling to suppress the Society and he would never do so? What if, I say, that pontiff had answered thus—the pontiff whom the Spaniards were saying was entirely theirs and whom they deemed hostile to the Jesuits, a pontiff who enjoyed such a great reputation with them for integrity and learning? Clearly the kings would be forced to grasp and admit that their demand was most unfair and could not be granted in justice and that they should abandon all hope of receiving it. And so they would be yielding, unless I am very much mistaken, to his authority and would abandon their undertaking. In short, with the suppression despaired of, they would demand some abasement of the Society; and content with that, they would be making no other major attack.

Nor was it more fitting for any pontiff other than Ganganelli to speak with priestly earnestness and firmness. For he was a religious, born in the Papal States, who had no nephews on his brother's side, who had no other entangling relations. He had no ambitions or fears either for himself or for his own. But he was a man who relied excessively on his own sagacity and was not accustomed to share anything with others. He preferred to follow clever designs rather than truthful ones. As the saying goes, he shot himself in the foot. For he answered the legates in a wordy, roundabout discourse, interjecting ambiguous terms. Although he was not really promising anything, nonetheless he could appear to be going along with what they demanded. He sent them off full of positive expectations. Certainly the kings believed the Pope had pledged his faith, and in order that they not seem toyed with, they forced him finally to make good on his promises, though unwillingly and reluctantly.

From these beginnings, very many were making dire predictions about the Jesuits although the pontiff communicated to no mortal his inner designs. To this was added an unusual event. Although it happened by chance, still it was taken as an ill omen since people are generally superstitious. For many the event seemed to portend the certain ruin of the Society.

Clement Takes Possession of the Lateran Church

There is a custom that new pontiffs on a set day go with a large cavalry train to take possession of the Lateran church. It is a very big celebration in the city and has the appearance of a triumph. It is not unlike those triumphs which Roman generals had when returning victorious from the provinces, [125] and in which they used to be carried to the Capitol, crowned with laurel. The route from the Vatican palace to St. John Lateran stretches for three miles. Along the way, windows are decorated with silk. Houses are covered with banners and bunting. In some places triumphal arches are erected. In other places you might see suitably displayed paintings, emblems, and inscriptions in honor of the new pontiff.

The dignitaries of the city go first on horseback in a very long line. They bring along almost an army of servants. The pontiff follows, riding on a white horse, very beautifully caparisoned. In addition to a large number of youths very stylishly dressed, two ranks of Swiss guards, gleaming in flashing armor, flank the pope. Four leading officials whom the Romans call *"conservatori"* stand, dressed in golden mantles, at the horse's bridle. The cardinals follow behind, riding on mules and dressed in old-fashioned greatcoats. Then there follow the patriarchs, bishops and department heads of the Vatican and the Roman Curia. Each is marked by his distinctive insignia and dressed in the traditional, conservative way. Light-armed horsemen carry up the rear of the procession, gleaming with their feathers and helmets and carrying the long spear in hand. Then there are some men dressed in mail, bearing drawn swords, and some companies of infantry with rifles.

What especially contributes to the festivity of that day is the fact that people flock from the entire surrounding region to see it. There is such a throng that you would scarcely find a place amid the jostling and pushing crowd. As the pontiff passes, all fall to their knees and applaud him with repeated, heartfelt acclamations. Ganganelli himself used to tell the story of how, barely ten years before, he struggled through the crowd to get a glimpse of this procession and after much shoving ended up on some filthy balcony. Now he alone was attracting to himself the eyes of the packed throng; the eager shuffle was to see and venerate only him. Thus in human affairs fortune toys with us, especially at Rome.

But an unexpected mishap marred Ganganelli's moment of glory. For when he had already ascended the Capitoline amid countless cheers of the populace, his horse suddenly balked on the descending road in a spot near the Mamertine Prison where once Peter the Prince of the Apostles was detained. The horse began to rear up and tried to shake off the rider until he threw him headlong and left him prostrate upon the ground. This seemed scarcely believable because there were four *conservatori* of the Roman people at the bridle. These were nobles, men skilled in the equestrian arts. Yet not one of them stopped the fall. They even say that one of the spectators ran forward to aid the falling pope, but a Swiss guard stoutly blocked him and forced him to stop in order that a common man [126] not touch the pontiff irreverently and defile him with the contact. However that may be, the pope finished the rest of the journey in a litter. He was, as he himself remarked, "confused, but not contused." From this event many drew an ill omen about his future pontificate. Some recalled that Clement V had experienced an accident on the same occasion and that he had suppressed the Order of the Templars. Hence they predicted the Society would certainly be suppressed by Clement XIV. But these were empty prophecies of the idle.

Jesuits Consider their Future

The heavenly signs on which Jesuits were relying were no truer, however. You will marvel, I believe, brother, that mature, educated, and experienced men would be deceived by old wives' tales. But they saw no hope on the human side. And when other resources are lacking, these preternatural ones are generally available. No one ever gives up hope altogether. They had, as we pointed out above, already experienced false prophecies which promised that the Society either would not be expelled or would be quickly restored. New prophecies began to spread in the reign of Ganganelli which were removing all fear of suppression. And still some of the graver Fathers put faith in the prophecies and sustained themselves and the tottering state of affairs with them. To speak now of no others, at Valentano, easily the leading city of Castro, a little old lady—pious perhaps, but certainly simple and unsophisticated—was said to know future events by a divine presentiment. A group of Sicilian Jesuits had been deported to that town and to their inquiries, she gave the following encouraging words: "They should not be downhearted. Let them hope for better things. With God's favor the ills will one day come to an end. Let them not be worried about a suppression. The pontiff will never come to that." The woman gave responses like this as the situation and time required. The Sicilians, thinking she spoke with divine inspiration, received her remarks as oracles sent from heaven. They disseminated them widely and sent them among the first to the Society's superiors. Once this report spread around, the Jesuits were fearing even greater evils, but had no concern about the suppression, as if that were an empty specter.

I, for my part, to tell the truth, did not fear this ultimate ruin. The authority of the Valentano prophetess did not influence me, but rather many grave reasons which I thought had to be weighed in a human way. Whatever the disposition of the pontiff, however inimical he might be imagined to be, [127] I could not convince myself that he would be willing, for the sake of the king of Spain, to deprive himself of a powerful branch of his militia and to hamstring himself, as it were. For while all religious orders are in the service of the supreme pontiff, the Society is considered his strongest and most faithful legion. This one consideration carried so much weight with me that I judged it certain that the pontiff would never have a mind to disband such a well-equipped, such a well-decorated unit and to cashier it despite its loyalty to the Holy See. Many wise heads, both in the Society and outside of it, thought the same thing. But other considerations were more weighty with Ganganelli than this one which seemed invincible. More will have to be said about these considerations elsewhere.

Ominous Events during Clement's Administration

Everything was becoming more troubled for us each day (1771). For the pope continued the policy he had initiated. He kept his plans to himself with an unbelievable silence. Outwardly he showed himself hostile toward us. He did this so convincingly that he seemed not to differ from a truly abominable enemy. He had already begun barring Jesuits from audiences. Now he was refusing them the customary blessing when he met them. If he saw any Jesuit kneeling and showing reverence as he rode by in the public streets, he would turn his eyes away. In addition, he forbade his staff and all Vatican officials to meet and deal with Jesuits. Not content with that, he seemed to be opposed not only to Jesuits, but also their friends and supporters. The view was growing that those who favored and supported Jesuits would not fare well with this pope and other seekers of honors would certainly be preferred to them. That this was no empty statement, he himself showed with several examples. I will relate one, known only to a few but to no one more than to myself.

Civil and foreign wars raged in Poland. The pontiff had appointed as legate there, Giuseppe Garampi, a singularly prudent and learned man.[17] He was replacing Angelo Durino, likewise an intelligent, accomplished man, but rather hotheaded. Durino had offended Stanislaus, king of Poland, somehow or other. When Garampi was on the point of setting out on this assignment, he picked out among other associates a certain friend of mine to serve as his private secretary. I have often spoken with you about him, brother. He was Francesco Cancellieri,[18] a talented young man, well-read, and someone who would be quite useful to Garampi for the conduct of business and for letter writing. But somehow the pontiff got word of the appointment. As soon as Garampi was in his presence, the pope clearly indicated that he did not approve his [128] choice of Cancellieri. He observed that he was a talented young man and of good character, but he is hopelessly devoted to the Jesuits. Those who are like that should not be placed in prominent places and definitely should not be employed in public tasks. Using the pope's order as an excuse, Garampi therefore scarcely returned home before he sacked Cancellieri although he had already been accepted on the staff.

But however that matter was, the pontiff had not yet completely won over the Bourbons. There still remained a suspicion that he was acting deceptively and that he wanted to appear more alienated from the Society than he really was. That saying of Orsini, that Ganganelli was a masked Jesuit, was still being bruited about. Therefore, he proceeded to graver measures which would remove that suspicion. A certain bishop had died just recently at Rome. His name was Pisani, a Maltese, and he was serving in the important post of Promoter of the Faith. In his will, he had made his heir one of his brothers who was far away in Malta. Since he had another brother, a Jesuit, at Rome, Pisani on his deathbed entrusted the administration of his property to him until the heir arrived. The Jesuit, a man of singular innocence and piety, was altogether ignorant and inexperienced in temporal affairs. So he passed the administration to another Jesuit, Casalio by name. He was a wise man and trained in business. Further he was Pisani's friend and he had a brother who was then governor of the City and is now a cardinal.

Casalio faithfully and carefully fulfilled his commission—which is to be expected in a nobleman and one who is also a religious. When, however, the heir arrived, he found the inheritance less than he had hoped for. Being a foreigner and born to a poor estate, he had formed an exaggerated idea of Rome's wealth. He had imagined there would be mountains of gold. Thinking that he had been defrauded of his inheritance, he brought a lawsuit against his brother, the Jesuit, for embezzlement of what was not rightfully his own and he dragged him into court. Rome stood in amazement at the man's impudence and condemned it. But what about the pontiff? When asked to assign an arbitrator, he chose a man who was not only openly hostile to the Society, but who was also dishonest, venal, greedy, lowborn, and low-mannered. I mean Alfani who rose from a vile pettifogger to become a bishop. In the previous pontificate he had been expelled from the city for some sort of judicial dishonesty. Even yet he was in ill-repute. Nor did Alfani disappoint expectations. Scarcely had he begun the case when he condemned the Jesuit Pisani for theft without a hearing. By some peculiar calculus of his own, he reckoned that seven thousand gold pieces had been stolen from the Pisani inheritance. To make good this loss, he put a lien on the property of the "The Mountains" as they call it. [129] This property belonged to the account of the Roman College, and from that account this judge and executioner, like a thief, took seven thousand gold pieces. He is said to have kept no small part of it for himself.

After this theft of Alfani (for people generally described the case thus), there was no doubt in anyone's mind that the pope was seriously and deliberately persecuting the Jesuits. I myself, to tell the truth, began to waver some. Nonetheless I did not change my view as I considered deeper and more important matters. While it was true that the pontiff assigned Alfani as judge for the Jesuit Pisani, still he had not committed the outrage of wanting to condemn an innocent man without a trial. Although he subsequently did us ill in other matters, I saw that he was acting not out of ill will, but only with this in view: to win the favor of the king of Spain by afflicting the Jesuits and thus be able to save the Society from destruction.

Hints of Clement's Latent Goodwill towards the Jesuits

Many considerations prompted me to think this of Ganganelli. In the first place, the third year of his pontificate was passing and he was still resisting the most powerful kings who were demanding the suppression of the Society with all earnestness and unanimity. He put off their demands and, in a way, toyed with them. This was all the more remarkable because with this one condition fulfilled and by one stroke of the pen he could have recovered the territory of Avignon and the Duchy of Benevento. He preferred to put up with reduced landholdings than to snuff out the Society. Would a truly inimical pope be doing that?

The following consideration carries no less weight. His predecessor Rezzonico had ordered that 12,000 scudi be paid out each year from the treasury to support the Portuguese Jesuits at Urbania. Very few knew about this. The task was assigned to Brasco, who was administering the pontifical treasury. Pope Ganganelli was not in the dark about this. Although he very much wanted to cut expenses and was carefully looking for ways to do so, still he was trying to cover up this generous largess and would do so until the ambassador of the king of Spain uncovered it. Despite the ambassador's protests, he did not stop the pension until after four years. His one fear seemed to be that his show of goodwill towards us would give the Spanish king's ambassador reason to take offense. Therefore he rejected bills of petition from the Jesuits unread. But if the name "Jesuit" were dropped from the petition, even if he knew who the petitioner was, still he readily granted the request. I myself know of many who, having used this one precaution, obtained not inconsiderable privileges and benefits from him. I saw these things with my own eyes. But there were other indications of why I should have thought well of his mind and disposition. [130]

In the year about which I am now writing, 1771, I took sick and retired to the Alban hills to brace myself with the country air and with leisure. For almost six months I enjoyed conversations and pleasant walks with friends. At that time several Roman notables were spending the dog days and especially the month of October at Albano. They heaped upon me signs of their good will, especially Cardinals Serbelloni and Fantuzzi. The former was bishop of Albano and the latter had a tasteful little villa there in which he took great delight. From them I learned many things about the election of Ganganelli which I narrated above.

But at this time my favorite companion was Felice Nerini, the dignified and learned Procurator General of the Hieronymites. He too had come there to pass time in the country and he was living quite comfortably in the Convent of St. Paul. I had a close tie of friendship with him which had grown strong by its long standing and our mutual favors. He was said to enjoy special favor with Ganganelli and would very soon be made a cardinal. The pontiff, when he was staying at Castel Gondolfo, which is about a mile from Albano, allowed no one an interview except ministers of the papal household. It is a fact that one Sunday he not only let Nerini in, but he also took him to an inner room and detained him there in intimate conversation.

I very much wanted to learn what the pope felt about the Society, what his thoughts were. For that reason I besieged Nerini almost daily. Whether I found him alone at home or was riding with him in a carriage, I brought up the pontiff in conversation. I tried to dig out from him what the pontiff's mind on the Society was. Nerini's answer was always one and the same without any ambiguity of wording: the Society is close to the pontiff's heart. He is looking for every way to preserve it. He wants it safe and sound if at all possible. But he is seemingly forced into great difficulties. He has placed all his hope on delay and in something unexpected happening. Accordingly, he drags matters out and makes no decision on this important subject. For the sake of our friendship, Nerini swore these things to me. I do not see what those who blabber on in their ignorance about Ganganelli's mind and intention can offer to counterbalance Nerini's authority. They are driven only by their pain and rage.

The next year, 1772, gave a better testimony on how matters stood. For that year Giovanni Carlo Vipera had come to Rome to preach. He was a man [131] most esteemed for holiness and one who was considered the outstanding preacher among the Conventual Franciscans. He was then in charge of the whole order; so he immediately went to pay his respects to the pontiff. In his earlier life, Ganganelli had not only been a fellow religious of his, but also a dear and intimate friend. After their exchanging some cordial remarks back and forth, Vipera observed, "Am I to believe, Holy Father, as rumor has it, that the Society of Jesus is on the brink of suppression and that at the hands of a pope who was a Franciscan?" The pontiff answered him, "Do not fear a suppression. But it is necessary for the Jesuits to suffer a lot if they wish to be saved."

Vipera reported these things to us in those very words. The remarks fitted marvelously the predictions that were widespread among us. Hence the spirits of everyone were steeled for further suffering, but all fear of suppression was removed. Ganganelli therefore was showing himself hostile to the Jesuits for a good purpose, and caused them vexations as opportunities presented themselves. He had determined to try everything before abolishing the Society. He inflicted lighter wounds in order to spare its life. In this respect he was similar to Pilate, who in order to save Christ from death, had Him flogged. But Clement did not advert sufficiently to the fact that the Society's enemies were not being appeased, but rather took heart and were the more inflamed to demand the Society's suppression. And so after inflicting these lighter wounds, Clement was forced to strike that last, lethal blow which the Bourbons wanted. In this too he was like Pilate, who, to placate the people who were becoming unwontedly ferocious, gave Christ over in the end to be crucified, though He was completely innocent.

The Lecchi Incident

But with that frame of mind that I have mentioned, the pontiff passed up no opportunity to show himself hostile to Jesuits. Let proof of this be his decision at the end of the year concerning Antonio Lecchi.[19] He was a well-known mathematician in Italy and so skilled in hydraulics that no one was considered a more experienced conduit-master than he. For this reason when Clement XIII decided to draw off stagnant waters in the area of Bologna and to dig a new channel for them into the Po, he summoned Lecchi from Milan and put him in charge of the work. It was a task of immense proportions. It was not only very beneficial for the public good, but also brought great honor and renown to Lecchi, for it came out well enough. Many acres of land that had formerly been under water were now being farmed and were yielding a very rich harvest of produce.

The pontiff was not unaware that the glory of this successful project redounded to the credit of a Jesuit. But out of regard for the public convenience, he had no thought of removing him from office unless some opportunity [132] presented itself. It happened that some disagreement arose between Lecchi and Ignazio Boncompagni,[20] an excellent and most distinguished youth who was prolegate of Bologna and supervisor of the project. The pope ordered both to Rome to plead their cases before the commission of cardinals which oversees matters of the water supply. Although the commission unanimously decided the case for Lecchi, the pontiff nonetheless ordered Lecchi dismissed. Because he dallied about the city and meanwhile spoke perhaps more freely on the topic than he should have, Cardinal Pallavicini, the pope's secretary of state, suddenly called him in. Lecchi was warned to leave the city within two days and to stop in Bologna for no more than two days.

This was a plain and simple way of declaring the exile. But it was not enough. Lecchi, out of a consideration for his reputation, had obtained a testimonial letter from Alessandro Cardinal Albani, the prefect of the waterworks commission.[21] In high-sounding words Albani thanked Lecchi in his own name and in that of the commission for the work he had done so painstakingly for the Apostolic See. He praised to the skies Lecchi's trustworthiness, application, and industry. Lecchi himself had dictated the letter and left a copy of it at Rome when he departed. But he scarcely had reached Florence when he was forced to return the original copy to the papal nuncio. Elsewhere these things were discovered by only a very few. I am sure of what I report since Cardinal Alessandro wished to communicate it to me. The harsher things which the pontiff did against the Jesuits in the following year, the Society's last, will be more fittingly discussed below.

But meanwhile, brother, that saying of Ganganelli was causing me great anxiety. It was the saying that I spoke of above: "It is necessary for the Jesuits to suffer many things if they wish to be saved." For I saw that, with the pope so minded, a certain great evil hung over us. I was unable to guess what sort of evil it would be. There was much discussion among us on this topic. Some thought the Society would have to be reformed and bound to laws of stricter observance. The power of the General Superior would have to be curtailed. His term of office would have to be limited to a fixed number of years. Others thought that the obligation of daily choir would be imposed on us as on other religious. Still others suspected a cowl would have to be added to the Jesuit cassock. My own fear was that the pope would reduce us to extreme need and thus to beggary. I was sensing that that was what envious religious were hoping for and urging. The Little Poor of the Mother of God especially wanted this. [133] They were aping us by letting down their cassocks to the ankle.

To be constantly afraid of what the future would bring, to grow pale at every shift of the wind, to live always under the knife, as it were, I considered a kind of death. To these anxieties of mind were added the inconveniences of poor health. Despite the long period of convalescence, I was still not very strong. For a tertian ague hit and regularly laid me low. It was also clear that some vestiges of my former illness were lingering still. These could not be completely cleared up unless I got away from Rome's climate. Accordingly, I thought a lot about returning to our homeland. I was only waiting for the passing of winter and the beginning of spring, at which season I could more easily undertake the long journey. All my friends advised me to follow that plan. Your very kind letters prompted me to do it the more readily and promptly.

Cordara's Departure from Rome

At the beginning of May, therefore, I began to prepare for the trip. I visited friends and bade them farewell till the next year. I took care that any writings in my desk that had dangerous themes were taken out and put in a safe place. Although I was going away with the expectation of returning, still in the midst of that troubled time, I thought every eventuality had to be feared. On the day before my scheduled departure, I went to ask Father General that he pray for me since I was setting out on a long journey and I was still sick (for I had taken to my bed the day before). In this meeting, which was my last with the very dear Father, both of us were deeply moved. He was sorry and unwilling to let me go. "I will miss," he said, "the best of friends whose conversation and company were a great comfort in my affliction." I, in turn, with a deep sense of pain, was abandoning him amid storms and waves. When he expressed doubt about my return, I made a solemn promise that I would return before the passage of a year and I pledged my word.

These were his last injunctions: that I was to commend him daily to God, that I beg for the King of Sardinia's support of the Society, and that I extend his kindest regards to you, brother. With these words, the sad man sent me off, sad too and almost crying. On the next day I climbed up on a coach, and with a servant boy at my side, I set out. I was leaving the city of Rome, that nourisher of my youth and my studies. I had been brought there as a boy of ten. In it I had lived most pleasantly for more than fifty years. I had a special love for it and for my very many dear friends there. I left never, as fate was to have it, to see it again. This at least went well. I was expecting on that day a new attack of fever and was carrying a supply of Peruvian extract with me. [134] But neither on that day nor on the following days did the fever return. Travelling through Tuscany by moderate stages, I stopped now and then to rest or to see friends. By the time I got to Turin, I was completely healed.

Let me not omit that I met at Leghorn a Frenchman, noted for his learning and for his fiery speech and writing, a man by the name of Caiveracchio. Pope Rezzonico held him in great favor for a long time. Since, however, he was defending the Jesuits more outspokenly than the time and situation could bear, he was ordered, on the request of the king of France, out of the Papal States. He was now on his way back to France and he accompanied me on my journey as far as Turin. [135]

BOOK VII

Persecution of the Society at Rome; Total Suppression

At Turin I found King Carlo Emmanuele wasting away, not so much from old age as from a lingering illness which in the end took him off. I immediately went to pay my respects to him. When I entered, he received me kindly, as was his wont. But he interrupted me as I began to commend the Society to his patronage. "I cannot see," he said, "why the king of Spain, when he has expelled the Jesuits from his realms, wants them crushed in other kingdoms too." He added that the pontiff has been placed in a difficult situation for this very reason. The pope was going to have difficulty wrestling with the force the Bourbons were bringing to bear. After he said more things in this same vein, he sent me off, partly uplifted with hope, partly dejected with fear. If anyone was, Carlo Emmanuele was a fair and wise prince, as knowledgeable in governance as any. He never appeared more well-disposed to the Jesuits. Yet while he kept using their services, he did not allow himself to extol them over other religious. Out of regard for the public good, to which he saw the Jesuits contributing greatly, he wanted them unharmed and was protecting them with his patronage. He shut his ears to any mention of suppression.

He had already been asked in the name of the king of Spain that he expel the Jesuits from his realm on the example of France, Spain, and Portugal. He replied, as befits a king, that he was not moved only by the example of other princes. If there were just reasons, he would do it. Since there were no such reasons, he did not think the Jesuits should be punished and he flatly refused the request. He was as tenacious as any king of his royal power and prerogative. He allowed no one but himself to rule in his house. He did not receive laws, but laid them down. But that high-minded and great-souled monarch, as was said, soon passed away.[1] His son, Vittorio Amedeo, succeeded to the throne. Although he was well-affected toward Jesuits, he nonetheless was married to the sister of the king of Spain and had given his daughter in marriage to the son of the king of France, the count of Provence. He had to have some regard for these princes who were joined to him by such close ties of kinship and who wanted the Society suppressed. He certainly did not think he should arouse their anger against himself for the sake of the Jesuits. [137]

Clement XIV Treats Jesuits Ever More Harshly

Meanwhile at Rome, the pontiff continued to show daily through ever harsher treatment how true his remark was that the Jesuits had to suffer a lot if they were to be saved. The Jesuits had eleven houses at Rome. Some were their own, others were entrusted to them by pontifical authority for the education of various nations' youth. Among the latter the foremost institution was the one they call the Roman College. There, large numbers of Roman clerics received free board. There was a larger number of noble youths who maintained themselves with monthly payments. This house can quite deservedly be called a rich and fertile seedbed of illustrious men. It counts among its alumni four popes, more than a hundred cardinals, eleven of whom are now living, and almost innumerable bishops.

Suddenly the pontiff, for no compelling reason, ordered a formal visitation of the Roman College and ordered that the Jesuits who were directing the youth gathered in that house be investigated.[2] As head of this visitation and investigation, he appointed Cardinal Marefoschi (for the pope had called him to be a cardinal among his first appointments in order to please the king of Spain). Marefoschi was a man who burned with an unquenchable hatred for the Jesuits. He knew well enough that no exception could be taken to the teaching. So he handed over the seminary's account books to an expert accountant (his name was Smuraglia) for auditing. He was in collusion with Marefoschi and laboriously pored over the books for the almost two hundred years of the institution's existence. He computed all the receipts and disbursements to the farthing and at the end, calculated that there ought to be a surplus of five million gold pieces and some small change. He asserted that the Jesuits had stolen this sum for themselves and perhaps had it hidden in some secret safe in the professed house.

The Jesuits laughed at this horrendous tale. They knew that the college was in debt and scarcely got by on the monthly payments of boarders. Marefoschi, however, reported the situation as if it were a fact. The pontiff not only deprived the Jesuits of the administration, but he also completely abolished the residential part of the Roman College, that source and training ground of virtue. He closed the house and then even sold it. A handsome reward was paid to the accountant Smuraglia for his service. However the tens of thousands of gold pieces, by which Marefoschi was so exercised, were nowhere to be found.

The Irish College was soon taken from us in the way that the Roman College was.[3] And again Marefoschi was the author of the injury. For he was a protector of the Irish people. [138] On that basis, he made a visitation of the college. He found so many grave abuses in it that he judged that the Jesuits should be completely removed from its administration. It is uncertain what he had in mind, but he ordered the proceedings of the visitation to be published and distributed. In them he raised special objections to two things which the Jesuits were doing. He accused them first of embezzling some of the college's income and turning it to their own use. (In this fashion a man of sterner stuff and very delicate conscience had regard for others' reputations!) His second objection against the Jesuits was that they were not taking proper care of the students and were sending them back to Ireland not well trained, but almost illiterate and ignorant. At best they were at the middle school level. I do not know what he meant by "middle school level." He evidently stood in horror of it as something monstrous.

It was not difficult to refute these charges. To pass over other things, there are extant excellent and quite recent testimonials of the popes on the Irish College. In them the popes approved and praised its entire administration, learning, and especially the first-rate courses of study. But Ganganelli, scarcely having received Marefoschi's report, removed the Jesuits as if they had been found guilty of some offense. He handed over the direction of the college to a group of Irish priests.

Justice Denied to Jesuits in Judicial Dealings

The Jesuits' lot at this time was clearly miserable. Due to the pontiff's favor, anyone who had judicial dealings with Jesuits, even if his case were less just, would win. I will give some examples of this sort of thing. The Jesuits used to own a large vineyard at Castel Gondolfo adjacent to a small farm belonging to the Irish College. The Jesuits had purchased the vineyard for a fair price a hundred years before. On it the Fathers General had constructed a villa for breaks in the country. Despite this long-standing possession of the property,

Marefoschi seemed to have spotted some flaw in the sale. Because of it the vineyard was to be returned to the Irish College. When the case came to court the judges decided it had been legally purchased and received by the sale. Nonetheless, Ganganelli, using, I think, the pontiff's universal right over all the Church's goods, ordered the vineyard returned to the Irish College.

At Macerata, the canons of the cathedral church had undertaken the building of a new edifice from the foundations. Until the construction could be completed, they requested the use of the Jesuit church for the conduct of religious services since it was bigger than other churches and more conveniently located. The Jesuits refused this imposition upon themselves. Still they were forced by order of the pontiff to allow the canons to use their church.

At Frascati, the Cardinal Henry, duke of York, who was also the local bishop, wanted to expand the space of his seminary. (For he did maintain a large seminary in that rather small diocese.) He asked that a small part of the Jesuit college be ceded to him. [139] When asked about the matter, the Pontiff gave to the Cardinal not just a small part, but the whole college with its attached church. Thus the Jesuits were evicted from a very old possession. The Jesuits were very pained by these events. But since, despite this treatment, the whole Society was still to be safe, they patiently endured all.

Through these stages Ganganelli, deceived by his hopeful assessment, was heading to the final act which he had intended to avoid. For the more he inflicted woes upon the Jesuits, the more urgently and insistently the Bourbon kings were pressing for the suppression of the Society. They were now demanding it not as a freely given benefit, but as a thing owed to them from the pontiff's pledged word. They were complaining that the matter was being dragged out to excessive lengths, that they were being put off unfairly with promises, that they were being made sport of. Thus, brought to an extremity, the pontiff undertook a plan that, if successful, would in fact deal with the Jesuits, but which could not be called a suppression. For he preferred anything to the issuing of a papal bull of suppression. He had many things to fear: the unpopularity of the deed, public turmoil, the scandal of the pious, the gloating and scoffing of the heretics. He did not think it in accord with the dignity of the Apostolic See to suppress an order which his predecessor Rezzonico had so recently confirmed and to counter a very recent papal bull with a new one.

What would happen if bishops, under the appearance of an apostolic visit, were to close the novitiates of the Jesuits, send the scholastics home, forbid the priests all sacerdotal ministry, and have the same power over them as over other clergy? If this were done everywhere, the Society would surely die out. But there would be no bull of suppression from the pope and since matters would proceed in a slow and roundabout way, certain things could happen in the meanwhile which might stop the course of events.

This was the plan he adopted and he kept things in the utmost secrecy. He wanted to make a first trial of his plan at Bologna since the archbishop there was Cardinal Malvezzi.[4] He was rather unfriendly to the Jesuits, and for that reason, not suspect to the Bourbons. This turned out differently than he expected. For although Malvezzi easily attained the objective of having the novices return to their homes, when it came to the scholastics, he could in no way persuade them to take off the Society's cassock. They were insisting that they had been called by God's will to the Society, that they were joined to it by the sacred bonds of vows, that they will not be separated from it against their wills unless the Supreme Pontiff, who is Christ's vicar on earth, ordered it. Let Malvezzi produce the orders of the pope if he had any such. Malvezzi denied [140] that he had to produce any instructions. He asserted that they ought to believe a cardinal who was declaring to them the pontiff's will. When the young men all the same persisted firmly in their stand, Malvezzi used force. Despite their protests and vain supplications for help from above, they were stripped of their religious garb by the hand of attendants and carried off to their homes. The people contemned the action and it stirred up hatred for Malvezzi.

An apostolic visitation of the Society followed at Ravenna and Ferrara. The task was entrusted to the cardinal legates of those cities. In both places the Jesuits were cooperative with the cardinals, which was fitting once they showed the pontifical letter. But the pontiff appeared to be extraordinarily troubled. For after the Bologna business, which was talked about throughout Italy and was offensive to all good men, he was hearing unfavorable reports on the matter.

Moniño Pressures Clement to Suppress Jesuits

In the crisis Moniño, who had succeeded the deceased Azpuru in the Spanish embassy, stepped forward.[5] He pounced on the wavering pontiff and drove him on the path he wanted. He pointed out that that gradual method of purging the Society was a road full of bumps and would never come to an end. If he were to proceed in that fashion, he would expose the pontifical dignity to ridicule and his authority to flouting. Everywhere the Jesuits cling tenaciously to their name and Institute. Assuredly, they will stir up riots in many places. When they have resisted so stoutly the Cardinal Archbishop of Bologna, what would they not dare in places where the bishop is of lesser standing? The business can and ought to be accomplished with one little page. Let him finally stop delaying. Let him publish the decree of suppression, which has been so ardently desired by so many kings, clearly promised, and so long delayed. Are the Jesuits as important as so many powerful monarchs? As the peace of the Church? As his own dignity? Finally, no middle ground is left. It is either the suppression of the Society or everlasting discord with the Bourbons.

The pope was thus placed in a bind. He promised he would do it provided the Empress Queen of Hungary agreed. That was the last dodge left to him. He was in hopes that Maria Therese, that woman of remarkable piety, would not at all consent to such a thing. For she had almost a hereditary benevolence toward the Jesuits from her ancestors. She had entrusted her sons and daughters to the Jesuits for formation in holiness and good character. Finally, she seemed to favor very much the Jesuits of her nation. But the queen handed the entire matter over to Count Kaunitz, her prime minister.[6] Somehow, the Spaniards had drawn him over to their side. And so when the papal nuncio made the proposal of suppressing the Society, he responded that the entire affair [141] rested upon the judgment of the pontiff and was entirely in his hands. The empress had no objections and would not refuse to consider valid whatever the pontiff had decided. Since the Austrians and Bourbons agreed (there was no need to doubt what the king of Portugal wanted), the pope saw that lesser princes would certainly follow the authority of these monarchs and he made the decision to suppress the Society.

Clement Seeks Danei's Support for Suppression

Still the pontiff, as before, was distraught with an unsettling concern. He delayed the decree and begged for heaven's light in pious prayers. He even proclaimed exercises of piety through the city and prayers of petition to be made in common. He decided he had to do something further to determine the will of God. There was living at Rome at that time a Paolo Danei from the town of Castelletto in the province of Alessandria.[7] Everyone considered him a saint. He was founder of a new religious order which derived its name from the passion of Christ. In order to consult such a man, the pope did not consider it beneath his lofty estate to enter a humble little domicile. He sat down with him there and spent an entire hour with no witnesses. No one doubted that he confided his plans about the suppression of the Society. He went away then much more cheerful than he had come.

The courtiers noted this and took it as a good sign. I think the venerable man, having heard the state of affairs, gave courage to the pontiff. With eloquent words, the priest persuaded the pope that if peace, dignity, and liberty could not otherwise be restored to the Church, he ought not fear to suppress the Society. He must conduct the affairs of the universal Church. This is the supreme pontiff's duty. He should entrust other matters to God. Religious orders, no matter how useful, no matter how holy, have been founded solely for the advantage of the Church. They can also be abolished if the advantage of the Church should demand it. I think Danei said these things or things similar to them. Accordingly, the pope went away with a cheered and buoyed mind. Certainly a short time thereafter, he ordered the brief of suppression, which had already been written before the visit, to be printed.

Through those times, I had retired to Calamandrana in the mountains to escape the summer heat and to enjoy some honest leisure with my friends. Then I received a letter from Rome which announced the sure and proximate suppression of the Society. A papal brief was in the press. All that remained was that it be sent out and promulgated to the Jesuits. I could scarcely bring myself to believe it. What did the pope achieve by troubling the Jesuits of Bologna so if he had it in mind to destroy all Jesuits with one blow? Fear and pain were troubling my mind. A letter to me from Father General, written on the feast of St. Ignatius, made me even more incredulous. In it, besides many other things, [142] were these very words, "We celebrated today with God's help the feast of Holy Father Ignatius with less splendor and pomp, but with an extraordinary turnout. They say this is the last celebration; but as I see it, St. Peter was freed from his chains precisely when Herod was going to drag him into court." When he wrote these words, he had perchance already recited the office of the next day when the feast of St. Peter in Chains occurred. He still hoped for better things in a reliance on certain prophecies. These predicted this very thing, that when the Society seemed brought to the very brink, then suddenly its fortunes would be changed and it would be freed not only from danger, but every annoyance. The good man, of course, had no idea that the fatal brief had started to be printed secretly ten days before. When it was published, it was signed under the date of 21 July.[8] Ricci was dumbstruck when the brief was produced, shown, and read. He had no suspicion of it. Asked by order of the pontiff whether he accepted the decision, he answered that what the Supreme Pontiff decided was sacred and ought to be obeyed by all. There was no need for his approval. But what transpired at Rome after this, I will tell below.

Publication of Papal Brief of Suppression

I, too, at the first sight of the papal brief which was brought to me as quickly as possible, was dumbfounded, blanched, and all but fell down in a faint. "In this way," I shouted out, "in this way did the Society of Jesus have to be destroyed? And that was done by a decree of the Supreme Pontiff whose greatest duty was to protect and guard such an order against all violence. Heavens, such is your good faith!" I could scarcely bring myself to read it. Yet I did read the brief quickly and with great trepidation. I was specifically afraid that the Pontiff in the document might level most serious charges upon us as grounds for destroying the Society. Countless books were full of such charges: Transacting business, betraying and slaughtering kings, lax moral teaching, corrupt instructing of youth, idolatry, obstinate disobedience to apostolic judgments, and other things of the kind. If that were the case, eternal disgrace would be being added to the pain of the Society's loss. Our accusers were certainly desirous of that. Tanucci, de Roda, Almada, Carvalho, and other ill-disposed parties were expecting it.

But Ganganelli, that noted enemy of the Society, burdened us with no crime, no punishment. He even had written up the matter in such a way that the Society's suppression seemed to be assignable not to any deserts of Ours, but to the tenor of the times. Accordingly, he detracted nothing from our honor and reputation. Finally, he used such moderate language that a friend of the Society or even one of the Jesuits, if he had been forced to compose such a brief, could not have used greater circumspection. This was so true that Tanucci, though he was glad the Society was suppressed, [143] still did not allow the brief to be promulgated in the kingdom of Naples. Hence came petitions of the Bourbons to the pontiff that he issue a new document and substitute a bull for the brief. It was not as if the bull would add greater weight to the matter, but they were not content with the suppression of the Society. They wanted its reputation and esteem overwhelmed with charges. However, they never obtained their request. But now let us quickly run through the brief.

The Substance of Dominus ac Redemptor

There are three just causes for suppressing an order. One is because it is split into factions by internal disagreements and divisions. The second is that it has

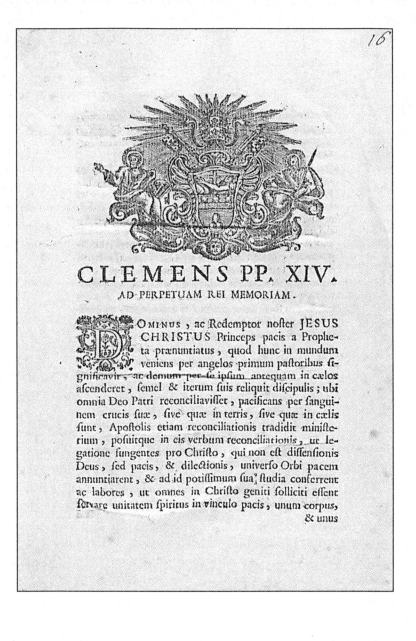

CLEMENS PP. XIV.

AD-PERPETUAM REI MEMORIAM.

Ominus, ac Redemptor noster JESUS CHRISTUS Princeps pacis a Propheta prænuntiatus, quod hunc in mundum veniens per angelos primum pastoribus significavit, ac demum per se ipsum antequam in cælos ascenderet, femel & iterum suis reliquit discipulis; ubi omnia Deo Patri reconciliavisset, pacificans per sanguinem crucis suæ, five quæ in terris, five quæ in cælis funt, Apostolis etiam reconciliationis tradidit ministerium, posuitque in eis verbum reconciliationis, ut legatione fungentes pro Christo, qui non est dissensionis Deus, sed pacis, & dilectionis, universo Orbi pacem annuntiarent, & ad id potissimum sua studia conferrent ac labores, ut omnes in Christo geniti solliciti essent servare unitatem spiritus in vinculo pacis, unum corpus,
& unus

Dominus ac Redemptor

been reduced to such small numbers that it is not deemed useful for the common good. The third, finally, is that it has notably departed from its original institute. Now because of lax discipline and poor example it labors under such public disgrace that it no longer should be endured or is to be corrected. The pontiff charged the Society with none of these three. He kept affirming that his sole aim was to restore her peace and tranquillity to the Church. This would not seem possible as long as the Society survived. He was maintaining that he valued the peace of the Church so highly that for the sake of preserving it, he would not hesitate to attack, to disperse, to destroy whatever he held particularly dear and which he could do without only with the greatest pain.

With that as a preface, he recalled several religious orders which at diverse times had been suppressed by apostolic authority. And after that he tried to show that because of the Society, the Church's peace had already begun to be disturbed from its inception. In the years that followed the Church continued to be constantly troubled. At its beginning, other religious had risen up against the Society, its laws and institutes, its privileges and its entire form of government. To these were added bishops, academics, and even the very kings. They had brought their outcries and complaints to the Apostolic See. However, the supreme pontiffs persevered unshakenly in approving and protecting it.

Next there sprang up very bitter doctrinal debates between Jesuits and other religious. These debates stirred strong emotions in the Christian republic and divided almost all of Christendom into factions according to their diverse inclinations. Then unfavorable rumors began to be heard about the Jesuits' excessive greed in acquiring resources and that they entangled themselves in the public business of princes. The Society's superiors thought they should meet this uproar with new and very holy directives. Further the Jesuits had often been accused before the Holy See of corrupting the faith by defending certain superstitious rites. They were also accused of laxity in doctrine and in the interpretation of pontifical decisions. [144] They were also often delated for 1) contumaciously resisting the bishops since the Jesuits have their privileges and exemptions; 2) quarrelling fiercely with the secular and regular clergy over that same matter; 3) giving occasion to all in Asia, Europe, and America, for riots, revolts, and conflicts. All this was true, but not to the extent of causing harm to the Society. As often as he was asserting that the Jesuits were accused, he was not also asserting that they were *justly* accused or that they were found guilty of outrage. He left it open whether they were guilty or innocent. He was handling the Jesuits very carefully unless you are so sensitive that you would take offense at the mere mention of a word apposite to a case.

Having touched upon some things with broad strokes, which could have been omitted and which seemed added only for the sake of juridical form (for Ganganelli was not unaware that similar things could have been said concerning each of the more famous orders), he came down to the true and only reason for suppressing the Society. He remarked that the Society had been expelled (he did not specify whether rightly or wrongly) from the kingdoms of Portugal, France, Spain, and the Two Sicilies. Those very powerful kings had conjointly begged his predecessor, Clement XIII, then himself, that the Society be completely uprooted and destroyed everywhere. They are still, even now, calling for this with all their effort and exertion. He could have added this, which, however, he judged should be kept quiet, that if they did not get their wish, they would never be reconciled with the Apostolic See or restore their original harmony with it. What the nature of that threat was I will take up later.

After that introduction, in which, in my opinion, nothing greatly opprobrious to our good name appeared, he suppressed in accord with the power committed to him by the divine Christ, the Society with its Constitutions and Institute, its laws and privileges. He declared it completely suppressed and extinct everywhere in the world. He deprived Father General and the Society's other superiors of all jurisdiction. He ordered that the colleges, houses, and novitiates be closed everywhere and that all Jesuits should take off the Society's cassock. Those who were clerics and priests, except those who entered another religious order, he subjected to the jurisdiction of the bishops. He ordered that an annual pension be given from the Society's property to priests for maintaining a decent living. If any of them should prefer to live together in some house of the Society either because of family need, or old age, or poor health, or any other legitimate reason, he left such decisions to the judgment of the bishops. The condition for allowing this, however, was that some prudent secular priest be put over them as superior; nor were they to be allowed to preach in public [145] or to hear confessions of the laity. He determined that others, provided that they seemed worthy, be permitted to administer the sacraments, to educate youth, and to be promoted to ecclesiastical dignities from which they had previously been excluded by their vows. He declared that the houses and property of the Society ought to be used only for pious purposes. He directed that his brief be promulgated by the bishops to the Jesuits in common. Because there were many who were exiles, driven from their homeland by their kings, he said they too were bound by his brief of suppression.

Towards individual Jesuits, however, he professed himself to be stirred by pastoral charity. He sternly forbade anyone to speak against them or to provoke them with insults and contumely. At the end he laid down that the brief should be promulgated all over the world and its contents be held firm and binding in perpetuity. As the penalty for opposing or criticizing the brief, he imposed an anathema. He earnestly requested princes that they would want in their own realms exact observance of what he himself had thought must be established for the peace and tranquillity of the Church.

This was the gist of the papal brief. As I said, it seemed to the ill-disposed tempered with excessive kindness. Perhaps it stirred the envy of many religious. Shortly afterwards, another document was promulgated in which the pontiff established a new commission of five cardinals.[9] To it all the business of the suppressed Society was to be referred, and he withdrew from any other tribunal the jurisdiction for dealing with those affairs.

Wide Range of Reactions to Suppression

Doubts were expressed on whether the professed of the Society were freed from their solemn vows by the brief, for the pontiff had not explicitly said so. But this debate seemed silly to me, nor can I see what difference, as far as obligation goes, there would be between the simple vows of coadjutors and the solemn vows of the professed since the Society had been suppressed. For all vows bind to the extent that the vower intends and prescribes for himself. Although the professed and the coadjutors as well wished to observe poverty, chastity, and obedience no differently than they had in the Society, still it necessarily follows that there was no obligation of the vows left. By this reasoning if one had vowed a pilgrimage to Our Lady's shrine at Loreto and if the shrine were totally destroyed, certainly no one would say that all the same the person is bound by vow to the pilgrimage or needs a dispensation of the pope. But that is a side remark and digression.

When the brief of suppression was read, as I was saying, I looked up to the sky for a moment as if very gravely pained. I held it certain that what Christ's vicar had ordered must be accepted as [146] a command from God. I judged that I must accede completely to the divine will. I also called to my aid the precepts of philosophy and especially that saying of Horace, "Whatever one is forbidden to correct becomes lighter with patience" (Odes 1.24.20). I then laid down a law for myself that I would never, or at least only with the greatest circumspection, speak of the suppression of the Society. I would not ever utter a word of pain or anger against Pope Ganganelli. If all Jesuits had observed the same reticence, our foes, I think, would soon be falling silent. Certainly they would not be continuing to rage so much against the remnants of the Society, as we have seen is done.

Finally, inasmuch as there is no kind of evil in this life that is not mixed with some good, I decided to enjoy what benefits the suppression brought to me. There were, to be sure, several and not unpleasant ones. How big a benefit was it, brother, for me to live henceforth with you, with your wife and children under a common roof? How big a benefit was it to be able to pass the final part of life—however long that period might be—in the most pleasant company of my relatives? I had many nominal brothers in the Society, but no real one except you. Bonds of blood were always more sacred and sweet to me than any others. With such mental preparation, I bore the bitterest of misfortunes with a cheerful and uplifted face.

Even at that time, I wrote letters full of jokes to my Roman friends. They thought that I was depressed and dejected by the misfortune. I kept the pain within and did not permit consoling gestures except from my closest friends. Thus I always am. I hate nothing more than to be considered worthy of pity. At that same time, in order to dispel and dissipate as best I could the gnawing sickness in my heart, I applied myself to writing that playful poem on the origins of Nizza Monferrato. Such as it is, you know well that it is charming and the most carefully crafted of all my works. I had spent two months at this work in Calamandrana when I learned that the brief of suppression had been duly promulgated both in the Turin College and in the other colleges of the province. I then went without delay to Alessandria. Here I took off the cassock of the Society; here I purchased for myself new clothes which were suitable for a nobleman priest; here I was transformed from a Jesuit into a diocesan priest. I returned to Turin and took up residence in the old college of the Jesuits, for that was still allowed for the space of one year.

Good God, what a college I found! How changed it was from that college where recently silence and the profoundest peace had reigned, where all had been regulated by religious discipline. The group was about fifty in number. [147] Part of the group consisted of select youths who were doing theological studies. The rest were older priests or coadjutor brothers. The superior of all was a nobleman, a prudent priest by the name of Father San Sebastiano. There were no rules for the house, no daily order except that at a set time all were summoned to the dining room by a bell and sat down there for the meal.

There was not even reading at table. For the rest each one passed the day as suited him. Their attitudes varied greatly. Many of the younger men were pleased with their new and elegant dress and also with the newfound liberty. They bore the Society's destruction with moderate feelings. Even some of the priests, who were holier and trained in solid virtue, rested in the divine will and spoke of the matter very sparingly and reflectively.

Intemperate Reactions against Clement

But there were others, especially those born in humbler stations, who observed no moderation in criticizing and complaining, in execrating and calling down dire curses upon Pope Ganganelli. There were some who, showing no respect for the pontifical power, were saying that Ganganelli was the most impure and criminal of men and deserving of a thousand crucifixions. There were some who falsely charged that he had been corrupted by simony as if he obtained the pontificate in exchange for the suppression of the Society. Certain ones took a legal stance and declared that he may not suppress the Society without its being very, very seriously at fault. I heard one of the graver Fathers openly pontificating as if from an oracle. He was maintaining that in the Christian era no more wicked deed had ever been done than the suppression of the Society. The pope ought to have been more ready to submit to every danger his life, his reign, the entire Church rather than to fetter himself with such a grave sacrilege.

Running about here and there, they dinned these views into the ears of their friends and certain pious women. Indeed they put a veil of piety in front of this undignified behavior and were using the public good as a pretext. They were shouting out that religion had been harmed, that divine worship was lessened in many places. Youth were deprived of suitable education, the people of mighty aids to eternal salvation. They were uttering other specious things of the sort as if they had responsibility for these and must render an account to God. Yet everyone understood that the poor fellows were aflame with anger and pain because they were being forced to leave the large Jesuit houses and to return to the hovels of their fathers, and especially because they had become accustomed to live with the noblest of men in a fraternal way and even to rise above them in certain cases. Now they were reduced to the status of ordinary priests and considered far below their former companions. They sensed that the people looked up to and revered that other group of priests, but held them in contempt. To this then came down their pain over the suppressed Society, to this came down their burning zeal for the common good. [148] They could not swallow the fact that such a distinction was introduced among brothers; so they continue to speak ill of Ganganelli even now.

Besides these, who seemed moved by an almost evil intemperateness, there were some who openly assailed the pontifical power. For despite whatever Ganganelli decreed in his brief, they unabashedly asserted that the Society remained against his wishes in Silesia and in Russia, where the local monarchs had not permitted the letter to be published.[10] These, in order to hold Ganganelli up for ridicule, flatly denied that the pope on his own authority can establish and end, found and destroy, bind and loose an order. Such a thing could be said only with the greatest rashness. Thus Jesuits, who were previously said to extol papal authority beyond, perhaps, due measure, now in their own case depreciated that authority much too unduly. Nor did they reflect even this much—that the trunk of the Society had been hewn in Rome and therefore its branches could not flower elsewhere. For what benefit was it for the Society to exist in Russia if it had been destroyed in Piedmont?

Some sought one alleviation for their pain, others another. For example, some said and confidently predicted that the Society was to be restored to its original state in a short time. They were saying that as Christ had risen from the grave within three days, so the Society would rise up with even greater glory after a very brief death. Once again optimistic prophecies began to spread. Again the prophetess of Valentano was brought on stage. While formerly she was said to have predicted that the Society would never be destroyed by a papal decree, now she was reported as announcing its imminent restoration. Such was the confidence in her prediction that one of the Fathers was ready to lay down money on a bet with me that the Society was to be restored before the end of the following year by a new brief of the pope. Some extended the time limit for a year, then for another year, as confidence waned.

Clement Increases Jesuits' Pain

Things occurred at the Turin College in my stay there against which, though I did not approve, or rather, which I thoroughly disapproved, still I did not dare to utter a word in order not, as they say, to stir up a hornets' nest. I have not learned what other Jesuits at Rome or those scattered through Italy were agitating. Inasmuch as all professed themselves most devoted to the Society and very many were moved by almost the same spirit, it is quite believable that several dared to speak and to do things similar to these and even worse. Certainly the pope, for scarcely any other reason [149] suddenly changed his tactics. The change greatly increased the pain over the Society's suppression. For when some rest was owed to Jesuits after such a dread, sorrowful shipwreck, strict investigations were being made into them. Even Ricci himself, the highest superior of the order, a very innocent and holy man, was shut up in Castel Sant' Angelo. The pope ordered that he be kept under close guard. A short time later, he imprisoned the five assistants, very dignified men of diverse nations and clearly the foremost members of the entire order. He put in the same jail at intervals other Jesuits who had something of a greater or a suspect reputation in the city. Almost daily Rome echoed with reports of Jesuits' arrests and Castel Sant' Angelo was full of Jesuits.

What seemed worst of all to many was the fact that he put Alfani, that faithless and detestable man, about whom I have spoken elsewhere, in charge of jailing the Jesuits and keeping them in custody. Finally, the pope ordered that the prophetess of Valentano, the source of so many predictions and prophecies, be put away in a convent and to be kept there as in an honorable captivity and to be subjected to a strict scrutiny. Nor was that enough. Although he had previously permitted bishops to use the Jesuits they preferred for preaching and hearing confessions, he now sent around a letter in which he ordered that the Jesuits be kept from any ministry of this kind unless the Holy See had given prior authorization. What reasons the pontiff had for decreeing such things, we will expound in a more leisurely way below. Now let us pursue things closer to hand.

Cordara's Return to his Native Alessandria

It was now towards the end of the year that had been granted to us to live in the Turin College. No prince was more generous to the Jesuits than Vittorio Amedeo. He offered to us the opportunity of living a common life in one of the three colleges in his realm: Chieri, Saluzzo, and Alessandria. Then I, brother, weighing everything carefully, preferred Alessandria to Turin, and a religious house to your home. In addition to the fact that I was loathe to abandon the silence and solitude of a religious' cell, to which I had become accustomed from my youth, I was intending to pursue my former studies for the rest of my life. That would be very difficult amid the noise and bustle of a secular house. Further, I liked Alessandria very much. It is a fairly large city with a good climate. Its site is excellent; it is well-populated and prosperous. I had a lot of friends there and some of its noblemen were related to me by marriage. Also the college building provided very comfortable living because of its layout and the relaxed daily order. [150] I knew there would be only a few living there. I was especially moved by the fact that it was only a four-hour trip from there to Calamandrana where I was intending to spend some part of the summer and fall each year with my relatives. Finally, I decided to finish my life there where by chance I had been born. For our parents, as you know, when our native Nizza Monferrato was being swamped with armed soldiers because of the war with France, had retired to Alessandria, as a safe refuge. Here mother gave birth to me.

Therefore at the end of the year, I came to Alessandria and took up quarters in the old Jesuit college, as if in a tranquil port. The most comfortable room in the house, which had been the rector's, was assigned to me. Nearby was a valet who saw to my needs and was immediately at my beck and call. There was no superior in the house. There was no strict discipline except that meals were taken together and our needs sufficiently met at the king's expense. There were no more than seven living together there. They were all priests of respectable families and of excellent character. Yet some of them still denounced Ganganelli. They grieved inconsolably the suppression of the Society, and wanted to appear to be still Jesuits as far as dress and exterior appearance went. I applied myself to writing now this work in hand, now other things. I led a life that was no different from the very quiet existence of a noble priest. Yet no one was more attached to the Society than I was. None of my companions from this province was as prominent in the Society as I had been. No one except me was forced to exchange Rome for Alessandria. But let us let the matter drop.

Last Days of Clement XIV

Meanwhile Pope Ganganelli, although he had a strong constitution and was not on in years, survived the extinction of the Society only for a bit over a year and a half. In the meantime, he rejoiced to see the princes mollified, Avignon returned by the king of France, and Benevento returned by the king of Naples. To please the king of Spain, he summoned Cardinal Malvezzi to Rome. For his good services at Bologna he made Malvezzi his prodatary for handing out patronage, but in such a way that he retained the see of Bologna. Since a Holy Year was approaching, the pope opened the treasuries of the Church and declared for the following year solemn indulgences for sins.

But while he was doing these things, the specter of the extinct Society of Jesus hovered over him. It frequently occurred to him how much harm had been done to the Church by that move, how much disgrace fell upon himself, and how much unpopularity he had generated with that brief. A great bulwark and column had been taken from the Apostolic See. [151] A select and hard-working band of laborers had been taken from Christ's field. Catholics were offended. Heretics exulted in joy. The Christian commonwealth, disturbed throughout the world, was tottering. And day and night this concern ate into him to such an extent that he sometimes raved in his discomfort and seemed to be out of his mind. Let this be a proof: at times he thought he heard at night the Jesuits' bronze bell, which, however, no one was ringing.

To these anxieties of mind was added an equally serious illness of body. For a long time he was suffering from a harmless rash. The boils, which used to break out and spread across the skin without injury, suddenly turned inward and infected the blood. Whatever means the doctors could think up to draw the infection to the surface of the skin were in vain. Warm compresses accomplished nothing. Though it was August, braziers were brought into the room to increase the summer's heat. That was for nothing too. And so as the malady outstripped the remedies, he paid his debt to nature on 22 September, surrounded by a group of priests. He was then passing through the seventieth year of his life, the sixth of his pontificate. When he was close to death, the palace cardinals, and especially Malvezzi, asked him to reveal the names of the cardinals whom he had created but had kept *in petto*. (There were eleven such.) He positively refused to do so. Nor could he be cajoled into doing it by any entreatings and coaxings.

The body was wasted for the reason I mentioned above. It began to discolor immediately and in a short time totally decayed. It emitted through the various apertures such a foul stench that no one could bear it. Hence that very powerful Franciscan, Bontempi, who was the closest of friends to the pontiff and who shared in all his affairs, spread the vicious rumor that the pope had been carried off by poison and that it was the doing of the Jesuits. Yet the more prominent of the Jesuits were being detained for more than a year now in Castel Sant' Angelo. The others were not so dim-witted that they would dare such an outrageous crime nor would they want to undertake it so late, when the whole situation was beyond repair. But the prestige of one friar was not such that he persuaded anyone to believe the charge. Certainly the cardinals, whose task it was to probe carefully the serious matter, scorned the rumor as a poorly contrived calumny and did not want any investigation into the matter.

Retrospective on Clement XIV

Thus Clement XIV ended his life; thus he ended his brief pontificate. He was, if truth were told, a pope who was more unfortunate than evil. He would have been an excellent pontiff if he had met with better times. He appealed to many, and not just ordinary people, with his endowments of intellect, learning, and virtue. He was remarkably [152] sagacious, the highest ranking gift, in my judgment, for a prince to have. Next, he was, despite his high station, both humble and equally moderate. He was mild, affable, frugal, never precipitous in judgment, never excessively angry. From his very lofty position he seemed to take nothing for himself except the insignia of the office and the cares of governance. He certainly gave nothing to his relatives. He had only one nephew on his sister's side. His name was Fabro. He was a young man who was both respectable and needy. The pontiff maintained him at Rome with a small outlay. He never admitted him for a visit.

Ganganelli happened upon princes who were full of Febronian ideas and who accordingly held papal authority in less esteem. To lessen the harm these princes might do, he inflicted upon himself and the Church two wounds. One was, as we said, the suppression of our Society. The second, a graver and more incurable wound, was the discontinuance of reading the bull *In Cena Domini*. That was a very sacred constitution on which papal authority in the Catholic world especially rested. When he ceased proclaiming it in a solemn manner, it was tantamount to suppressing the bull. He set an example which his successor Pius, though otherwise a courageous pontiff, was forced to follow. These two things make the pontificate of Ganganelli remarkable, and indeed it is a pontificate always to be remembered with pain and grief.

Who could determine whether any other pope would have done the same in the circumstances? The princes conspired closely against the rights of the Church. If you were to offend one, all were irritated. No one, which was unusual, came to the pontiff's aid. In this state of affairs, it seemed better to Ganganelli to concede something willingly rather than to reduce everything to a crisis stage. For although the supreme pastor has the greatest legal power over the entire flock, and therefore, over the kings themselves inasmuch as they are sons of the Church, still he can not exercise it over unwilling and resisting kings. At this ruinous time, the rights of kings far prevailed over the pope's. If what he did was bad, Ganganelli should not be thought to have acted out of a bad intention. But let us restrict our comments to the suppression of the Society, which is my sole theme.

I maintain this first of all, Ganganelli always lived his personal life in such a way that he was considered a good, God-fearing monk. There are some who go farther and call him a real saint and would assert his holiness was proven by miracles. But I think such claims are made out of partisanship and some extol him excessively because others disparage him excessively. He was by nature lively and used to joke in his personal encounters. (I knew the man when I was living in Piceno.) His character was upright. His close friends, his fellow Franciscans, gave witness to this. [153] If anyone accuses Ganganelli of a lax life, he is clearly lying and must needs admit he is being motivated by mere ill will. He was not only innocent in his life and always far removed from any crimes, but also he was so dedicated to higher studies that he excelled among his fellow religious because of his learning. He also whiled away leisure time with painting. An example of this hobby is a very large canvas drawn by his hand and representing St. Bonaventure. It can be seen today at Soriano nel Cimino in the house of the Albani family.

Clement XIV's Attitude toward Jesuits

I also add this point: He was always very fond of the Society. Jesuits themselves formerly acknowledged that at Milan, at Bologna, at Rome where he taught theology for the Franciscans and maintained acquaintances with Jesuits. It is clear enough that wherever he was, Ganganelli got on very well with Jesuits and was always reckoned among their friends. Once at Milan he was going to defend publicly some theological theses. He wanted them dedicated to the founder of the Society, St. Ignatius. He used the occasion to have a laudatory oration on the Society be printed and prefixed to the theses. That eulogy is extant even now and there is no finer commendation of our order.

Ganganelli was transferred from Milan to Bologna and then summoned by Annibale Cardinal Albani to Rome.[11] He was put in charge of the famous college of his order, St. Bonaventure by name. He used to report that he had received that position thanks solely to the kind offices of a certain Jesuit (his name was Urbani). For Urbani had obtained this favor from Annibale with whom he had some sort of blood tie. Ganganelli, accordingly, out of a sense of gratitude, used to visit Urbani often and he sought to accommodate him in whatever ways he could. When Urbani was in the throes of a slow, persistent illness, not a day passed without Ganganelli's coming to greet and console him. He moved about among the Jesuits with such familiarity that he seemed one of them. But why more on these matters?

Pope Rezzonico, when he made Ganganelli a cardinal, stated openly, as I said before, that he was making a cardinal out of a Jesuit clothed in a

Franciscan's habit. The Jesuits themselves were convinced of this. I for my part do not deny that after that time Ganganelli appeared alienated from us and was commonly considered anti-Jesuit. For from then on he refrained from all contact with our men. He undertook support of Palafox's cause and he maintained close relationships with de Roda, the ambassador of the king of Spain. But having obtained the cardinalate, he began to look to the papacy. This itch affects almost all the cardinals. He was wise enough to see that an open supporter of the Jesuits was not going to be named pope. [154] And so he went over to the opposite camp. However, he changed only the appearances, not his inner attitude, not his will. He deserved to be called "a masked Jesuit" as he was by Cardinal Orsini. We saw that above, but let us finish up the rest of the material that pertains to this theme.

It has been shown well enough, I think, that no deal concerning the suppression of the Society was struck in Ganganelli's election. Yet, you will say, he did suppress it. Yes, of course; but he put it off to the fifth year of his pontificate. He examined every way of avoiding the suppression. He acted not on his own will, but out of necessity. That is evident from the facts we have touched upon here and there in our work. But in the end, he acted unwillingly. There is a still more evident proof, which, as far as I can see, cannot be refuted. That was that to the first letter of the king of France, requesting the suppression of the Society, Ganganelli wrote back that he was most loathe to do it. Besides other reasons why he should not do it, he gave the excuse that the order had been approved by the Council of Trent. If he were to suppress it, the Gallicans, who put the authority of a general council above that of the pope, would not accept the decree. Thus he expressed his mind at that time and there is a copy of the letter available in Guerra's *Collection*, published at Venice.

Nonetheless he suppressed the Society. But he suppressed it in such a way that the suppression could not have been done more gently and considerately. Contrary to what our adversaries were wishing, he laid upon us no charge. He branded us with no mark of ignominy. He presented no other reason than the peace and tranquillity of the Church. That was a value that we ourselves had to aspire to, no matter the danger to us. He completely spared the honor and reputation of the Society. He was not unaware that some of us were from poor families and others were weakened by illness and old age. He had consideration for both groups and allowed the latter to continue to live together in some house of the Society and for the former he directed that a fair pension be given from the Society's property. In the end, he did indeed suppress the Society; but after it was done, he was almost mad and beside himself. He got

Pope Clement XIV presents a copy of the Decree of Suppression of
the Society of Jesus to Spanish ambassador Giuseppe Moniño.

no rest night or day. Gradually he wasted away with illness and grief. This grief
was that infamous "poison" injected into his veins. In a sense, then, it could
be said that the Jesuits did him in.

Analysis of Good and Evil Effects of the Suppression

Some say he ought not to have decreed the suppression for any human reason, for any proposed good whatever, for it was a thing injurious to the undeserving and for that reason evil in itself, a slanderous and unjust act. They cite
appositely to this the old saw, "Evil is not to be done so that good may ensue."
You would at times hear the less learned interjecting remarks like the above.
For modesty did not [155] prevent them from judging and condemning their
own judge. At least they should have reflected that Ganganelli was an excellent theologian and accordingly knew what was licit and what was not, and he
certainly did not want to commit an obvious crime as all the world looked on.

I ask of men such as these, "What injury did he inflict upon Jesuits when
he suppressed the Society?" He dissolved that sacred bond of association by
which many men had come together for a common life under the laws and
Constitutions of St. Ignatius. The men themselves, however, he preserved

from injury. Some individuals among them had opted for a humble and abject life in the Society. Out of love for Christ, they had renounced wealth, honors, the comforts of home, and the most precious of possessions, their liberty. Now, as far as he could, Ganganelli restored these things to them. Would you say this is an injury? Other religious, if they could obtain the same favor, would not think they had received an injury, but the greatest of benefits. I know what you will say: "The other religious return home freely and willingly; they are not forced to go against their will." That is, of course, a big difference. But I still do not see in what way a benefit, even when conferred on the unwilling, can be called an injury.

Next I ask this: May not a king, when public interest requires it, disband, dismiss, and remove from the ranks one of his legions, even if it is serving faithfully and enthusiastically? May he not send each of the soldiers to his home, especially if each one's honor is saved, if his pay is protected? The argument gives them pause and snares them as in a noose. For they see the analogy of the military legions fits religious orders very closely. As legions are subject to a king, so orders are subject to the pope.

The objectors then jump from human considerations to divine ones and start a new discussion. They observe that religious are men given over to divine worship, withdrawn from the cares of passing things, organized under the watchful care of their superiors. Thus, within the protective walls of religion, they have become accustomed to living piously and with holiness. But to bring them back into the secular world, to subject them again to the alluring delights of the world, and to free them from every restraint is to run the risk of their turning to license and finally rushing off into eternal ruin. And so the Society could not have been suppressed without the greatest impiety.

Thus these malcontents make Ganganelli guilty of the gravest outrages as if those rather troubled youths, whom Father General now and then used to dismiss from the Society for serious reasons, but with no formal hearing, were not being subjected to the same dangers of a laxer life and eternal damnation. Would they say that the pontiff was not allowed for the peace and tranquillity of the Church to do what the general thought was permissible to himself for maintaining the serenity and reputation of the Society? And each person [156] must look to his own salvation by careful observance of the divine laws. But there are dangers everywhere, even within the cloister. There are aids for eternal salvation everywhere, even in the world. And nothing at all prevented those who had been Jesuits from entering another religious order and living in it a life protected from the dangerous temptations of the world. Finally, as I see it, God's help ought to be expected more by those who, by order of the pope, that is, by the manifest will of God, became secular priests than by those who by their own choice had made themselves religious. For I am convinced that in those choices which have only the appearance of piety, there is very often intermixed much human convenience.

Few are like Aloysius Gonzaga who, though he was born in a noble and rich home and was the oldest son, still scorned the allure of a large fortune and hid himself in the cell of a religious. Everyone, when he joins a religious order, says that he is embracing a poor and humble life out of zeal for his eternal salvation. But many could have found humility and poverty much more easily in their own homes and were never less poor than when they professed voluntary poverty. They do, indeed, get up at night to sing the office. They wear a coarse garment. They eat sparingly. Sometimes they have to obey a harsh superior. But in their own homes, they barely repulsed hunger with dry bread. They were with difficulty warding off winter's cold in a wrap of coarse cloth. Perhaps they were being subjected to an even harsher master at home. They were sweating out a much more strenuous toil in the field and in the shop than in the monastery.

What about the fact that the cowl generates a certain kind of nobility? At times we see seated at the table of patricians one whose father or brothers rub down the horses in the stable or wash the pots in the kitchen or pull the plow in the field. All indeed are not lower class, all are not working-class people. Indeed in some orders there are very many nobles, many upper-class people. But for some there was a poor home, for others many brothers, slight incomes, and very often such a straitened condition that one had to live in sad bachelorhood. I do not mean to exclude their consideration of their eternal welfare in embracing religious life. I mean to say that the eternal salvation of the soul is generally not the only consideration nor always the most important. I mean we can never be so certain about the will of God as when we obey a superior, especially Christ's vicar. But let us return to the theme from which the warmth of my feeling has distracted me.

Legal experts imagine a city besieged by a very powerful enemy and about to be stormed shortly when its walls and ramparts are knocked down. The general, especially irate with a certain one of the citizens, demands that the citizen be handed over to him to be put to death. The citizen is otherwise upright and innocent. The general promises that the city will be spared on this condition. [157] But if it is not done, he threatens slaughter, burning, all the destruction of war. The legal experts teach that in such a situation that citizen ought to offer himself of his own accord to the enemy. If he should refuse, he would be subject to the death penalty for he put his own safety ahead of that of the state. For that reason it is permissible for the magistrate to hand him over to the enemy to be slaughtered.

If that is the case, return now to our subject matter. Four very powerful kings were implacably incensed at the Jesuits. Because of the Jesuits, the kings were at odds with the Supreme Pontiff. Some of them had invaded the fiefs of the Roman Church with their armies. They were threatening in menacing fashion the capital itself, the very city of Rome. Other kings openly and publicly assailed the rights of the pope. All were in agreement on this: they would never renew their earlier favor and good will with the pope unless he were to suppress and abolish the Society. There was in question the entire Church, the kingdom of Christ. It had to be weighed whether this kingdom ought to be split or at least troubled forever, or ought the Jesuit order be destroyed. Which then would Jesuits prefer? Without a doubt, to avoid so many evils for the Church, they should willingly and most gladly agree to their suppression. If any had judged otherwise, for that very reason they deserved the suppression as a punishment for their insane ambition. Whatever were the Jesuits' preferences, the pontiff justly assessed that he had to grant the kings' petition. He inflicted no injustice on the Jesuits. But this is enough on the topic.

Rationale for Clement's Treatment of Ricci and Other Fathers

Still many accuse Ganganelli because he shut up in Castel Sant' Angelo, first Ricci, the Society's Father General, then the leading fathers of the order, his assistants. He ought rather to have heaped honors and favors upon them as an alleviation for their pain. Yet he kept them shut up in prison for more than a year. Then through the letter to the bishops which I mentioned, he wanted to forbid to the Jesuits every ministry of preaching and hearing confessions. From this they charge that his attitude toward Jesuits was unjust. But first of all, everyone knows he took these two steps at the request and instigation of the kings. It is no big surprise that when he had suppressed the Society for their sakes and yielded on this much more serious point, that he did not want to refuse these lesser requests. If you have cut off the master's head, why should you be afraid to cut off a finger? There were good, or at least, understandable reasons, for doing what he did. I will now undertake the explanation of them.

First, the kings who saw to the suppression of the Society imputed to it many and serious perversions. These charges were leveled not at this or that

Jesuit, but at the superiors of the order. It was fitting both for the importance of the case and the dignity of the kings, that at least these superiors be subjected to examination and that some investigation be made of them. [158] For that purpose the accused had to be kept in custody. If they were released from the prison after a few days since their innocence was sufficiently proven, it would be unseemly for the kings who had weighed them down with so many grave charges. Accordingly, although the chief investigator Andreotti absolved Ricci and his companions on every charge, and remarked that never before had more innocent defendants been brought before him, still it was decided to drag the judicial procedure out for a year and even more. Then Ricci died in prison.[12] The embarrassment of the kings was the prior cause of that unexpected and long captivity.

A second, perhaps more just cause, was added. Everyone knows how much Jesuits boast about their name, how tenacious they are of their own things. There were, indeed, very many who, still after the suppression and in defiance of the papal brief, wanted to be considered and called Jesuits. If Ricci were set free, these undoubtedly would continue to reverence him as their superior and to extend to him their deference and obedience. It was therefore to be feared that, given such attitudes, the pontifical authority would be held up for ridicule and serious storms would rise up in the Church because of dissenting judgments. Because of those things the pontiff deemed that Ricci should be kept in strict confinement even though he deserved no punishment. He used that strict precaution that Benedict VIII had once used. In order to head off the danger of a schism, Benedict put his predecessor, Celestine, away in a high tower. Celestine was quite innocent and a very holy man who had willingly abdicated the pontificate. Benedict did not let Celestine out of the tower until he died. But it is also clear that Ganganelli's concern was that the innocent Fathers, and Ricci by name, be treated most humanely and honorably. If that was not done, it should be attributed not to the pontiff's attitude, but to the wickedness and crudity of Alfani who was in charge of the imprisonment.

Rationale for Forbidding Jesuits to Exercise Sacred Ministries

A second heading in the accusation of Ganganelli concerns the circular letter with which he forbade the Jesuits to exercise sacred ministries. The reasons for this were almost the same as for the imprisonment. We have stated before how unbecomingly and intemperately many of the Jesuits received the decree of suppression. In their boldness they were reviling Ganganelli with wranglings and cursings. They were speaking no more moderately or reverently about the king of Spain, the author of the suppression. These were from the dregs of the Society, men of little talent and less learning. They certainly were not remarkable for prudence or religious virtue. Nonetheless, seeing that the Jesuit name and image were great everywhere, they got a large faction of people behind them and got many to agree with them, both from the ordinary people and from the nobility.

Add the fact that many of these Jesuits in accord with the Institute of Ignatius, desired nothing more eagerly than to hear confessions of the faithful [159] as before, and to keep people attached to themselves in the tribunal of penance, nobles especially and pious women. As far as they could, they would be speaking on divine matters from that higher place. For hence had come their former prestige. Hence the ability to stir the feelings of simple folk. When the Bourbon ambassadors, who were keeping careful watch on all at Rome, and Moniño especially, noticed these maneuvers, they clamored that the boldness of the Jesuits, who even after the suppression were acting so insolently, must be checked. They brought this up to the pope time and again. What was the pope to do? He threw one of the more talkative ones into chains at Rome. By making an example of one, he cowed the others who were in his jurisdiction. But he did not see how he could repress others who were scattered through Italy and subject to other princes. One thing he could do was to forbid them to preach and to hear confessions. If the Jesuits had guarded their tongues, if they had accepted the destruction of the Society with appropriate reserve, the pope was not going to think of any such measure.

This defense of Ganganelli, as I see, will not please many. There will undoubtedly be some who will accuse me of being ignoble because I have undertaken the defense of the Society's destroyer. I would like them to recall what Ignatius used to impose upon us in that *Letter on Obedience* which was read each month at table. He wrote, "One must obey not only with his will, but also with his intellect, as if obeying God and not men. Whatever the superior has commanded, even if it seems to us less just, must be considered just. As in matters of divine faith, so here somehow or other reasons are to be sought for defending his commands whatever they may be." This directive especially pertains here. When I find reasons, I obey the Holy Founder, I show that virtue by which Ignatius wanted true sons of the Society to be distinguished from other religious. I think I am doing something more pleasing to him than are those who fast on the vigil of his feast.

Three Remaining Questions

Yet I do not defend Ganganelli in such a way that I do not leave some of his deeds indefensible. I admit I cannot contrive a defense for all. First of all, I do not understand and marvel the more why he did not reveal his mind immediately from the beginning of his pontificate, but undertook a tactic of subterfuge and vacillation. If he had not given his word to the kings, if he had eloquently and freely declared that while he was not a friend of the Jesuits, he still could not and wished not to suppress the Society, he would have shut off all access to new petitions and would have stopped the movement in the very beginning. What could King Charles of Spain reply to that pontiff whom he esteemed highly, whom he considered learned, holy, completely devoted to himself [160] and finally very hostile to Jesuits? Surely the other kings would settle down once the Spanish king was appeased.

Next I do not understand why he deliberated on the suppression of the Society only with himself, or at most with Bontempi. He did not consult the cardinals or bishops. He did not at least have the subject debated in a meeting of theologians. It was a matter of such grave importance that it could not warrant too much consideration.

Finally, I wonder at the almost unbelievable pliability of Ganganelli. He wanted to pay for the peace of the Church with the destruction of the Society. Yet he took no measure for obtaining the true and stable peace of the Church. He did nothing in the matter, but handed it over completely to the judgment and good faith of the kings. What peace did he gain in the end? Avignon was returned to the Roman See. Benevento was returned. Is this the whole peace of the Church which had to be purchased at so dear a price? The kings continued to reject the bull *In Cena Domini*, to lay their profane hands on property consecrated to God, to violate in many matters the divine rights of the popes. But no royal edict which was doing harm to the liberty and immunity of the Church was rescinded. But no less was war continued against other orders of the Church. He did not, therefore, obtain the peace of the Church which was to be the just recompense for the loss of the Society. The pontiff sensed that he had been duped, but too late. Hence that incurable sadness, hence that constant anxiety of mind, from which first he lost his mental capacities, and later caught a fatal illness and succumbed. [161]

BOOK VIII

Analysis of Reasons for the Suppression

Although we see that great fires are often started from small sparks, still prudent men are not easily convinced that causes of great events were not themselves great. The suppression of our Society was one of the most memorable events in Church history. Many think that it did not happen by chance. Rather it had been conceived of long before, was plotted with concerted deliberation, and brought off in a set order. These same people reflect on the many and varied causes for it. The causes are all important and it is worthwhile to examine them at this point.

Contrivance of Royal Ministers

First there are some who imagine for themselves a certain contrivance on the part of the royal ministers. These wanted to take revolutionary steps in the Church contrary to traditional ways. They thought they had first to bring down the Society since it was the firmest bulwark of the Church. With it standing, they could achieve their goal only with the greatest difficulty. Thus our flatterers were speaking to us on the matter. Thus they were playing up to our sense of importance as if the cause of the Society and the Church was one and the same. Indeed in many of Ours this very boastful view had taken hold. The fact that a Portuguese was the first to put his hand to the implementation they ascribed to the fact that Carvalho was bolder than the rest of the ministers. He was less afraid of the deed's violence and men's adverse judgments. Indeed, he thought it attractive to be the torchbearer and to lead the way in a business of such weight. Thus some Jesuits think.

But I, for my part, will readily concede that the Jesuits have always fought and definitely would have fought most strenuously for the rights and power of the Church. However, I do not see at all how they could retard the royal ministers' initiatives and break their power. I see many steps taken in many places against the authority of the Church, though the Jesuits were still in existence and protesting in vain. Their shouting could perhaps bring it about that more abuses would not occur, but it could not exclude them altogether.

Next, the very series of deeds clearly excluded that conspiracy of ministers. For Charles was king of Naples (and afterwards of Spain) at the time when Carvalho was harassing the Society in Portugal. Charles was favorable to Jesuits then. [163] When he was transferred to Spain, he declared war on Portugal and made an armed invasion of her. Finally, the Jesuits of Paraguay, whom Carvalho was especially attacking, Charles not only absolved from every charge, but also approved their work and sent new Jesuits, as we saw, to Paraguay at his own expense. He never would have done that had there been an agreement between the ministers of the two courts to destroy the Jesuits.

Jansenist Attacks

Others attribute the whole destruction of the Society to the Jansenists. They are moved especially by the fact that the first waves of the storm were stirred in the pontificate of Benedict XIV. He was considered little favorable to Jesuits and not so hostile to Jansenists. This view has some semblance of the truth. For before his pontificate, Lambertini had been heard to remark that much of Jansenism is a mere specter of the Jesuits and that the bull *Unigenitus* had been extorted by their sinister crafts. With remarks such as that, the very learned, but often too outspoken man, had given reason why the Jansenists thought him on their side although he hated nothing worse than that sect.

To this was added the fact that scarcely had his pontificate been announced when suddenly a fierce war against the Jesuits broke out at Rome. The war was waged with the weapons that are usually found in the Jansenists' arsenals. For the first to go into battle was that Capuchin Norbert, who was secretly sent from France. Mention has been made of him elsewhere. He was no less bold than he was remarkably ignorant. He stirred up the dormant controversies on the Chinese rites in published books that were dedicated to the pontiff. He charged the Jesuits who were exercising pastoral care for the Christians in that country with an impious and superstitious cult. He portrayed them as recalcitrant and stubbornly resistant to pontifical decrees. He shamelessly loaded them down with countless other charges.

Daniele Concina, a son of the Dominican religious family, succeeded Norbert. He was an eloquent speaker and not unlearned. Perhaps he had too much self-assurance, and certainly he was overly trusting in his admirers. He renewed the old charges of the Jansenists that the Jesuits were lax in their moral teaching. He found a thousand monstrous errors in the printed works of rather prominent Jesuits and branded them with the mark of intolerable laxity. Benedict was taking books of this sort, though they were filled with calumnies and insults, as a joke. Yet in them the reputation of our order was openly and freely being attacked. Benedict scoffed at us and our adversaries equally. If any of Ours secretly published a reply (for this was not allowed without permission of superiors), it was a criminal act though self-defense is a natural right. Such a person was said [164] to have acted illegally and would not get off unpunished. The Dominicans, who were censors of all publications, were keeping a close watch.

When they saw what was happening, many of Ours made a fairly good guess that this whole storm had been raised by the Jansenists. Having gained the opportunity, the Jansenists wished to get vengeance for all the blows they had often suffered from the Jesuits. Many even now persist in that view. I would not deny that the Jansenists have contributed much to the situation. There were many of that sect at Rome, living at the expense of their group. They lost no opportunity to put down Jesuits or to lift up their side. But our men used to call almost all our adversaries Jansenists as if they had no other foes but them.

Other Anti-Jesuit Forces

Besides these there were in the city very many from every order, but especially from the monks who either openly or secretly were striving for our destruction. The Poor of the Mother of God, whom they call the Scolopi (Piarists), were taking a hostile stance towards us not so much, I think, out of hatred towards us but from an eagerness to show off. There is no creature so small as to lack a sting. Thus they went about the business of charging us in anonymous pamphlets and in conversations.

Perhaps these could have been scorned, but we were also under attack in the congregation they call the Holy Office. That is the most important and most sacred council of the world where grave matters of religion are debated. The Dominicans, natural enemies of the Society, and those who were subject to the influence of the Dominicans, are almost in sole control of the Holy Office. The members certainly welcomed nothing from Jesuits. What was worst was the fact that at that time there were sitting on the congregation three cardinals, Passionei, Spinelli, and Tamburini. They were among the most outstanding in the College of Cardinals because of their talent, their learning, and the integrity of their lives. But by bad luck they were hostile to us. To their number was added next the Dominican Orsini. Hence the Jesuit Berruyer[1] was condemned with such forceful language as never had been used for Luther or Calvin or any other founders of sects. But if the four cardinals were contriving, as I think they were, the destruction of the Society, they did not enjoy the fruit of their labor and did not see their prayers answered, for they all died within a space of less than three years.

In the reign of Benedict, therefore, there was great animosity towards us in the city and it was increasing daily. There is no doubt in my mind that at these meetings in Rome the suppression of the Society was first conceived and pondered. But the pontiff himself—whatever his mind toward us which could never be clearly grasped—certainly was not going to suppress the Society. [165] Nor was he going to allow it to be harassed so undeservedly and fiercely in other realms since he had great influence with the kings. For he himself was an exceptionally learned man and an excellent judge of scholars. For that reason he esteemed Jesuits highly. Let this be a proof.

He conceived the idea of reforming the Roman breviary (a project that he did not complete) and established a special commission of learned men for that task. He had intended that I be the editor for the readings of the saints. He had ordered that the secretary of the commission, De Valentis from Trevi (who later was made a cardinal), be advised of that appointment.[2]

Further he surveyed all the orders of the Church from the highest vantage point. Consequently he praised not only the learning of the Society, but also its apostolic labors, its morals, its Institute. He did this not only orally but also in public letters, copies of which remain to the present generation. What about the fact that he expelled the Capuchin Norbert from the city and from the entire papal realm? Norbert was a bold-faced reviler of the Jesuits. He forced a public retraction in writing from Concina when he learned that Concina had painted many false pictures about Jesuits. What about the fact that he resurrected, promoted, and almost, in his incredible zeal, brought to completion the cause of Bellarmine?[3] That cause had been set aside for a long time and was languishing. And finally, on his deathbed, he approved in a solemn decree the virtues of venerable Francesco de Geronimo. Some, reflecting on this last act of Benedict, remarked appropriately, "He loved them till the end." To sum up, Benedict perhaps desired that the great wealth of the Jesuits be curtailed and their enormous power be somewhat reduced. But he wanted not only the Institute of the Society, but also its reputation and esteem to be unharmed. That can be seen clearly in his letter to Saldanha, about which I spoke in its proper place.

There are some, finally, who place the cause of the Society's suppression in our wealth. Such a view seems not only false, but also unjust to the Bourbon family. They are such rich and powerful kings that they would not want to snap up in their great abundance of everything even these little crumbs. Who would believe this of the king of Spain for whom America generates such wealth? Yet he was the principal author and instigator of the suppression. I admit that on the whole the Society could have been said to be wealthy. Many of the colleges were endowed with an adequate income. That should have been the case if common life was to be observed exactly. But the wealth was greater in appearance than in fact. Much of it was turned to the adornment of churches. When people saw in our churches so many valuable vestments and so much worked silver, [166] they thought the Jesuits were richer than Croesus. But the Jesuits themselves were living very frugally. They were very careful about money matters. In addition, in some places they barely had enough to live on. In France, out of the great wealth of the Society, scarcely enough to maintain a schoolmaster was found and an annual pension had to be paid out to the Jesuits. Finally, whatever the wealth of the Society, none of it could end up in the princes' treasuries. For it is property consecrated to God and ought to be used only for pious purposes.

Cordara's Opinions on Possible Reasons for Suppression

Now that I have expounded the common opinions for the cause of the suppression, it remains for me to propose my own. I am accustomed to judge even more serious matters in a natural, straightforward manner. From my reading of history and the observances of human affairs, I have learned that major events often follow from the slightest beginnings. I think that initially there was no thought of suppressing the Society. But gradually it came to that as if through certain stages. I think that Carvalho for personal reasons began to be injurious to Jesuits out of anger. In the course of time he inflicted harsher measures out of malice. Finally he wanted Jesuits outlawed and expelled from all of Portugal. He acted out of that fear of vengeance that a person who has injured another must necessarily feel.

Once the example was given of doing what seemed very difficult, then I think all the other powerful royal ministers got the idea of expelling the

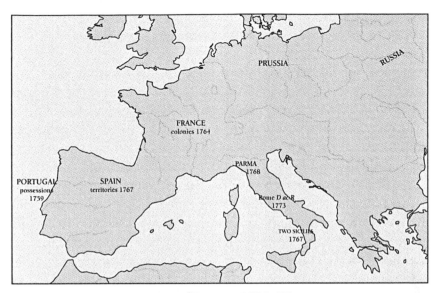

Map of Europe, 1750–75

Society. They made a certain agreement on the matter, either out of private hatred or for no reason that can be assigned other than their desire to flatter the philosophers of this world to whom all tradition was abhorrent. After they had expelled the Jesuits from their individual realms, then they bestirred themselves to press for the ultimate ruin of the Society. For unless the Society had been completely brought down and destroyed, they felt that without a doubt, when times had changed, it would return to its original homes. And through this march of events, it was easy to proceed to the further step once the first ones were successful. Malevolent and hateful people pressed the matter. Thus I think events came to an outcome which hardly anyone would have dared to conceive of before. But the mind must now be lifted a bit higher, away from human considerations.

God's Punishment for Jesuits' Sins

When I was at Turin and participated in many conversations about the suppression at daily gatherings of Jesuits, on a certain day various people were venting their indignation and rage. One of the younger men remarked, "God wanted to punish us for our sins." One of the Fathers was incensed at this remark, and raising his voice said, "Aren't you the bold one! Watch what you say! God wished to punish the human race, not [167] us who did nothing to deserve the Society's destruction." The young man demurely bowed his head and remained silent. I stood in amazement at the colossal ignorance and arrogance of the older man, but I remained silent too. Especially so since quite a few of the Fathers seemed to agree with and to applaud the crazy statement. I was saying to myself: a good Christian imputes to himself whatever ills befall him, and recognizes in them punishment from God for his sins. Who is free of stain? Or what offense against God is so slight that it can be expiated by any human punishment? Were only the Jesuits free of guilt so that they could not have been punished by God with their suppression? I think not.

These reflections I made to myself in silence, not openly, in order not to give occasion for a quarrel. But now, since I am in solitude with myself, nothing prevents me from saying what I think. A certain blot had settled in among us, invisible to man perhaps, but certainly manifest to God's gaze. I have not the slightest doubt that because of it God willed the suppression of the Society. It is uncertain what the nature of this blot was which so inflamed the divine wrath against us. I would like to look into and investigate it a bit more carefully. The judgments of God are hidden and removed from the perception of men. For this reason they are more to be revered than to be probed with curiosity. It is, however, a pious and useful idea to interpret them for the growth of the soul and the correction of sins.

Many and various charges were being laid upon us, which can be read in countless pamphlets. But all these charges were false, or at least certainly exaggerated and not common among Jesuits. I will pass over the more atrocious charges of regicide, sedition, and poisoning, which not even the adversaries who write them up believe. I will pass over the preposterous story about the Paraguay republic, the tyranny over the provinces, and the persistent war waged against two very powerful kings. Those who read of such in the Portuguese proceedings, cannot refrain from laughing and hold such charges only in contempt. The calumny about our business transactions, contained in those same Portuguese proceedings, has been sufficiently refuted by me in its proper place. I will omit these, as I say, and will take up charges that are more credible.

Jesuit Avarice

Many ascribe avarice and an insane desire for riches to the Society. They keep repeating that we besiege cities, that we hunt legacies with our sinister cunning, that the voraciousness of Jesuits is insatiable. They are influenced by the fact that the Society has grown due to truly large bequests. In a short time it has matched or even surpassed the wealth of older orders. What should have been attributed to the generosity of the faithful, they were attributing [168] to our greed and astuteness. But I note, not to deny that at various times and places many rich inheritances have been left to the Jesuits, that other legacies have been turned down by these alleged profligates. I do not know whether other religious could boast of such about themselves. To mention nothing earlier, we saw in our lifetime a very large inheritance, which Tuzzi left to the Sora College, refused and even a larger one left to the Montesanto College by Guarnerio Marefoschi. I say and resolutely affirm that, to the contrary, none can be said to be less greedy than the Jesuits and no other religious order has been further from the spirit of avarice.

To show that I am not speaking rashly, I submit this for the reader's consideration. Other orders without exception take stipends for masses. In the space of a year that amounts to quite a sum. The Society used not to accept stipends. Other religious, when they receive anyone into their ranks, require a certain amount of money either for the religious habit or for sustenance during the novitiate. The Society used to receive its candidates empty-handed. It did not demand a cent. Further, if later any were dismissed, the Society kindly sent them home with a gift of a new suit of clothes and travel money. In the other orders, if the relatives refused to pay the assigned dowry, legal action was taken to recover the money. The Society had surrendered that right in perpetuity.

I pass over the profitable administration of parishes. Other orders have them; the Society does not. Could the Society still be said to be greedier than other orders? What am I to say about the poor whom publicly and privately the Society treats well and kindly? How many, who were disgraced by poverty, have the Jesuits aided with secret gifts? How many dowries have they provided? How much of their own money have they paid out either to relieve the need of the poor or to support laboring men? Even today when there are not any Jesuits anywhere, many miss their generosity and complain that they do without many sources of relief for their need.

Jesuits' Laxity

Many accuse the Jesuits for propounding moral teaching that was too lax and too accommodating to human passions. By this device, they kept saying,

Jesuits inveigled entrance into the courts of monarchs, attracted large follow-ings for themselves, and everywhere subjected people to their influence. The Jansenists were the first to make these charges against us. Our other foes took up such charges with approval and protracted the brouhaha to these latter days. But those who use Jesuits as spiritual guides note that they are generally not lax or tepid, [169] but to the contrary, they excel others in their integrity, piety, and innocence of morals. Who would believe that those who walk the straight and narrow themselves would lead others astray? Then, too, the very foes of the Jesuits were conceding this to them—that they were living piously, chastely, and with strict morals. Who could convince himself that those who opted for a stricter path for themselves would want to show to others one laxer than is right?

While Jesuits professed kindness toward their neighbor, it was the kind-ness which our Divine Teacher taught by word and deed. They condemned severity, but only the severity which Christ himself reproached in the Pharisees who demanded that the minutest detail of the law be observed. They exhort-ed to the more perfect, they did not require it. They did not, as many now do, create new laws on their personal authority. They treated no one roughly, no matter how much he was weighed down with sin. They denied the sacra-ments to no one provided he was penitent and sorrowful. They drove no one to despair over the forgiveness of his sins and hope for his salvation. For that reason great throngs of penitents flocked to them. Many chose them to be their spiritual directors.

There is no doubt that some authors of the Society at times erred and leaned toward an excessive leniency in moral matters. But Franciscan and Dominican authors had led the way. The Jesuits were following their lead. Also, when they were writing on the topics, matters were still open to discus-sion. The supreme pontiffs had not yet interjected their judgment. Once the popes decided, you would find no Jesuit who stepped the least bit out of line.

Finally, many found fault with Jesuits because they lived too closely bound-together, and seemed animated by almost the same spirit. Foes were saying that from this close-knittedness it resulted that if you provoked one Jesuit, they all would be irritated and would rise up together to his defense. They blamed us for something that should be considered praiseworthy. For that was the mutual charity and union of souls which were so praised in those early Christians when, "there was one heart and one soul in the multitude of believers" (Ac 4.32).

There lurked beneath the accusation something equally hateful and false, a presumption that the Jesuits found in their ranks nothing reprehensible and therefore would defend their companions even in baser enterprises. Yet no one undertook the defense of Lavalette's business transactions. But on the other hand, I have often observed that our adversaries heap the crime of one Jesuit on them all. An example of this is Concina. Because Benzi[4] held it was not in itself a mortal sin to touch a woman's breast, [170] Concina attacked the entire Society and truculently smeared all with the stain of debased teaching. All Jesuits are justly irritated by such provocations and they rose up not so much to defend a single companion as to defend the esteem and reputation of them all.

The charge about the Chinese rites was more truthfully founded. For a long time, the Society stuck to the defense of certain superstitious rites. But if that was a fault, it belonged to other religious as well, very many of whom took the Jesuits' side in the dispute. The supreme pontiffs themselves suspended judgment for some time since the matter had not been sufficiently studied. But once the Apostolic See ended the dispute with a judicial decision, the Jesuits went no farther; they did nothing contrary to the decree. Pope Benedict XIV gave testimony to their obedience. He not only destroyed the calumny about intransigence that was weighing down on the Jesuits, but he also ascribed to them the undying credit for being the first to enter China, the first to establish a permanent residence there, the first to bring the Christian faith to that people.

I do not see in the points that I have raised up to now what could provoke the divine wrath against us more than against other religious. To the contrary, examining our affairs closely, I think I see many reasons why the Society should be more pleasing to God than other orders. The morals of the Jesuits were certainly chaste and above reproach. No failing of this sort went unpunished among us. Youths who had any tendency to unchasteness were immediately dismissed from the Society.

Poverty was not only required, it was also strict. Possessions were held in common; no one had anything of his own. It was forbidden to spend more than three scudi without the superior's permission. It was forbidden to buy food or clothes for oneself from private resources. The table was economical; the clothing decent. The furniture in the rooms was clean and adequate, but not luxurious, not more than what was necessary.

Jesuits wanted their obedience to be perfect, even beyond that which the French senators reprimanded.[5] Unless a superior had commanded something manifestly sinful, Jesuits were to accede to his bidding as if they were blind men. So the three vows, on which the virtue of religious men especially rests, were being kept.

Next there was no ambition among Jesuits, no seeking after honors. They are prohibited by vow from seeking offices outside the Society. Inside the Society, the Father General alone appoints the minor and major superiors of the order. There was no chapter, which is often a fertile seedbed of hatred and division. Jesuit discipline, while mild and seasoned with civility, is everywhere the same and relaxed nowhere, not even in tiny colleges. There are set times for prayer during the day. [171] There are times for silence, times for recreation. All must assemble at the sound of the bell. They go out of the house only in twos, and you would notice modesty linked with reserve wherever they went. By sundown they would return home.

But perhaps all these things are common with certain other orders. What is proper to the Society is this—that no one of us is completely unoccupied, no one is retired no matter how old he is, no matter how long he has served. As long as he is alive, each contributes his part to the common good. Those who are unable to undertake major apostolates can at least preach to a sodality of merchants or workingmen or hear confessions. And so one little college of the Society (may this be said without rousing envy) at times was more beneficial to a city than six or ten monasteries of other male religious.[6] Hence, since people usually measure things by the yardstick of their own advantage, there was everywhere such love for and esteem of the Society that, if the matter were to be decided by the people's vote, they would prefer other orders to be abolished rather than the Society. Yet Almighty God rejected this Society. Everyone judged that nothing was holier, nothing was more useful for the common good than the Society. The other orders, however, were spared; God willed the Society alone be extinct. One must conclude that there was lurking in it some hidden fault which particularly provoked the divine indignation.

As I thought about this, it occurred to me that while the Society matched or even surpassed the probity of other orders, still it was less holy than its own Institute and the profession of individual Jesuits required. Surely its founder Ignatius wished all his sons to be apostles. They were to be tireless workers who entered the fields and continually bore the sun and dust, who shirked no labor, no danger for the salvation of souls. But not all were apostles, or at least some had a comfortable apostolate. There were some who opted for a quiet, leisurely life in the colleges. They thought they had worked hard enough if they spent the entire morning in hearing the confessions of some pious little old ladies.

No Jesuit, as was said, is entirely free from work. But some jobs are not at all strenuous and demand neither physical effort nor mental strain. The elderly men used to undertake that sort of work so that they seem not completely worn out and inactive. Now, some of the more vigorous took these jobs for themselves. Some preferred handling finances to teaching. Some gave the people a half-hour sermon from the pulpit once a week; [172] the rest of the week they devoted to their physical well-being, or they passed their time with visits to friends and in frivolous conversations. I know that some of these "apostles" were more fastidious than women. They had to have chocolate in the morning, a full hour's siesta after dinner. If even a little of their customary food or sleep were cut back, they would perish, they would be reduced to nothing. They were not men born or brought up to this pampering. Indeed they were raised in rather Spartan households. They had developed this softness in the Society. They were types who, while being decent enough, were not fulfilling the ideal of the Holy Founder and were not attaining the holiness of their vocation.

There were also, it must be admitted, very many hardworking, tireless men. They met every need night and day. They rushed off to sickbeds and to jail cells. They passed through villages and towns to give missions. They worked strenuously for the salvation of their neighbor in the schools, in the seminaries, from the pulpit, on the street corners. They could truly be called apostles.

But who could answer for their mind-set and attitude? Unless the intention is right, unless the soul is moved by a spirit of divine charity, the works, before God, are vain and of no value, no matter how excellent they are in themselves. Cain also was presenting his sacrifices and offerings to God. But because his mind was impure and his intention insincere, God did not look upon his offerings favorably. Who now, as I was saying, could guarantee that those dedicated teachers of youth, those eloquent preachers of God's word, those tireless laborers for the gospel were looking only to the glory of God and the salvation of souls? Might they also, perhaps, have been seeking as well and even more so, the honor of the Society, the approval of men, personal gain, and fame for themselves?

We had magnificent adornments for our churches. The feast days of the saints were celebrated splendidly and with much pomp. Was this only for religious celebration? Or was it rather for pride and a display of power? The answers are hidden to men who see the bare exterior of things, but not so to God who searches the inmost thoughts of men. Men are influenced by appearances, but God weighs everything at its true importance. As Sacred Scripture shows, he found depravity even in the very angels. Pride is a very subtle fault. It insinuates itself into just and pious deeds so that at times it can scarcely be distinguished from virtue. It does not, however, deceive the penetrating gaze of God who sees all inner secrets.

Jesuits' Pride

The discourse has finally been brought to the point where I touch upon the hidden sore spot for the Society and I uncover that fault for which God especially [173] willed the Society to be punished with extinction. My former Jesuit companions will have to pardon me. Unless they wish to be falsely complacent, they have to admit along with me that there was much pride among us. The masters of novices quietly instilled it in us. They kept preaching that a vocation to the Society was God's greatest gift. They presented no models to imitate except our own Jesuit ones. They spoke of the Society's ways and procedures in such a way that it seemed nothing could be superior or even imagined to be. Once they had imbued our minds with such a high esteem for the Society, in vain were they trying to instill humility and deference. The good young men only thought that they were superior to other religious.

In the same spirit as the novices, the scholastics were formed when they took up studies. They heard no writers cited or praised except those of the Society. When they rattled off the names of Suarez,[7] Bellarmine, Petau,[8] Segneri,[9] and others of the sort, they thought more learned men were scarcely to be found elsewhere. Once they had formed that opinion, some of them never did discard it thereafter. I know some of the more simple-minded who, even when they were men of very advanced age, seemed convinced still that very little or nothing praiseworthy is found outside the Society.

There were among us many glorious things which easily bred and fostered pride. There was outstanding learning of every kind. A characteristic of the Jesuits was that no one was completely illiterate. There were many renowned for their sanctity and accomplishments. Very many were of noble and prominent birth. There were signal successes everywhere. On the basis of these things, nobles and common men everywhere were eagerly following us and generally preferred us to other religious. Many things inspired a sense of pride in our minds. Such, for example, were the apparent success of our undertak-

DENIS PETAU
Jesuite
Né à Orléans, en 1583, Mort à Paris, le 11 Décemb.
1652.

Denis Petau, S.J.

ings, the magnificence of our buildings, the splendor of our churches, the trappings of our feasts, the gatherings of nobles such as not to be found elsewhere. Wherever the eye fell, it met with provocations to pride. Add the fact that the Society differed in many respects from other orders and that Jesuits were bragging about these differences as if they were marks of excellence. Many Jesuits wanted nothing in common with other religious and considered these far below themselves.

You would hardly believe it, but even the lay brothers whom we call temporal coadjutors were puffed up with a certain air of self-importance. They put themselves ahead of other religious, even those who were priests. They yielded to no one on the score of dignity. At this point I have decided to relate a story that is hardly believable, yet it is true. From it one can guess what the rest were like. There was a lay brother at Albano who was born in the country and took care of the large farm of the Roman College. [174] The citizens of Albano showed him every sign of respect since he was the administrator of considerable resources. He conducted himself as one of the powers-that-be. He had the use of horses and the direction of servants. His daily drink was chocolate and no other beverage pleased him as much.

When I was staying there on the same farm for the sake of my health, I marveled at what it was that made this rough-bred man seek out luxuries and conduct himself like a satrap. But my wonder was greatly increased when I heard him saying that the Conventual Franciscans, who have a monastery nearby, invite him to dinner on more important feasts during the year. They seat him in the dining room at the place where the superior customarily sits. I thought the man's arrogance should be gently corrected; so I admonished him mildly that he should take the first place among the lay brothers, not among the priests; for what he was doing seemed improper. But he responded in anger, "You speak as if the brothers of the Society were not worth as much as priests of other orders." Without another word, he walked off. Thus our men extolled themselves in comparison with other orders.

The Jesuits have a particular rivalry with the Dominicans. This rivalry could have been praised if it had only the scope of stirring each side to do its best work. Yet many of Ours were contending that the Society had matched or even surpassed the glory of the Dominican order in learning, holiness, and the magnitude of its accomplishments, and that, despite the fact that the Society was born so much later. They did not reflect on the Dominicans' long-standing glory of thoroughly crushing the incipient Albigensian heresy. Often the Dominicans eradicated errors that were cropping up elsewhere. In

Paolo Segneri, S.J.

addition to hundreds of saints, the order produced four Supreme Pontiffs and almost innumerable cardinals. If it did nothing else, the order did give to the schools the master of all teachers—Thomas Aquinas.

The Jesuits were not, as I say, reflecting on all these facts. They were even boasting that they were the only ones to break the power of that mighty order, that they were the only ones to obscure a bit its glory. For granted that the Dominicans carry some weight and stand out at Rome because of certain professorial chairs and appointments, still the Jesuits are prominent all over the world and have no little influence in the royal courts. These boasts were made here and there among us. Our flatterers, and there was a crowd of them, whispered such words in our ears. Hence the general run of the Jesuits became so puffed up that, while they saw some grounds of rivalry with the Dominicans, they haughtily scorned other orders as far inferior to themselves.

This sense of self-importance cost us dearly. In the royal courts, [175] where Jesuit power was the greatest, pride was on a par with power. In God's providence, it was there in the courts that the Society's ruin was found. Perhaps the religious were the first to join in this royal conspiracy for the Society's destruction. In the hour of their greatest peril, the Jesuits thought the Dominicans were their only enemies, but they had many others who were more hostile, especially those whom they had disparaged the most. For these religious were irritated by the contempt shown them. They gave a push to the reeling Society by means of slanderous publications and secret plots. They looked on with incredible joy as the Society was completely uprooted and ruined. But God in his higher plan directs all human passions, no matter how base, to the goal he wants. Thus he wanted to punish our pride, but he permitted their evil designs to prevail and to meet with success.

An Even More Subtle Pride

And yet, to state openly what I feel, there was another, more subtle kind of pride among us, a pride that was far more hateful to the divine will. I do not know whether I ought to assert that because of it the divine wrath was especially stirred against us. Jesuits value chastity very highly, to such an extent that they seem to put it before other virtues. They were self-satisfied about their observance of it. They were bragging that by it they were set off from the rest of the crowd of religious. They were hearing many scandalous stories spread about concerning other religious. They were hearing many bad reports. Nothing of the sort was ever heard of them. Perhaps, therefore, they took from this the opportunity to think highly of themselves and to contemn others as the dregs of humanity.

But they were not reflecting that chastity is vain in the eyes of God unless it is joined with humility. Bernard said, "Virginity is praiseworthy, but humility is more necessary. The former is recommended; the latter is required." How would it be if they were not only self-complacent about their innocence and chastity, but also if they were to attribute it to themselves and their own virtue and did not consider it as a freely given gift of a merciful God? What if they were boasting as if they had not received it? What if they were converting this gift from heaven, which ought to make men humbler, into an increase of pride? They follow the example of those, "who trust in themselves as if they were just and who scorn others." I am afraid that the chaste, but far from humble, Jesuit would sometimes close his meditation with those famous words of the Pharisee: "I give you thanks, Lord, because I am not like the rest of men."

All pride, as is known, is hateful to God and men, whether it is born of nobility, wealth, excellence of talent and learning, beauty, or of any natural gift at all. The pride that is derived from divine gifts is so detestable that this passage should be understood as speaking to it, "God resists the proud; to the humble, [176] however, he gives favor." Some impure person, who derives a reason for humbling himself from his sins and impurities, will more readily obtain the divine mercy than a very chaste and law-abiding person who vainly boasts of his virtue and haughtily disdains sinners. Christ has taught us this very thing in that well-known parable about the Pharisee and publican. He concluded the parable with the memorable saying, "Everyone who exalts himself will be humbled; everyone who humbles himself will be exalted."

Perhaps some Jesuits will not want to hear such things and will be angry at me because I exposed their weak spots. Surely those will be angry who do not wish to admit any human defect in the Society on account of which God wanted the Society afflicted with its suppression. Those will be angry who are wont to admire or praise nothing outside the Society, who think that along with the Society, religion is destroyed everywhere, piety is routed, all is lost. They think that there is no learning or apostolic spirit left in the Church, and no one can fill in for the Jesuits. Above all others, those will undoubtedly be angry with me who do not wish to admit that after the suppression they had been assimilated to ordinary priests and are in no way different. Rather they retain the titles, dress, and customs of the Jesuits as much as they are allowed, and they never stop cursing Ganganelli. Those will definitely be angry with me. But as soon as they show such a great, incurable pride in their terrible depression, they are confirming that I have spoken the truth, and though I have named no one, they will be, by their actions, making a confession.

But I expect no criticism from those who are truly pious, who are truly sons of Ignatius. They accepted the destruction of the Society with appropriate self-possession. They deemed that they must accede completely to the divine will. They observe that Ignatius, when assailed by opponents, left it in writing that if the Society were by chance destroyed, the Society which he had founded with so much labor and so many tears and sighs, he would pray for a while and within an hour he would put aside all anxiety and worry about the matter. Indeed, he would rise from his prayer in peace and calm as if nothing unto-ward had happened. These Jesuits put before themselves the model of this excellent parent (and I think there were very many of them). They will not only not feel anger toward me, but I expect that they will readily agree with my view, especially if they make an unprejudiced appraisal of what I have said.

The Suppression: God's Will or Only Permission?

It would be possible at this point to debate whether God willed the suppression of the Society or only permitted it, but it would be useless. I call the debate useless [177] because in either case we must yield to the divine will without which nothing can be done. Yet, in order to express my view on this topic too, a certain fatal series and concatenation of events seem to me to have occurred. As I study the events from their beginnings, it seems to me that it follows that the suppression was not simply permitted, but decreed and pre-pared for by a definite plan of God.

At the beginning, Queen Mariana of Austria dies in Portugal. While she was alive, Carvalho did not dare to attack the Jesuits. Then at Rome Pope Benedict dies. If he had survived a little bit longer, Cardinals Saldanha and Atalaja would scarcely have been publishing those decrees against the Jesuits. The decrees prepared the way for the expulsion.

France follows the Portuguese proscription. When the debate was heating up in the Paris Parlement, there died one after another the Dauphin, heir to the throne; his wife; and the Queen Mother. When bereft of these patrons the Society was helpless and was outlawed.

Spain next took up the debate. The death of Queen Amalia of Saxony was very bitter. She was protecting the Society vigorously, but her death left the way open to the king's ministers to accomplish their goal. There was still hope in Elizabeth Farnese, the king's mother, but she too died at the very point at which the movement for expulsion was taking shape.

These numerous deaths occurred at a time that was inauspicious for us, but favorable for our enemies. For due to them, the Society was stripped of all human aid. The deaths show clearly that God was angry with us. For they happened not by human trickery, but by the will of God.

After the expulsions, discussion about the complete suppression began. Suddenly Clement XIII dies. He was a pontiff who had confirmed the Society in a quite recent constitution.[10] He would never suppress it. Wise men think that the supreme pontiff, who is the vicar of divine power among men, is chosen by a certain inspiration from God. When the cardinals were on the point of electing a successor to Rezzonico, they suddenly changed their minds and elected someone whom they previously did not want at all: Ganganelli. He was the Spanish king's man entirely. Though he delayed for a while, in the end he thought the Spanish king should be denied nothing, and most reluctantly he suppressed the Society. Are these not clear indications of the divine wrath?

Yet I add something further. Ignatius in heaven, Xavier, Borgia, Aloysius Gonzaga, and other Jesuit saints knew what our enemies were instigating against us at Rome and elsewhere. They were very much concerned that the Society always be safe and flourishing. These saints, however, although [178] they must be thought to be powerful before God, either did not think they should beg that the suppression be averted or they were not heard. Whichever way you say it was, the suppression was decreed. The decision of God stood unshaken. There definitely was some fault in the Society, on account of which God determined to remove the Society from our midst. I make no certain judgment on what sort of fault it was. We have shown what we conjecture to be the truth of the matter.

Possibility of Restoration of the Society?

Perhaps now someone will ask me what I think about the restoration of the Society. In the beginning many of our men were proposing it as a glorious certainty. They were relying on some prophecies which were being spread about on the matter. I know of one man who put his cassock in a wardrobe with the intention of putting it back on at the earliest possible moment. After a space of six years, I think, the cassock had been eaten by moths and he abandoned his hope. And now confidence eluded many as the prophecies failed of fulfillment year after year.

Nor do I see any grounds for hope in the present. Two of the kings who expelled the Jesuits from their realms, namely the Portuguese and French monarchs, have died in the intervening time. Two of the royal prime ministers who could be said to be the primary persecutors of the Society, Carvalho and Tanucci, have been removed from office and reduced in rank. To Ganganelli succeeded a pontiff who could not be fairer or more desirous of restoring the Society. I know Braschi. I know his high regard for us. Braschi, however, after he was made Pius VI, has an overview of the entire Church. He makes no move concerning the Society, nor does it appear that he will in the future. He thinks that the kings are not to be irked because of the Jesuits nor is the peace of the Church to be disturbed. Any Jesuit, I believe, would think the same if he were made pope.

Meanwhile year after year passes by and the restoration of the Society becomes daily more difficult. Many of its friends are dying. The zeal of others cools due to the long delay. On the other hand, our foes, as long as religious orders survive, will be strong in number and resources. Everywhere other ministers of the sacraments fulfill the function which Jesuits used to perform for the salvation of souls. People gradually grow accustomed to these ministers so that the Jesuits seem to be missed less now. Add the fact that the Society's wealth has been scattered and turned to other uses for the common good. In many places other religious have taken over the college buildings for their use. If the Society were to revive, the Jesuits would be unable to find places where they might live. [179]

Yet in human affairs, hope is the last thing to go. One may always hope for the better. Hope itself is a good which a person, no matter how wretched and overwhelmed with woe, may enjoy. I, at times, hope that the Society is to be restored. Malevolent people would begrudge me this pleasure in vain. No one, even if he be the most powerful, could ever remove it. My hope, however, is not based on those predictions that come from old ladies and are now circulating. I have hopes because it is to the public's interest that the Society be restored to its original condition and flourish once again in the Church.

Nothing holier or wiser than our collection of laws could be devised. All prudent men give Ignatius credit for his legislation. He made selections of the best to be found in other orders. He discarded other material and gathered the best laws for the one Society. The Institute was constantly proven in use and by experience of every nation through two centuries. There will be better times, with God's favor, when princes will remember the Society's excellence. What the Society accomplished all over the world for the salvation of souls, for the glories of literature, for the increase of religion and piety will live in the memory of the centuries. None of them will be forgotten.

The princes will have a sense of how much harm they created for their realms when they wanted the Society suppressed. They will understand that the Jesuits were unjustly accused, attacked with unadulterated calumnies, overwhelmed by sheer force and malice. They will not refuse to let them return to their original homesteads. The pontiff, whoever he is going to be, will be eager to rearm this column to face his attackers, to recall to arms this branch of his military, even if not for love of us, but only out of self-interest. Nations, recalling the Jesuits' past good services, will most eagerly embrace them on their return.

The mind predicts these things will certainly happen. Would that it be soon while I am alive to see it. But as I write this, I am past seventy-four. I think I am too close to death to be able to see with my own eyes such a delightful turn of events. In addition, I do not think the Society is to be restored before that self-importance of Ours is completely deflated and there is no one left who is not resigned to his present lot, whatever it might be, and no one is left who would still curse Ganganelli. I realize we are a long way from that—such is the stubbornness of men.

Yet the Society will rise up from the ashes in its good time. Restored by the divine will, it will remain till the end of time. One may rightly think that St. Teresa spoke from divine revelation, [180] when she predicted that at the last times the Society will join ranks with the Dominican order and will wage a joint war against the Antichrist. I doubt very much whether the Society will get back its original resources or power. I hold for certain that the Jesuits who will follow us will be more cautious. Schooled by the calamities that befell us, they will avoid the hatred of men, especially of religious. They will never extol themselves above others with a sense of self-importance. They will always keep themselves within the boundaries of modesty. [181]

ENDNOTES

Giulio Cesare Cordara, S.J. (1704–1785)

1. The letters of Cordara to Cancellieri have been published by Giuseppe Albertotti in *Lettere di Giulio Cesare Cordara a Francesco Cancellieri (1772–1785)*, 3 vols. in 2, Modena, 1912 (vols. 1 and 2) and 1916 (vol. 3 with extensive bibliography). In letter 198, vol. 1, p. 140, Cordara wrote, "Io penso d'estrarre tutta l'Istoria della soppressione della Compagnia e farne un' opera a parte" ("I am thinking of extracting all the history of the Society's suppression and making of it a separate work"). The result of Cordara's distillation is his monograph *De suppressione Societatis Iesu*, translated into English in the present work.

2. *Beiträge zur politischen, kirchlichen und cultur-Geschichte der sechs letzen Jahrhunderte*, 3 vols. Wien, 1862–82. The Cordara material is the first item in volume 3: introduction, pp. vii–xxviii; excerpts: pp. 1–74.

3. *De suis ac suorum rebus aliisque suorum temporum, usque ad occasum Societatis Iesu Commentarii*, Giuseppe Albertotti and Agostino Faggiotto, eds., published in *Miscellanea di storia italiana* LIII, Turin, 1933.

4. *De suppressione Societatis Iesu Commentarii*, 2 vols. in 1, Padua, 1923 and 1925. The excerpts came almost entirely from Books 9 to 16 of the longer *De suis temporibus*. This publication continues the extensive Cordaran bibliography which Albertotti had begun in the 1916 volume of the letters to Cancellieri.

5. The commentaries *De suis temporibus* constitute a detailed autobiography. A modern retelling of the events in Cordara's life, based on this work, is Giuseppe Castellani's, *La Società romana e italiana del Settecento negli scritti di Giulio Cesare Cordara*, Rome, 1967. A more popular biography from the pen of Mario Cavallotto appeared the year before under the title *L'abbate Giulio Cesare Cordara dei Conti di Calamandrana*, Alessandria, 1966. Luigi Buchetti's

1804–05 Venice edition of *Opere latine e italiane dell' Abbate Giulio Cesare Cordara dei Conti di Calamandrana* in four volumes begins with an essay, *"De vita et scriptis Julii Caesaris Cordarae e Societate Jesu quamdiu ea stetit Commentarius."* M. Vigilante has written the biography of Cordara in the *Dizionario biografico degli italiani.* The life with bibliography is in volume 28, pp. 789–92.

6. Data about the Society are very conveniently found in the *Synopsis historiae Societatis Iesu,* Louvain, 1950. This work will be referred to hereafter by the initials *SHSI.*

7. *De tota graeculorum huius aetatis litteratura* was placed on the Index by Clement XII on 13 April 1739.

8. Agostino Faggiotto did a short survey of Cordara's personages in "Papi, cardinali, e principi romani del sec. XVIII nei *Commentarii de suis* di G.C. Cordara" in *Atti del II° Congresso nazionale di studi romani* II (1931), pp. 305–12.

9. Almost the same might also be said of modern accounts. Apart from brief accounts in survey histories of the Society of Jesus, the only detailed description of the suppression as a whole in English is Sydney F. Smith's in his nineteen installment articles appearing in *The Month* in vols. 99 and 100 (1902) and 101 and 102 (1903). Other accounts, both contemporary and subsequent, treat of the suppression in Portugal, or in Spain, or in the Spanish colonies, or in France, but not as a whole. Volume 16 of Ludwig Pastor's *Geschichte der Päpste: im Zeitalter der fürstlichen Absolutismus von der Wahl Benedickts XIV bis zum Tode Pius VI (1790–1799)* (Freiburg im Breisgau, 1931–33) remains an important source for the suppression of the Society of Jesus; but he treats of course many other things in the reigns of Benedict XIV, Clement XIII, and Clement XIV. Pastor frequently cites Cordara in his narrative.

Introduction: A Momentous Event

1. Bracketed numbers in the text of this translation indicate the ends of pages in Albertotti's 1923–25 edition of Cordara's Latin *De suppressione Societatis Iesu Commentarii.* The Latin text runs from page 13 through page 181. The references are given for the convenience of anyone who might wish to check the original.

2. The nine saints canonized before 1773 were Sts. Ignatius Loyola, Francis Xavier, Francis Borgia, Aloysius Gonzaga, Stanislaus Kostka, John Francis Regis, Paul Miki, John de Goto, and James Kisai (*SHSI,* col. 716).

3. The exact time frame is from 1540 to 1773.

4. The three Jesuits made cardinals by Clement XI were Giovanni Battista Tolomei (1712), Giovanni Salerni (1719), and Alvaro Cienfuegos (1720) (*SHSI*, col. 285).

5. The monarchs who figure in the suppression of the Society of Jesus were Charles III of Spain (1759–88), Joseph I of Portugal (1750–77), Louis XV of France (1715–74), Ferdinand IV of the Two Sicilies (1759–1825), and Duke Ferdinand of Parma (1765–1801). All but Joseph I were Bourbons. Cordara does not use numbers when referring to any of these kings, though he does for popes.

Book I: Portugal, Part I: Carvalho's Enmity; Saldanha's Visit

1. Cordara, in fact, uses the name Carvalho throughout, and never Pombal. The kings, popes, and major statesmen who appear in Cordara's narrative have complete biographies written about them. The churchmen, at least the major ones, can be found in the monumental *Enciclopedia italiana* (*EI*); others are found in the *Enciclopedia Cattolica* (*EC*). For the French, the *Grand Larousse* supplies basic information (*GL*). Fuller presentations for many are to be found in *La grand encyclopédie* (*GE*). The more prominent of the Jesuits have articles in Ludwig Koch, S.J.'s *Jesuiten-Lexikon* (Paderborn, 1931). Those who were authors can be found in C. Sommervogel, *Bibliothèque de la Compagnie de Jésus* 12 vols. Paris, 1890–1960 (Sommervogel). The lesser figures are not to be found, and for the most part Cordara tells us all we need to know about their parts in the story. The Spanish statesmen are almost all to be found in the *Gran enciclopedia Rialp* (*Rialp*).

2. Cordara actually wrote, *"Gulielmo Enrico Annoverano Angliae Regis filio."* This mistake was corrected by P. A. Monti, S.J., in the errata he supplied for Professor Albertotti. The correct relationship in the Latin is *"Angliae Regis fratri."* The correction is what is translated here, "brother of the king of England."

3. José Moreiro was confessor and spiritual guide for Joseph I from 1740 to 1757. It was he who recommended Carvalho to Joseph's favor (cf. Alfred Weld, *The Suppression of the Society of Jesus in the Portuguese Dominions*, London: 1877, pp. 10–11).

4. Gabriel Malagrida lived from 1689 to 1761. He entered the Society in 1716 and served as a missionary to Brazil (1721–53). Cordara will describe his recall to Portugal, his spiritual work upon his return, and his execution on 21 September 1761 (Koch, *Jesuiten-Lexikon*, s.v.).

5. Filippo Acciaiuoli's dates are 1700–66. He served for ten years as apostolic nuncio to Switzerland, 1743–53. He held the same position in Portugal

(1753–60). He finished his days as bishop of Ancona (*Dizionario biografico degli italiani*, s.v., and Charles Berton, *Dictionnaire des Cardinaux*, Paris, 1857, col. 286 *[DdC]*.

6. Luigi Centurione was born in 1686 and entered the Society in 1703. He served as General Superior of the order from 1755 until his death on 2 October 1757 (Koch, *Jesuiten-Lexikon*, s.v.).

7. Timoni served successively as provincial of the Roman Province (1748–51), procurator general (1756–58), secretary of the Society (1758–61), Italian Assistant (1761), and vicar-general as described here (2 Oct. 1757–21 May 1758) cf. *SHSI*, col. 631–40.

8. The full title of Ludovico Antonio Muratori's (1672–1750) work is *Christianesimo felice nelle missioni de' Padri della Compagnia di Gesù nel Paraguai*. It was first published in 1743 and 1749.

9. Francesco's name is also Anglicized into Francis Jerome and Latinized as Francis de Hieronymo. He lived from 1642 to 1715, and entered the Society as a priest in 1670 (Koch, *Jesuiten-Lexicon*, s.v.).

10. Francesco António Saldanha lived from 1713 to 1766. Benedict XIV made him a cardinal in 1756 and he became patriarch of Lisbon in 1758 (*DdC*, col. 1459).

11. Domenico Passionei was born in 1682 and died in 1761. He did diplomatic service in France where he was exposed to Jansenism. In 1738 he became correspondence secretary and prefect of the Vatican Library. He was firmly opposed to the Society of Jesus (*DdC*, col.1350–52).

12. Joseph-Manuel de Atalaja, made a cardinal by Benedict XIV in 1747, served as apostolic protonotary in Portugal. As the text indicates, he died in 1758 (*DdC*, col. 286).

13. Gianfrancesco Albani, 1720–1803, was a staunch supporter of the Jesuits. He led the opposition to the French as they pressured and imprisoned Pius VI. Cordara was on very close terms with him and Albani is the source of much of Cordara's "inside knowledge" (*Dizionario biografico degli italiani*, s.v. and *DdC*, col. 202–3).

14. Guidobono Calvalchini, 1683–1774, had wide legal experience and served in various capacities in the Roman Curia. He supported the Jesuits at first, favoring, for example, the beatification of Robert Bellarmine. At the end, however, he changed positions and advocated the suppression to humor the Bourbon princes (*EC*, s.v., and *DdC*, col. 643).

15. Paul d'Albert de Luynes lived 1703–88. He was made bishop of Bayeux in 1729 and archbishop of Sens in 1753. He was raised to the cardinalate in 1753 (*DdC*, col. 1162–63).

Book II: Portugal, Part 2: Anti-Jesuit Cardinals; Assassination Attempt

1. Giuseppe Spinelli hailed from Naples and was made a cardinal in 1735 by Clement XII. He was a staunch opponent of the Jesuits (*DdC*, col. 1539, and Enrico Dammig, *Il movimento giansenista a Roma nella seconda metà del secolo XVIII*, Rome 1945, pp. 232–33) (Dammig).

2. Cordara uses the expression *"primarius . . . Administer,"* which seems to indicate something like the current secretary of state.

3. Alberico Archinto lived 1698–1758. He served as nuncio to Poland (1746–54) and thereafter as governor of Rome. He was made a cardinal in 1756 and served as secretary of state. He was, as Cordara indicates, mildly anti-Jesuit (Vigilante, *Dizionario biografico degli italiani*, s.v., and *DdC*, col. 257).

4. Carlo Rezzonico (1724–99) was made a cardinal in 1758. He served as bishop of Porto and Papal Chamberlain (*DdC*, col. 1445).

5. Fortunato Tamburini, O.S.B., was abbot of St. Paul at Rome and hailed from Modena. He was made a cardinal in 1743 (*DdC*, col. 1545; Dammig, pp. 162–63).

6. Neri Corsini belonged to the family of Clement XII. His dates were 1685–1770. Much of his life he spent in travel, looking after his family's financial interests. In general, he was anti-Jesuit and pro-rigorist, supporting people such as Almada and Pagliarini (*DdC*, col. 767, and *Dizionario biografico degli italiani*, s.v.).

7. Urbino Tosetti (1714–68), a Piarist, was a teacher and rector at the Nazarene College. His scholarly work was mostly in the physical sciences (*EC*, s.v.).

8. St. Joseph Calasanctius was born in Spain in 1556 and lived till 1648. He opened the first free public school in Europe in 1597, and in 1621 the teachers were afforded full rights of religious (Clerks Regular of Christian Schools), which, however, were subsequently revoked and only gradually returned. He was beatified in 1748 and canonized in 1767 (*New Catholic Encyclopedia*, vol. 7, pp. 1115–16).

9. Augustin J. C. Clement (1717–1804) was a canon of Auxerre and travelled widely to support Jansenist positions (Dammig, pp. 359–62, and *Nouvelle biographie général*, vol. 10, col. 778).

10. Ludovico M. Torrigiani was born in 1697 and was made a cardinal in 1753. He tried to protect the Society from its attackers (*DdC*, col. 1567).

11. Giralamo Spinola's dates are 1713–84. He was made a cardinal in 1759 and, as the text indicates, served as papal nuncio at Madrid (*DdC*, col. 1541).

12. The attack took place during the night of 3–4 September 1758. "(1759)" appears in the text of the *De Suppressione*, p. 45. I have corrected the year in the translation.

13. Jaô Alessandro Souza was a veteran missionary. He was born in 1703, entered in 1718, and died in 1772. His offense seems to have been making his return voyage from Brazil in the company of some members of the Tavora family (Francisco Rodrigues, *Historia da Companhia de Jesus na Assitência de Portugal*, vol. 4, p. 208).

14. Jaô de Matos, another white-haired missionary, was born in 1693 and entered in 1707. He was imprisoned with Malagrida in 1759 because he was related to one of the suspected noble families. Presumably he died in prison (Sommervogel, vol. V, col. 725).

15. The Latin text reads, *"denariis singulis . . . assignatis."* Christoph G. von Murr in his *Geschichte der Jesuiten in Portugal unter der Stattsverwaltung des Marquis von Pombal* (2nd edition, 1923, p. 67) gives *tostâo* as the Portuguese monetary allowance. It would come to four or five cents.

16. Hermann Busenbaum was born in 1600 and entered the Society in 1619. His handbook of moral theology entitled *Medulla theologiae moralis* was extremely popular, having some 200 editions by 1776. He is criticized for his teaching on regicide and for laxism in general. Busenbaum died in 1668 (Koch, *Jesuiten-Lexikon*, s.v.).

17. Giuseppe Orsi, O.P., lived from 1692 to 1761. Clement XIII made him a cardinal in 1759. His major work, *Istoria ecclesiastica*, had reached twenty volumes and covered only up to 600 A.D. His main interests were clearly scholarly (*DdC*, col. 1293–94).

18. Antonio Maria Erba Odescalchi was born at Milan in 1715. Made a cardinal in 1759, he was shortly thereafter made vicar of Rome. He died in 1762 (*EI*, s.v., and *DdC*, s.v. Erba Odescalchi, col. 871).

19. Andrea Andreucci's dates are 1684–1771. He was director of a sodality for priests and was the author of numerous works (Sommervogel, vol. I, coll. 353–65).

Book III: Portugal, Part 3: Trial of Malagrida

1. Albertotti's printed Latin text (1923–25) reads 1761 for the date, but that is clearly a mistake. Cordara may have been thinking of Malagrida's trial, which did take place in September 1761.

2. Cordara wrote, *"Henricum Magnum,"* by which he means Henry IV (reigned 1589–1610).

3. Carlo De Gros and Abbate Capriata are discussed in Dammig, pp. 144–46. De Gros was expelled from Rome in 1762 and went to Naples where he continued his anti-Jesuit polemics. Capriata wrote *I lupi smascherati nella confutazione del libro intitolato 'Monita secreta Societatis Iesu'* which Dammig considers the most virulently anti-Jesuit pamphlet of the period.

4. Vincenzo Maria Dinelli, O.P., was a student of Concina. He was exiled from Rome in 1760 (Dammig, pp. 190–91).

5. Jean-Thomas Boxadors, O.P., was born in Barcelona in 1705. He was made a cardinal by Pius VI in 1775 and passed away in 1780 (*DdC*, col. 590). He was general of the Dominicans from 1756 to 1777.

6. Martino Natali, a Piarist, lived from 1730 to 1791. He was a prolific author with Jansenist leanings (*EC*, s.v.).

7. Tommaso Maria Mamachi, O.P. (1713–92) accused the Jesuits of laxism, but at the end, also opposed Jansenist positions (Dammig, pp. 186–89; *EC*, s.v.).

8. Norbert, who is also known as Pierre Curel Parisot and Abbé Platel, lived from 1697 to 1769. His attack on the Chinese and Malabar rites of the Jesuits took form in his two-volume work of 1744 entitled *Mémoires historiques sur les missions des Indes orientales* (Koch, *Jesuiten-Lexikon*, s.v. Parisot).

Book IV: France

1. Some authors use the form La Vallette. Antoine Lavalette was born in 1709 and entered the Society of Jesus in 1725. In 1742 he went to the Antilles and eventually was made superior and apostolic prefect (1753). He died, dismissed from the Society, in 1767 (Koch, *Jesuiten-Lexikon*, s.v.).

2. The courts, in fact, of both Marseilles and Paris ruled in favor of the bankers. The Jesuits decided to appeal to the Paris Parlement, relying on friends and alumni among its membership.

3. Marthurin Germain de Forestier was born in 1697 and entered the Society in 1717. He served as provincial of France in 1734. His death occurred in 1780 (Sommervogel, vol. III, col. 887–88).

4. *Extraits des assertions dangereuses et pernicieuses, que les soi-disant Jésuites avoient déclarées* was the title of this collection of alleged errors (*SHSI*, col. 339).

5. An assembly of the clergy of France issued the "Declaration of 1682," which contained four points of a somewhat mitigated Gallicanism. The points were 1) rejection of the extreme parliamentary position that denied any papal intervention in temporal matters; 2) admission of papal authority but also subjecting papal authority to conciliar supremacy; 3) demand that the ancient canons and customs of the French Church be recognized by the popes, and 4) denial of papal infallibility apart from the consent of the universal Church (*New Catholic Encyclopedia*, vol. 6, pp. 265–66, s.v. Gallicanism). A group of Jesuits accepted these points to the chagrin of Clement XIII and Ricci.

6. Jean Antoine Cerutti was born in 1738 and entered in 1753. He was out of the Society by 1768 and eventually allied himself to the insurgents in the French Revolution. He died in 1792 (Sommervogel, vol. II, col. 1003–06).

7. Daniele Concina, O.P., was born in 1687. He entered the Dominicans in

1707. He was a friend of Spinelli and was a rigorist. He died in 1756 (*Dizionario biografico degli italiani*, s.v.).

8. This witticism is usually ascribed to Voltaire, who, however, can scarcely be described as a friend or defender of the Society.

9. Philippe-Onufre Desmaretz lived from 1700 to 1780. He was confessor to Louis XV from 1752. He was intransigent vis-à-vis Madame de Pompadour (*Dictionnaire de biographie français*, vol. 10, col. 1451).

10. Jean-François Rochechouard was born in 1708. He served as bishop of Laon and was made a cardinal in 1761 (*DdC*, col. 1465).

11. Louis XIV also proposed a vicar-general for France, and so Louis XV was repeating an idea of his grandfather (cf. William V. Bangert, *A History of the Society of Jesus*. 2nd ed., St. Louis, 1986, p. 300).

12. The Paris Parlement's condemnations of the Society were passed on 1 April 1762 and 6 August 1762 (*SHSI*, col. 339).

13. Some measures were in fact taken both by the Parlement and the revolutionary government. The topic is discussed by D. G. Thompson in his article "The Fate of the French Jesuits' Creditors under the *ancien regime*," *English Historical Review* 91 (1976), pp. 255–77.

14. Christopher Beaumont (1703–81) had previously been bishop of Bayonne (1741) and Vienne (1743). In his tenure as bishop of Paris from 1746, he was in conflict with the Paris Parlement (*GE*, s.v.).

15. Yves André was a mathematician who was born in 1675, entered the Society in 1695, and died in 1764. Cordara refers to his *Essai sur le Beau dans le physique, dans le moral, dans les ouvrages d'esprit et dans la musique*, Paris, 1741 (Koch, *Jesuiten-Lexikon*, s.v.).

16. The new approval and confirmation of the Institute of the Society of Jesus were in *Apostolicum pascendi* of 7 January 1765 (*SHSI*, col. 345).

17. René Maupeou lived from 1714–92. For seven years (1768–74) he served as chancellor of France and revised the makeup of the Paris Parlement (*GE*, s.v.).

18. The princess Marie-Louise, one of Louis XV's six daughters, became a Carmelite at age thirty-three. She lived in the convent for sixteen years and passed away in April 1770. She reproached her father for allowing the suppression of the Jesuits in France. (Cf. G. P. Gooch, *Louis XV: the Monarchy in Decline*, New York, 1976 reprint, pp. 131–36.)

19. Conde de Aranda (Pedro Pablo Abarca de Bolca) was primarily a military man. His dates are 1719–98 (*Rialp*, s.v.).

20. Ludovico Valenti's dates are 1695–1763. He was made a cardinal in 1759 and among other positions served as bishop of Rimini (*DdC*, col. 1597).

21. Prospero Colonna Sciarra (1706–65) served as chamberlain and was made a cardinal by Benedict XIV. Since he was protector of France, he absented him-

self from the conclave of cardinals called by Clement XIII on 3 September 1762 to discuss the measures taken by the Paris Parlement against the Jesuits (*DdC*, col. 311 and *Dizionario biografico degli italiani*, s.v.).

22. Joseph-Henri d'Aubeterre's dates are 1714–88. In addition to being ambassador to Rome, he also served in that capacity at Vienna and Madrid (*GE*, s.v.).

Book V: *Spain and Naples—Two Sicilies*

1. François Cardell was born in 1717 at Prague and entered the Jesuits in 1733. He died in 1768 at Prague (Sommervogel, vol. II, col. 732–33).

2. Marqués de la Ensenada (Zenón de Somodevilla y Bengoechea) lived from 1702 to 1781. He served Charles III primarily as a financial minister (*Rialp*, s.v.).

3. Cordara wrote, *"in oppido agri Clusini,"* which would not necessarily have to be in Chiusi itself, but certainly in the area. Tanucci, however, was born in Stia, some distance further south and east (see *EI*, s.v. Tanucci).

4. Conde de Campomañes (Pedro Rodrígues) was born in 1723. He worked for school reform, trying to break the nobles' stranglehold on education and career advancement. He devoted himself to the study of law and history. He died in 1802 (*Rialp*, s.v.).

5. Mario Marefoschi (1714–80) spent most of his career in the Roman Curia, working in the congregations for rites and propaganda. He was made a cardinal in 1779 (Dammig, pp. 234–36; *DdC*, col. 1167).

6. Manuel de Roda y Arriata was a friend of the Augustinian Vazquez (see note 9 below) during his tenure as ambassador to Rome. In 1765 de Roda was made minister of justice by Charles III (*Diccionario enciclopédico espasa*, s.v.).

7. Joachim-Ferdinand Portacarrero was made a cardinal in 1743. He was the titular patriarch of Antioch (*DdC*, col. 1422).

8. Venerable Juan de Palafox was born in Spain in 1600. He served as bishop of Puebla, Mexico, till 1649. Then he was made bishop of Osma, where he died in 1659 (*New Catholic Encyclopedia*, s.v.).

9. Francisco Xavier Vazquez, O.S.A., was a Peruvian. Before coming to Rome to serve as his order's procurator general, he taught theology in Spain. After eighteen months as procurator general, he was elected general in 1753. He befriended Spanish officials such as de Roda and Moniño, with whom he had a four-hour meeting upon Moniño's arrival at Rome, no doubt to discuss the complete suppression of the Society (Dammig, pp. 149–55).

10. Domenico Orsini was duke of Gravina and made a cardinal in 1743. Previously he had represented Queen Maria Amalia, Charles III's wife, at the

pope's court. He worked for the Society's suppression, cooperating with Azpuru and de Bernis. Cordara mistakenly thinks he was pro-Jesuit. He passed away in 1789 (*DdC*, col. 1297, and *EC*, s.v.).

11. The Society of Jesus does not, in fact, have a Third Order.

12. François Philippe Mésenguy (1673–1763) produced several editions of his *Exposition de la doctrine chrétienne* (*Dictionnaire de spiritualité*, s.v.) and Dammig (pp. 348–56) discusses in detail the vicissitudes of the Italian version of the catechism.

13. Thomas Azpuru y Ximenes (1713–72) was bishop of Tortosa and in 1770 appointed archbishop of Valencia but he never took possession of the see since he was in Rome at the time, serving as Charles' agent. Obviously, Cordara is mistaken about his attitude toward the Jesuits. He worked closely with Azara for the complete suppression of the Society (*EC*, s.v.).

14. Lazaro Opizio Pallavicini was born at Genoa in 1719. From 1760 to 1767 he served as nuncio to Spain and was made a cardinal in 1766. Clement XIV made him his secretary of state, an office which he continued to hold under Pius VI. He died in 1785 (*EC*, s.v., and *DdC*, col. 1292).

15. The Spanish form of the name is Esquilache. Leopoldo de Gregorio, Marqués de Esquilache, was born in Messina, Sicily, around 1700. He entered the service of Charles in 1748 and followed him to Spain in 1759. He was sent back to Naples after the sombrero riots. He died in Venice in 1785, while serving as ambassador there (*Rialp*, s.v.).

16. The decree of expulsion was issued on 17 February 1767, almost a full year after the uprising (*SHSI*, col. 356).

17. The pragmatic sanction was a separate document from the decree of expulsion and was issued on 2 April 1767 (*SHSI*, col. 356).

18. The disgrace was a charge that Charles III was illegitimate. The basis for Charles' suspicions was a forged letter of Ricci. Sydney Smith rejects the alleged illegitimacy as a cause of Charles III's anger toward the Society in part VI of his study on the suppression: "The Suppression in Spain (2)" *The Month* (July 1902), p. 7. More recent biographers of Charles III include the story of the forged letter of Ricci and the alleged illegitimacy (John Lynch, *Bourbon Spain: 1700–1801*, p. 283 and Anthony H. Hall, *Charles III and the Revival of Spain*, p. 139). They accept the charge as a possible motive of Charles' action against the Jesuits.

19. Cordara uses the capitalized noun *Synhedrium*, which probably means the General's consult, consisting of the various Assistants.

20. Francisco Saverio de Zelada (1717–1801) was made a cardinal in 1773 and served on the committee that was to oversee the suppression of the Society. From 1789 to 1796 he served as papal secretary of state (*EI*, s.v., and *DdC*, col. 1699–1700).

21. Antonio Maria Doria Pamphili Landi (1749–1821) was in charge of provisioning the city of Rome from 1778–80. In 1785 he and his brother Joseph were made cardinals (*Dizionario biografico degli italiani*, s.v. and *DdC*, col. 843).

22. The Aragon Province was renamed Holy Father Ignatius; Baetica, St. Francis Borgia; Castile, St. Francis Xavier; Chile, St. Cassian; Mexico, Holy Trinity; Paraguay, St. Joseph; Peru, St. John the Baptist; the Philippines, St. Tiberiacus; Quito, Sts. Joachim and Ann (*SHSI*, coll. 356-57). Obviously, the new names were not limited to saints of the Society of Jesus. Perhaps Cordara referred only to the Provinces of Spain proper.

23. Cordara wrote *Retzio*, but may have meant *Riccio*. Francis Retz was General from 1730 to 1750. Retz would have had to be having premonitions of the troubles subsequently faced by the Society.

24. Francisco Xavier Idiaquez was born in 1711 and entered the Society of Jesus in 1732. He was a rector and twice a provincial of Castille (1764–67, and 1773). He died at Bologna in 1790 (Sommervogel, vol. IV, col. 546–49).

25. On the night of 3–4 November 1767, the thirty-one communities in the territory of Naples were expelled to the Papal States (*SHSI*, col. 355).

26. Marquis Giovanni Fogliani Sforza d'Aragona was born at Piacenza in 1697. He held several diplomatic posts in the service of Naples and in 1759 was a member of the board that was to guide Ferdinand IV. In 1755 he had been made viceroy of Sicily. He died in 1780 (*Dizionario biografico degli italiani*, s.v.).

27. Marcantonio Colonna was born in 1724. He was made a cardinal in 1759 and served as prefect of Propaganda and as vicar of Rome. He died in 1793 (*DdC*, col. 700).

28. Henry Benedict Maria Clement Stuart is commonly known as Cardinal York. His dates are 1725–1807. Made a cardinal in 1748, he subsequently was bishop of Frescati from 1761–1803. At his brother's death in 1788, he became titular king of England with the name Henry IX (*The Complete Peerage of England, Scotland, Ireland, Great Britain and the United Kingdom*, 1987 edition, vol. 6, pp. 919–20, and *DdC*, col. 1693–96).

Book VI: Parma; Election of Clement XIV

1. Guglielmo du Tillot was born at Bayonne in 1711. He entered the civil service of Parma in 1730 and was highly influential until his fall from favor in 1771. He then retired to Paris, where he died in 1774 (*EI*, s.v. du Tillot).

2. Philip of Parma died on 18 July 1765, to be succeeded by his son Ferdinand who reigned from 1765 to 1801 (*EI*, vol. 26, p. 389).

3. Clement XIII issued his *Brevi Monitorio* on 30 January 1768, declaring du

Tillot's measures invalid and excommunicating those who issued them or cooperated with them (*SHSI*, col. 355).

4. During the night of 7–8 February 1768, some 150 Jesuits were expelled from the Duchy of Parma to the Papal States (*SHSI*, col. 363).

5. François Joachim de Pierre de Bernis (1715–74) studied humanities with the Jesuits. He was another of the French ecclesiastics who pursued a diplomatic career. He was made a cardinal in 1758 and sent as ambassador to Rome in 1769 where he died five years later (*New Catholic Encylcopedia*, s.v. Bernis; *DdC*, col. 516–19).

6. Cordara alludes to the sack of Rome in May 1527, when the German and Spanish troops of Charles V plundered the city.

7. Vitaliano Borromeo was born in 1720 at Milan. He entered the diplomatic service of the Vatican, serving as ambassador to Tuscany and Vienna. In 1766 he was made a cardinal and he died at Rome in 1793 (*Dizionario biografico degli italiani*, s.v., and *DdC*, col. 581).

8. Simon Bonaccorsi's dates are 1708 to 1776. He was made a cardinal in 1763 (*DdC*, col. 605).

9. Benedetto Veterani lived from 1703 to 1776. He was made a cardinal in 1766 (*DdC*, col. 1612).

10. Giovanni Ottavio Bufalini was born in 1709 and died in 1782. He served as the governor of Benevento and Loreto, nuncio at Lucerne, and bishop of Ancona. He was made cardinal in 1766 when he assumed the see of Ancona (*Dizionario biografico degli italiani*, s.v., and *DdC*, col. 604).

11. Fabrizio Serbelloni was born at Milan in 1695. He served as nuncio in several courts and as the governor of Ferrara, 1721–28. He was made a cardinal in 1753 and bishop of Ostia (*EC*, s.v., and *DdC*, col. 1513).

12. Gaetano Fantuzzi was born in 1708. He shared Cordara's interest in poetry, publishing verse as a young man. His main interest, however, was in canon law and he worked on several Rotas. In 1759 he was made a cardinal and died at Rome in 1778 (*Dizionario biografico degli italiani*, s.v., and *DdC*, col. 890).

13. Giovanni Francesco Stoppani was a Milanese, born in 1695. He served as governor of Urbino and was made a cardinal in 1753 (*DdC*, col. 1541).

14. Giuseppe Maria Castelli lived from 1705 to 1780. He was made a cardinal in 1759 (*DdC*, col. 642).

15. Surprisingly the *Dictionnaire des cardinaux* does not have an entry for de Solis. Smith's enstallments on the conclave of 1769 (*The Month* 100 (1902), pp. 517–36, 581–91, and 101 (1903), pp. 48–61) stress de Solis's importance in the election of Ganganelli. He mentions that de Solis was archbishop of Seville, which see he held from 1758 to 1785. Smith also states that de Solis was subsequently Patriarch of the Indies.

16. Pozzobonelli is also missing from the *Dictionnaire des cardinaux*. Cordara uses the Latin form *Puteobonellus*. As the text indicates, he was representing the interests of the Holy Roman Emperor and Austria at the conclave of 1769.

17. Giuseppe Garampi was born in 1725 at Rimini. He became a canon at St. Peter's in Rome and a Vatican archivist. He was made a cardinal in 1785 and died in 1792 (*EI*, s.v., and *DdC*, col. 969).

18. This is the same Francesco Cancellieri referred to in the section entitled "Giulio Cesare Cordara, S.J. (1704–1785)" in this translation (p. xv). He was Cordara's pupil and longtime friend. He lived from 1751 to 1826 and made his mark as poet, scholar, and librarian (*Dizionario biografico degli italiani*, s.v.).

19. Antonio Lecchi was born at Milan in 1702. He entered the Society in 1718. Clement XIII entrusted him with many projects, but as the text indicates, Clement XIV did not favor him. He died in 1776 (Sommervogel, vol. IV, col. 633–38).

20. Ignazio Boncompagni was born at Rome in 1743. Pius VI made him a cardinal in 1775. He died in 1790 (*DdC*, col. 535).

21. Alessandro Albani, the younger brother of Annibale, was born in 1692. He and his brother were made cardinals in 1712. He filled various curial offices and was legate to Vienna in 1720. He died in 1779 (*Dizionario biografico degli italiani*, s.v., and *DdC*, col. 202).

Book VII: Persecution of the Society at Rome; Total Suppression

1. Carlo Emmanuele III died on 20 February 1773 and was succeeded by his son Vittorio Amedeo III (*EI*, vol. 39, pp. 508–09).

2. The visitors of the Roman College were Cardinals York, Marefoschi, and Colonna. They were named on 7 May 1771. Cordara reverses the order of the visitations of the Roman College and the Irish College (*SHSI*, col. 363).

3. Cardinal Marefoschi had been named visitor of the Irish College on 6 March 1771 (*SHSI*, col. 363).

4. Vincenzo Malvezzi of Bologna was born in 1715. As early as 1733 he was made a cardinal. He died in 1775 (*EC*, s.v., and *DdC*, col. 1183).

5. José Moniño y Redondo (1728–1808) was especially competent in financial matters. He was sent as ambassador to Rome in 1772, explicitly to work for the suppression of the Society. As a reward, he was made secretary of state in 1775 and given the title Conde de Floridablanca (*Rialp*, s.v. Floridablanca).

6. Wenzel Anton, Count Kaunitz (1711–94), was the directing force of Austrian foreign policy from 1753. He was prominent until 1793 (*Der Neue Brochkaus*, s.v.).

7. Paolo Danei (Paul of the Cross) was born in 1694. The fundamental

documents for his founding the Passionists date from 1720 to 1721. He died at Rome in 1775 (*EC*, s.v. Paolo della Croce).

8. *Dominus ac Redemptor* was dated 21 July 1773 and promulgated 16 August 1773 (*SHSI*, col. 361 and 363).

9. The commission of five cardinals was set up by the letter *Gravissimis ex causis* of 13 August 1773. The five cardinals were Corsini, Marefoschi, Carafa, Zelada, and Casali. Macedonio and Alfani were also on the commission as secretaries (*SHSI*, col. 361, and William V. Bangert, *A History of the Society of Jesus*, 2nd ed., St. Louis, 1906, p. 574).

10. The monarchs in question were Frederick II of Prussia and Catherine the Great of Russia. The brief was promulgated in the former country in 1780 (*SHSI*, col. 374), but not in Russia, where a remnant hung on and conducted congregations which elected vicar-generals (*SHSI*, col. 378).

11. Annibale Albani was born in 1682 at Urbino. He studied under the Jesuits at the Roman College. He was a nephew of Clement XI and entrusted with many diplomatic missions. He was made a cardinal in 1712 and died at Rome in 1751 (*Dizionario biografico degli italiani*, s.v. and *DdC*, col. 202).

12. Ricci died 24 November 1775. Pius VI ordered that he be buried with his predecessors in the Gesù after the funeral mass at San Giovanni dei Fiorentini (*SHSI*, col. 371).

Book VIII: Analysis of Reasons for the Suppression

1. Isaac Joseph Berruyer was born at Rouen in 1681. He entered the Society of Jesus in 1697. His principal work, *Histoire du peuple de Dieu*, appeared in three parts and multiple volumes. All parts were placed on the Index. Berruyer died at Paris in 1758 (Koch, *Jesuiten-Lexikon*, s.v., and Sommervogel vol. I, col. 1357–70).

2. Luigi De Valentis was born in 1695. He served as bishop of Rimini and was made a cardinal in 1759. He passed away in 1763 (*DdC*, col. 1597, s.v. Valentin).

3. St. Robert Bellarmine was born at Montepulciano in 1542. He entered the Society of Jesus in 1560. Made a cardinal in 1599, he served as bishop of Capua from 1602 to 1605. However, much of his later life was spent in Rome as a special assistant to the pope. He died in 1621 at age seventy-nine (Koch, *Jesuiten-Lexicon*, s.v.; *DdC*, col. 335–485; and Sommervogel, vol. I, col. 1151–1254).

4. Bernardin Benzi was born at Venice in 1681. He entered the Society in 1705. Both his *Praxis tribunalis conscientiae* and *Dissertatio in casus reservatos* were placed on the Index. He died in 1768 (Koch, *Jesuiten-Lexikon*, s.v., and Sommervogel, vol. I, col. 1315–16).

5. Cordara alludes to the Paris Parlement's criticism of the Jesuits' blind obedience to a foreign Father General.

6. This rather bumptious statement might perhaps be tempered by comparing it to what Cordara wrote to Fabrizio Carafa: *"Un solo piccolo collegio di dieci o dodici Gesuiti in una città, possiamo ben dirlo fra noi, rendeva più servizi al publico che molti, o molto più numerosi conventi di altri regolari"* ("A single little college of ten or twelve Jesuits in a city, we can say this between ourselves, was giving more service to the public than many, or much more numerous, convents of other regulars"). The letters of Cordara to Carafa were published by Giuseppe Albertotti under the title *Nove lettere inedite di Giulio Cesare Cordara all' Abbate Fabrizio Carafa* in the *Atti del reale Istituto Veneto di scienze, lettere, ed arti*, vol. 82, part 2 (1922–23), pp. 1051–1103 and vol. 83, part 2 (1923–24), pp. 183–233. The text cited in this note appears on p. 1061. The nine letters cover in Italian much of what Cordara has to say about the causes of the suppression in Book VIII of the *De suppressione*.

7. Francisco Suarez was born in 1548. He entered the Society in 1564 and had an illustrious career as professor of theology at Segovia, Valladolid, Rome, and Coimbra. Benedict XIV and others referred to him as *doctor eximius*. He died at Lisbon in 1617 (Koch, *Jesuiten-Lexikon*, s.v., and Sommervogel, vol. VII, col. 1661–87).

8. Denis Petau was born at Orleans in 1583 and entered the Society in 1605. For twenty-two years he taught theology at the college of Cleremont. He died in 1652 (Koch, *Jesuiten-Lexikon*, s.v., and Sommervogel, vol. VI, col. 588–616).

9. Paolo Segneri was born in 1624 at Milan. He entered the Society of Jesus in 1637. He was the foremost preacher and mission-giver of his age. He died at Rome in 1694 (Koch, *Jesuiten-Lexikon*, s.v., and Sommervogel, vol. VII, col. 1050–89).

10. Cordara alludes, of course, to the bull *Apostolicum pascendi* of 7 January 1765 (*SHSI*, col. 345).

BIBLIOGRAPHY

Primary Sources

Cordara, Giulio Cesare. *De suis ac suorum rebus aliisque suorum temporum usque ad occasum Societatis Iesu Commentarii.* Giuseppe Albertotti and Agostino Faggiotto, eds. Published in *Miscellanea di storia italiana* LIII. Turin, 1933.

————. *De suppressione Societatis Iesu Commentarii.* 2 vols. in 1. Giuseppe Albertotti, ed. Padua, 1923 and 1925.

————. *Lettere di Giulio Cesare Cordara a Francesco Cancellieri (1772–1785).* Giuseppe Albertotti, ed. Modena, 1912 (vols. 1–2) and 1916 (vol. 3).

————. *Nove lettere inedite . . . all' Abbate Fabrizio Carafa.* Giuseppe Albertotti, ed. *Atti del reale Istituto Veneto di scienze, lettere, ed arti* 82.2 (1922–23), pp. 1051–1103 and 83.2 (1923–24), pp. 183–233.

————. *Opere latine e italiane dell' Abbate Giulio Cesare Cordara dei Conti di Calamandrana.* 4 vols. Luigi Buchetti and Mauro Boni, eds. Venice 1804–5.

Döllinger, Johann J., ed. *Beiträge zur politischen, kirchlichen und cultur-Geschichte der sechs letzen Jahrhunderte.* 3 vols. Wien, 1862–82.

Secondary Sources

Albertotti, Giuseppe. "Gli ultimi anni di G. Cesare Cordara da un ms. inedito." *Atti del reale Istituto veneto di scienze, lettere, ed arti* 86.2 (1926–27), pp. 867–910.

————. "Su alcuni scritti di G.C. Cordara che si ritenevano perduti." *Atti del reale Istituto veneto di scienze, lettere, ed arti* 82.2 (1922–23), pp. 469–74.

Astrain, Antonio. *Historia de Compañía de Jesús en la Asistencia de España.* 7 vols. Madrid, 1902–25.

Backer, Augustin de. *Bibliothèque de la Compagnie de Jésus.* Louvain, 1960.

Bangert, William V. *A History of the Society of Jesus.* 2nd ed. St. Louis, 1986.

————. "The Second Centenary of the Suppression of the Jesuits." *Thought* 48 (1973), pp. 165–88.

Benzo, Paola. "Bibliografie essenziali ragionate: G.C. Cordara." *Rivista di sintesi letteraria* II (1935), pp. 296–310.

Berton, Charles. *Dictionnaire des Cardinaux.* Paris, 1857.

Boero, Giuseppe. *Osservazioni sopra l'istoria del Pontificato de Clemente XIV scritta dal P. A. Theiner.* 2 vols. 2nd ed. Monza, 1854.

Campbell, Joseph. *The Jesuits: 1534–1921.* New York, 1921.

Carayon, Auguste. *Charles III et les Jésuites de ses états d'Europe et d'Amerique en 1767.* Paris, 1868.

————. *Le Père Ricci et la suppression de la Compagnie de Jésus en 1773.* Poitiers, 1869.

Castellani, Giuseppe. "I Commentarii di G.C. Cordara." *Studia romana* 5 (1957), pp. 553–64.

————. *La Società romana e italiana del Settecento negli scritti di Giulio Cesare Cordara.* Rome, 1967.

Cavalloto, Mario. *L'abbate Giulio Cesare Cordara dei Conti di Calamandrana.* Alessandria, 1966.

Cicchitto, L. "Il Pontifice Clemente XIV . . . della *Storia dei Papi* di L. von Pastor." *Miscellanea Francescana* 34 (1934), pp. 198–231.

Crétineau-Joly, Jacques. *Clement XIV et les Jésuites.* Paris, 1847.

————. *Polemique sur le Pape Clement XIV; lettres au Père Augustin Theiner.* Liege, 1853.

Dammig, Enrico. *Il movimento giansenista a Roma nella seconda metà del secolo XVIII. (Studi e Testi* 119). Rome, 1945.

Delplace, Louis. "La Suppression des Jésuites (1773–1814)." *Études* 116 (1908), pp. 69–96 and 228–47.

Dudon, Paul. "The Resurrection of the Society of Jesus." *Woodstock Letters* 81 (1952), pp. 311–60.

Dunne, Peter M. "The Expulsion of the Jesuits from New Spain, 1767." *Mid-America* 19 (1937), pp. 3–30.

Egret, J. "Le Procès des Jésuites devant les parlements de France (1761–70)." *Revue historique* 204 (1950), pp. 1–27.

Enciclopedia Cattolica. Città del Vaticano, 1948–54.

Enciclopedia italiana di scienze, lettre ed arti. . . . Rome, 1929–39.

Faggiotto, Agostino. "Giulio Cesare Cordara e papa Clemente XIV." *Atti del reale Istituto veneto di scienze, lettere, ed arti.* 95. 2 (1935–36), pp. 25–46.

————. "Papi, cardinali, e principi romani del sec. XVIII nei *Commentarii de suis* di G.C. Cordara." *Atti del II° Congresso nazionale di studi romani* II (1931), pp. 305–12.

———. "I precedenti della edizione veneta delle opere di G. Cesare Cordara." *Atti e Memorie dell' Academia di scienze, lettere, ed arti in Padova* 35 (1919), pp. 207–34.

Fonqueray, Henri. *Histoire de la Compagnie de Jésus en France des origines à la suppression (1528–1762).* 5 vols. Paris, 1910–25.

Frammelsberger, Karin. "*Dominus ac Redemptor:* die Aufhebung des Jesuitenordens im 18. Jahrhundert." *Geist und Leben* 63 (1990), pp. 373–82.

Gran enciclopedia Rialp. Madrid, 1989.

La grand encyclopédie. Paris, 1885–92.

Grand Larousse. Paris, 1960.

Gross, Hanss. *Rome in the Age of the Enlightenment.* New York, 1990.

Harney, Martin P. *The Jesuits in History: The Society of Jesus through Four Centuries.* New York, 1941.

Holt, Geoffrey. "The Fatal Mortgage, the English Province, and Père La Vallette." *Archivum Historicum Societatis Iesu* 38 (1969), pp. 464–78.

Koch, Ludwig. *Jesuiten-Lexikon.* Paderborn, 1931.

Kratz, G., and P. Leturia. *Intorno al 'Clemente XIV' del Barone von Pastor.* Rome, 1935.

Leturia, P. "Ancora intorno al 'Clemente XIV' del Barone von Pastor." *Civiltà cattolica* 85.4 (1934), pp. 225–40.

Lopes, Antonio. "D'Alembert et la suppression des Jésuites." *Christus* 38 (1991), pp. 367–77.

Monti, Alessandro. *La Compagnia di Gesù nel territorio della Provincia Torinese.* Chieri, 1915.

Murr, Christoph G. von. *Geschichte der Jesuiten in Portugal under der Staatsverwaltung des Marquis von Pombal.* 2nd edition. Freiburg im Breisgau, 1923.

Padovani, Umberto A. *La soppressione della Compania di Gesù.* Naples, 1962.

Pastor, Ludwig. *Geschichte der Päpste: im Zeitalter der fürstlichen Absolutismus von der Wahl Benedickts XIV bis zum Tode Pius VI (1790–1799).* Vol. 16 in 3 parts. Freiburg im Breisgau, 1931–33.

Ravignan, Gustave. *Clement XIII et Clement XIV.* Paris, 1854.

Rochemonteix, Camille de. *Le P. Antoine Lavalette à la Martinique.* Paris, 1907.

Rodrigues, Francisco. *Historia da Companhia de Jesus na Assitência de Portugal.* 4 vols. in 6. Porto, 1931–50.

Rosa, Enrico. *I Gesuiti dalle origini ai nostri giorni.* 3rd ed. Rome, 1957.

———. "Giulio Cesare Cordara nella sua vita e nelle sue lettere." *Civiltà cattolica* 64.4 (1913), pp. 433–70.

———. "Gli ultimi anni di G. Cesare Cordara." *Civiltà cattolica* 78.3 (1927), pp. 540–50.

————. "Intorno al Pontificato di Clemente XIV." *Civiltà cattolica* 86.1 (1935), pp. 17–35.

Smith, Sydney F. "Suppression of the Society of Jesus." *The Month* 99 (1902), pp. 113–30, 262–79, 346–68, 497–517, 626–50; 100 (1902), pp. 20–34, 126–52, 258–73, 366–77, 517–36, 581–91; 101 (1903), pp. 48–61, 179–97, 259–77, 383–403, 498–516, 604–23; 102 (1903), pp. 46–63, 171–84.

Synopsis historiae Societatis Iesu. Louvain, 1950.

Theiner, Augustin. *Geschichte des Pontificats Clemens XIV nach unedirten Staatsschriften aus dem geheimen Archive des Vaticans.* 2 vols. Leipzig, 1853.

Thompson, D. G. "The Fate of the French Jesuits' Creditors under the *ancien regime*." *English Historical Review* 91 (1976), pp. 255–77.

————. "General Ricci and the Suppression of the Jesuit Order in France 1760–64." *Journal of Ecclesiastical History* 37 (1986), pp. 426–41.

————. "The Persecution of French Jesuits by the Parlement of Paris 1761–71." *Studies in Church History* 21 (1984), pp. 289–301.

Vigilante, M. "Cordara, Giulio Cesare." *Dizionario biografico degli italiani* 28 (1983). pp. 789–92.

Weld, Alfred. *The Suppression of the Society of Jesus in Portuguese Dominions.* London, 1877.

INDEX OF PERSONS

With a few exceptions, the Index of Persons contains only those persons who lived in the eighteenth century and to whom Cordara refers in his text. The notations "n." and "nn." refer to the number(s) of the endnote(s) where the name appears.